ALSO BY SELMA R. WILLIAMS

*Kings, Commoners, and Colonists:*
*Puritan Politics in Old and New England*

# DEMETER'S DAUGHTERS

*The Women
Who Founded America
1587-1787*

# Selma R. Williams

# DEMETER'S DAUGHTERS

## The Women Who Founded America 1587-1787

ILLUSTRATED WITH OLD ENGRAVINGS

AND PAINTINGS

Atheneum 1976 New York

Library of Congress Cataloging in Publication Data

Williams, Selma R
Demeter's daughters.

SUMMARY: Details the varied activities of
colonial women, the extensive legal rights they
enjoyed, and the difficulties they faced in a new
land.
Includes biographical sketches of representative
women of that period.
Bibliography: p. 323
Includes index.
1. Women—United States—Biography.   2.
United States—History—Colonial period, ca. 1600-
1775.   [1. Women—History,   2. United States—
Colonial period, ca. 1600-1775]   I. Title.
HQ1416.W54   920.72'0973 [920]   75-13773
ISBN 0-689-30494-3

*To Burt*

# Contents

vii

# List of Illustrations

# Changing the Focus

Colonial women set the pace for twentieth-century feminists. And the modern "Ms." has yet to catch up. Even that title—Ms.—is a hand-me-down from colonial times. There was no distinction in address between married and unmarried women. All were called "Mistress," frequently abbreviated to "Mrs."

Like the ancient Greek goddess Demeter, females of early America were responsible for supplying society with earth's blessings: food, marriage, children—and civic harmony. The story of these women—heroines, victims, and at least a few out-and-out scoundrels—is the story of the founding of the United States.

Early in the writing, *Demeter's Daughters* took on a direction of its own, casting aside narrative history in favor of chapters and sections that followed in a logical rather than a chronological sequence. Next, the book began developing five major themes that recur and intertwine throughout, as in a mosaic: (1) The actual settlement of colonial America, in which women play the lead. This is a long-neglected aspect of our history, frequently nudged out of the limelight by exclusive emphasis on war and politics. (2) The special concessions and privileges, unheard of back home in Europe, that women won in return for their indispensability in the era of colonization. (3) Concurrent and contradictory setbacks and suffering.

(4) Well-documented contributions of women to fields too often treated as exclusively masculine. (5) The growth of American self-sufficiency and independence, which was simultaneous with the dawn of feminism.

From beginning to end, women reverse their usual role in history books, here playing the starring parts with men in the background.

The lives and achievements of specific women are described, not for purposes of biography or heroine-worship, but to illuminate various aspects of society and to illustrate the development of patterns of colonial life that are part of America today. Thus most, though by no means all, notable American women of the seventeenth and eighteenth centuries are portrayed, using their own words wherever possible. Overall, however, there has been a conscious attempt to deal with women of every socioeconomic class, not just those wealthy enough to attract history's attention or sufficiently articulate to leave behind their writings for posterity.

The English and the thirteen colonies occupy center stage because, of course, they were the nucleus of the future United States. However, occasional attention is given to other areas and to immigrants from other countries, and there is special emphasis on the role of the blacks, who were the second largest group in America at the time of the Revolution.

The Indian women, who contributed so much to successful colonization of the New World only to find themselves excluded from the mainstream of American society, begin the story with a prologue all their own. Also, they appear from time to time on the periphery, unhappily just as they did in the course of actual settlement by the English.

# DEMETER'S DAUGHTERS

---

*The Women
Who Founded America
1587-1787*

# Native Americans

Women joined the welcome for Columbus when he arrived to discover America in 1492. "Naked as their mothers bore them," women as well as men, Columbus commented to his journal. Except for the woman who "had a piece of gold in her nose."

They were the most beautiful men and women he had yet seen, Columbus decided after two months of sailing from island to island in the Caribbean. And the gold he saw surrounding them everywhere was exquisite, too.

But to get that gold there had to be promise of human survival. Practical adventurer that he was, Columbus seized on the solution for survival very early in his travels. On December 21, 1492, referring to himself in the third person, he noted that the women "were the first to come and give thanks to heaven, and to bring what they had, especially things to eat—some of which the Admiral ordered to be preserved, to be taken to the Sovereigns." He concluded pointedly: "The women did not do less in other ports."

The pattern was set for all of the next century: Old World men explored. New World women fed them—or showed them how, where, and what to plant, as Renaissance Europe's traditions proved frighteningly useless in coping with primeval America.

Among native Americans, food planting and gathering

"A chiefe Herowans wyfe of Pomeoc and her daughter of the age of eight or ten years" by John White, 1587. *Courtesy of the British Museum.*

"A Chieff Lady of Pomeiooc and daughter." An engraving
after John White. Notice how the engraver who had not seen
Indians substituted Caucasian features. *Courtesy of the Fogg
Art Museum, Harvard University, Bequest of Francis Calley
Gray.*

were female responsibilities, so that the skills the women
transmitted, first to explorers and later to colonists, included
sowing and harvesting corn and potatoes (two of the world's
basic staples today), catching and cooking shellfish, and cultivating berries and herbs for use as medicine to prevent or cure
almost any illness from French pox to stomachache. In addition, they introduced such strange new foods as artichokes
(the roots of which could be used in stews), peanuts, peppers,
and pumpkins. As a matter of fact, the early New England
colonists became so dependent on pumpkins that one anonymous rhymester cheerfully bewailed substituting the new diet
for the one he had known and loved back in England:

Instead of pottage and pudding and custards and pies,
Our pumpkins and parsnips are common supplies;
We have pumpkins at morning—and pumpkins at noon,
If it was not for pumpkins we should soon be undone!

There was a definite division of labor between native women and men, though for certain tasks the work was shared. Reflecting a universal pattern, women were in charge of keeping house, providing meals and medical care, and bearing and rearing the children—while men's particular responsibilities were to protect the family from natural catastrophes (tasks that included constructing forts and dugouts and making weapons), to fish and to hunt, and to fell trees in order to clear the land for cultivation. The fish that men caught women cooked. Men trapped and killed animals; women cooked them. Another process, tanning, was usually man's work, but the next step, fashioning fur and leather into clothing, was woman's duty.

The basic need for shelter was another shared responsibility. Men procured poles and bark for the living quarters, which the women then constructed—covering the family lodge by fastening oak, chestnut, or birch bark tightly to the framework in an overlapping, shinglelike pattern, and finally placing the poles over the bark to help keep it in place.

Besides sharing labor with the men, many native women played a special role in their society—arising from the commonsense observation that, while fatherhood was at best uncertain, there could be no doubt about the claim of motherhood. Thus certain large tribes—for example, the eastern Iroquois and the western Navajo and Hopi—were set up on a *matrilocal* basis (literally, home is where the mother lives), meaning that the new husband moved into his wife's lodge. In addition, these tribes were *matrilineal* (that is, children belong to the mother only), so that all descent was traced through the mother, not the father. William Penn, who founded Pennsylvania in 1682, described the consequence of these traditions in a letter written to the Society of Traders in London:

> Their government is by kings . . . and those by succession, but always of the mother's side. For instance, the children of him that is now king will not succeed, but his brother by the mother, or the children of his sister, whose sons (and after them the children of the daughters) will reign; . . . the reason they render for this way of descent is that their issue may not be spurious.

In this instance, Penn was referring to the Iroquois, who had lived on the east coast of America for at least ten thousand years before the coming of the English and the French. Always, among the Iroquois, older women chose the sachems (chiefs) who sat on the tribal council and participated in ruling the tribe. Each of these women, as grandmother or great-grandmother of all members of her clan—every clan in the tribe was composed of a number of related families—was the founding mother, common ancestor. Almost invariably she named one of her own sons as sachem. Furthermore, she, not a man, chose representatives for League councils (at various times five or six tribes or nations belonged to the League of the Iroquois). And for carrying out lesser duties and tasks she could replace her own kin, who had been killed in combat, with prisoners-of-war, over whom she had absolute power of life or death.

Though she herself did not govern, she was in effective control, even after a chief had been chosen. For she had the power to initiate proceedings to depose him should he fail to perform his duties. In addition, the public treasury—consisting of such resources as corn; furs; meal; fresh, dried, and smoked meats; and strings and belts of wampum—was under her jurisdiction.

In all Iroquois clans, the female line determined disposal of goods and property, owned tools used in raising food, and maintained peace and order in the longhouse (communal dwelling house). Also, mothers traditionally arranged marriages for their children.

One modern scholar, Peter Farb, finds the Iroquois "as close to being a matriarchate as any society in the world." And another recent scholar, Carolyn Thomas Foreman, adds that "among the Iroquoian tribes—the Susquehanna, the Hurons, and the Iroquois—the punishment for killing a woman of the tribe was double that exacted for killing a man."

On the other side of North America, Hopis, Navajos, and Zuñis, on the continent for at least twenty thousand years, gave women a strong position in every phase of life—economic, political, religious, and social. And, like all matrilineal tribes, they exalted women in the myth of the Earth Mother.

In blackness and nothingness, this myth recounted, there emerged the seeds of growth, as well as sun, light, and the seas on which the earth floated. With the warmth from the sun, green scum began forming over the waters, solidified, and finally divided into Earth Mother of the Four Directions and Sky Father who covered the universe.

The union of Earth Mother and Sky Father conceived all of earth's creatures. But before the actual birth of these living things and beings, Earth Mother and Sky Father separated to prepare the world. Earth Mother supervised the rising of mountains to divide land from land and to enclose the world by providing an outer rim. Drawing milk from her own breasts, she made nurture of children forever possible. And she made clouds emerge from the waters. At the same time, Sky Father breathed and caused fertilizing rain to fall from these clouds, and also blessed the breasts of the Earth Mother, decreeing that food for their children would spring from her body. Thus the world lived happily ever after, with warmth and life flowing from Earth Mother, while fertilizing rain and cold, which strengthens men, came from Sky Father.

Hopis, Navajos, and Zuñis further believed that corn, their chief crop, came to them from Corn Mother, the daughter of Earth Mother and Sky Father. In these tribes, custom dictated that women owned the houses, the furnishings, and the crops, which they shared communally. Hopis and Zuñis practiced dry-land farming, locating their gardens at the mouths of streams in order to catch runoffs from rains. Women's responsibilities included gardening, cooking, and nursing the sick. And though game was a decidedly secondary source of food, wherever possible the men hunted for meat, which the women then preserved and stored for the winter.

Marriage was allowed only between a man and a woman belonging to different clans. Divorce was easy and initiated by the woman. She would simply put all the husband's belongings outside the door, a sign that he was to return to his mother's home. The husband-father was considered of no great importance in disciplining children or teaching sons to stalk animals or catch fish. These responsibilities belonged to the mother's brother.

In contrast, tribes that depended on animals as their chief source of food tended to be patrilineal and patrilocal.[1] This enabled brothers to band together in hunting areas with which they were familiar. Moving to his wife's home would put the man in alien territory, away from the lands he had known since birth. Likewise, where there were frequent wars, the need for cooperation among males precluded any major role for women.

---

[1] Perceptively, Anne Grant, memoirist who lived in New York State from 1757 to 1768, commented about Indian societies she herself had observed or had learned about through conversations with others: "Wherever man is a mere hunter, woman is a mere slave. It is domestic intercourse that softens man, and elevates woman; and of that there can be little where the employments and amusements are not in common."

Recent scholarship establishes that even in male-dominated tribes, native women seldom suffered abuse. However, early explorers and settlers tended to see Indian women through European eyes. Men used their superior strength, one wrote in 1648, not to labor for the good of the family, but "to keep the wife in subjection and oblige her to every kind of drudgery." Reporting this early observation, Thomas Hutchinson in his 1764 history of Massachusetts added some double-edged chauvinism (in almost the same words used by William Wood 130 years before in his *New England's Prospect,* 1634) to cut down native men while sharpening the chivalrous image of Englishmen: "The [Indian] men commended themselves for keeping their wives employed and condemned the English husbands for spoiling good working creatures."

Similarly, in 1651, New England's enthusiastic historian Edward Johnson, writing his *Wonder-Working Providence of Sion's Savior in New England,* found that the Indian women "are generally very laborious at their planting time, and the men extraordinarily idle, making their squaws to carry their children and the luggage beside; so that many times they travel eight or ten miles with a burden on their backs, more fitter for a horse to carry than a woman. The men follow no kind of labor but hunting, fishing, and fowling."

Of all Indian women, the most famous is, of course, Pocahontas. John Smith, the dauntless explorer and propagandist who doted on mixing accurate observation with racy imagination, credited Chief Powhatan's daughter with saving him from death in Virginia by throwing herself on him at the crucial moment. If this escapade is only legend, other events in Pocahontas's short life probably did occur as reported. For example, she was almost certainly kidnapped by Governor Thomas Dale of Virginia, who staved off a war with the Indians by holding her as hostage. And there are definite records showing that later she was converted to Christianity, baptized as Rebecca, and married to John Rolfe, who took her to

London where she died of smallpox in 1617 when she was about twenty-two years old.

John Smith related the Pocahontas story as further exaltation of his own importance, not for glorification of Indian womanhood. Subsequently, the myth-making school of history latched onto the legend, always mentioning her marriage to John Rolfe.

Unfortunately, the legend of Pocahontas has continued to burn so brightly that it obscures the roles, accomplishments, and contributions of her sisters over thousands of years. Furthermore, the frequent retelling of the fairy-tale marriage of the royal Indian and the white commoner has muffled the conscience-searing cry of Pocahontas's father Powhatan on behalf of his descendants and his successors—three brothers, two sisters, and their two daughters:

> Why will you take by force what you may quietly have with love, or to destroy them that provide you food? What can you get by war, when we can hide our provisions and fly to the woods, whereby you must famish, by wronging us your friends? And why are you jealous of our loves, seeing us unarmed, and we both do and are willing still to feed you with that you cannot get but by our labors? Think you I am so simple not to know it is better to eat good meat, lie well, and sleep quietly with my women and children, laugh, and be merry with you, have copper, hatchets, or what I want being your friends; then be forced to fly from all, to lie cold in the woods, feed upon acorns, roots, and such trash, and be so hunted by you that I can neither rest nor sleep. . . . Then must I fly I know not whither, and thus with miserable fear end my miserable life, leaving my pleasures to such youths as you, which, through your rash unadvisedness, may quickly as miserably end, for want of that you never know how to find? Let this therefore assure you of our loves, and every year our friendly trade shall furnish you with corn; and now also if you would come in friendly manner to see us,

and not thus with your guns and swords, as to invade your foes.[2]

On a completely different level, the nearly neglected legend of the squaw sachem of Massachusetts serves to illuminate a hidden area of Indian society. The heroine was an Indian queen—a title never used by Indians, though frequently bestowed on native female rulers by contemporary English settlers to whom a ruler was synonymous with royalty.

Detective work by historians over the centuries has uncovered enough scattered references to reveal something of who and what she was. She began as the wife of Nanepashemet, once sufficiently powerful to have ruled over most of the tribes in areas that are today part of Massachusetts, Maine, and New Hampshire. Nanepashemet maintained dwellings in present-day Salem, Lynn, and Marblehead, Massachusetts. However, intense hostility between the Tarrantines of Maine and Nanepashemet erupted into sporadic warfare over the four-year period from 1615 to 1619. Nanepashemet, always on the run attacking or repelling his enemy, saved the lives of his wife and children by sending them to live with friendly Indians. In 1619, he himself was killed by the Tarrantines, who then returned to Maine.

Nanepashemet's vast authority was badly eroded by the four years of warfare with the Tarrantines. But his wife was determined to exert power over the three tribes that remained loyal to her husband's memory—the Naumkeags, the Saugus, and the Winnisimmets. Grouping them together under the old federated name of Massachusetts, she placed her three sons

[2] This rare report of an Indian's inner feelings and reactions to European colonization found its way to England in a book written by six of John Smith's good friends and fellow adventurers in 1612. It is generally conceded to be authentic—though ignored at the time by Englishmen eager to impose their will and rule over the New World.

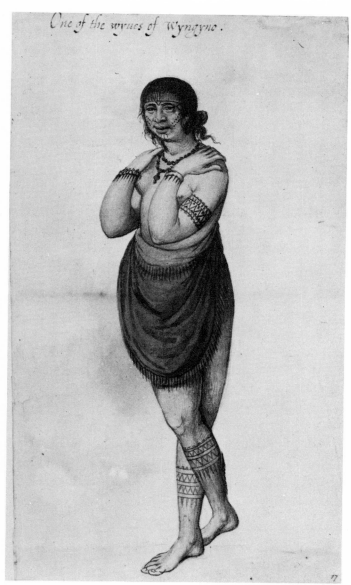

One of the wyues of Wyngyno.

An Algonkian woman of Virginia—of the same linguistic family as the Indians of Massachusetts, by John White, 1587. *Courtesy of the British Museum.*

over the three tribes and herself assumed the title: Squaw Sachem of Massachusetts.

For more than twenty years she held together her late husband's domains, including areas considered increasingly valuable by white colonists—parts of modern Arlington, Belmont, Cambridge, Medford, Melrose, Somerville, and Stoneham, Massachusetts. Then, in 1643, she let herself be hurled into civilization along with other New England sachems, including Massasoit. They each agreed to a treaty with the English settlers, promising to obey colonial laws and to take instruction in the Bible. In addition, the squaw sachem allowed Captain Edward Gibbons, a Boston trader, to win first her friendship and then her consent to a properly English deed to her land.

All this occurred just six years after the Pequot War of 1637, the first military confrontation between New England Puritans and Indians. Puritans justified the war as self-defense, but as a result won unlimited control throughout New England. Already greed for land had replaced gratitude for survival lessons—greed rationalized into the need to convert the "heathen." In words any seventeenth-century Britisher would have understood and accepted without question, the contributors to *Mourt's Journal* in 1622 laid out the scenario for Europeanizing Indian America. Conversion, they declared, could take place only if "we go to them or they come to us; to us they cannot come, our land is full; to them we may go, their land is empty."

# · *Part I* ·

---

# SETTLEMENT

---

"Brides for Virginians." *Courtesy of the New York Public Library.*

# CHAPTER ONE

# Newcomers

B y the 1620s England had stumbled on the winning method of New World colonization—settlement by self-motivated, privately financed family groups.

More than a century earlier Spain had made a half-hearted attempt at government-supported, family colonization. King Ferdinand decreed that Spanish officials leaving for America must take their wives along, and could obtain royal permission to sail only with the consent of the wife if she decided to remain behind. However, Spanish officials whose wives agreed to take up New World residence tended to return home to Spain after completing their terms of service. Thus few Spanish women became permanent colonists. In fact, at the end of the eighteenth century, after three hundred years of Spanish colonization, German scientific explorer Alexander von Humboldt estimated that less than one out of ten European-born Spaniards then living in Mexico City were women. And the number was even smaller in provincial towns.

The fate of the very first woman colonist was a bad omen for Spanish women in the New World. She was Francisca Hinestrosa who landed at Tampa Bay on May 25, 1539, with her husband Hernando Baustista, one of explorer Hernando De

Soto's soldiers.[1] Less than two years later, in March 1541, she died in a confrontation with the Indians of north Mississippi.

One immediate result of the shortage of pure-blooded Spanish women was intermarriage between Spanish explorers and natives, at first quietly condoned and later officially favored. A striking example of this was the wife of Juan de Oñate, the explorer who in 1595 obtained the contract for conquest and settlement of New Mexico. Oñate's wife was granddaughter of Hernando Cortes, who in 1521 had conquered Mexico, and great-granddaughter of Montezuma, the Aztec ruler defeated and killed by Cortes.

The English, who entered the race for New World empire almost one hundred years after the Spanish, made a disastrous attempt in 1587 to colonize Roanoke Island on the Atlantic coast. The 117 settlers included 91 men, 17 women, and 9 male children. They tried moving in on land inhabited by a large Indian population not at all anxious to share their meager resources.

One of the women, Eleanor White Dare, was already five months pregnant when she left England with her sailor husband, Ananias Dare, and father, John White (the Virginia governor who left behind a journal history of the colony as well as sixty-three exquisite watercolors of New World natives, flora, and fauna). After sailing stormy seas for three months and living in the tropical wilderness of Virginia for one month, she gave birth on August 18, 1587, to the New World's first English child, a girl appropriately named Virginia.

Sadly, just nine days after excitedly announcing to his journal the birth of his granddaughter, John White was forced to

[1] Under Spanish law Francisca Hinestrosa kept her own maiden name and would have been allowed to retain personal ownership of her own property. This was also true in later Catholic settlements in Spanish Florida and French Louisiana, and among early Dutch Walloon colonists in New Netherland.

return to England because of an extreme shortage of supplies and need for help. But he no sooner arrived home than murderous rivalry between England and Spain again erupted into full-scale warfare. His superiors refused to allow his departure. And even after the summer of 1588 when the Spanish Armada was utterly demolished and the seas were open for England all the way to the New World, he was detained because of the near bankruptcy of his sponsor, Sir Francis Raleigh. Finally back in Virginia in August 1590, almost exactly three years after leaving, he looked everywhere for traces of his little family and the colonists, but found not even a human bone. In the end, thrashed by severe storms and starved for food, he was forced to give up the search "as luckless to many, as sinister to myself."

Scarcely more successful than the Roanoke colony was the English settlement at Jamestown. No women came that first year, 1607. But seventy arrivals the following year included Anne Forrest and her maid Anne Burras. (Fourteen-year-old Anne Burras had a further claim to record-making when, not long after her arrival, she married laborer John Laydon, one of the earliest colonists. This was the first English wedding in Virginia or, indeed, in any of the English colonies.)

A letter from the Spanish ambassador to England, Don Pedro de Zuñiga, written to King Philip III of Spain, March 5, 1609 is the source of the estimate that four to five hundred (nameless) men and women colonists left England in the "Great Supply" sailing of nine ships from England. They went in apparent response to a broadside soliciting both men and women for "the better strengthening of the colony." A later report noted that by the spring of 1610 only sixty still survived famine, plague, and Indian warfare.

The growth of the Virginia colony was excruciatingly slow, so that by 1616 there were only 351 colonists in Virginia, including 286 male adults and 65 women and children. A malaria epidemic made the settlers early sanitation fanatics, resulting in the publication of a warning to Jamestown women: "No laundress dare to wash any unclean linen . . . or throw out the water or suds of foul clothes in the open street, within the palisades, or within forty feet of the same." In addition, the town forced women to drag dirty pans and kettles to the riverbank or bring them, along with water, to a secluded area for cleaning, forbidding them to clean up after meals at the nearby well or pump.

Such extra responsibilities falling on female shoulders made Virginians conscious of the need for more women. Thus on July 31, 1619, the newly established House of Burgesses included in its journal the suggestion that wives should be given shares of land "because that in a new plantation it is not known whether man or woman be the most necessary."

Even so, the ratio of men to women remained at the discouraging level of six males to every female, a ratio fed by the continuing influx of indentured boy servants thirteen to fifteen years old. To remedy the situation, Virginia decided to import a hundred or so "young and uncorrupt" girls, forcibly put on ship to serve as wives and breeders in the New World. The move struck terror back in England, where a Somersetshire magistrate wrote to the Privy Council describing the flight of forty maidens from one parish to "obscure places, and their parents do not know what has become of them." The price successful suitors had to pay the Virginia Company for importing these maids was first 120 pounds, later 150 pounds "of the best leaf tobacco for each of them."

Ninety were sent out in 1620, followed by an additional fifty in 1621 and 1622. By late 1622 all 140 of these impressed young girls were married and there was a continuing demand for more. Men complained bitterly that they had no wife or woman servant to wash their clothes or to care for them in illness.

The situation was improved ever so slightly by 1624–1625, reaching a ratio of four (instead of six) men to every woman. An inpouring of colonists, following still another devastating combination of plague and Indian massacre in which seventy-five percent of the earlier residents were killed, brought the population to 1,225–885 men (432 free immigrants, 441 white servants, 12 black slaves), 233 women (176 free immigrants, 46 white servants, 11 black slaves), and 107 children.

However, the ratio was far from satisfactory, and completely out of line with what colonists had known back in Europe, where women substantially outnumbered men. With impressment of young girls increasingly frowned on, authorities resorted to publicists who concocted a sweet mixture of promise and propaganda. For example, as late as 1649, William Bullock in London held out the assurance of early marriage for all unwed women who would go to Virginia where "if they come of an honest stock and have a good repute, they may pick and choose their husbands out of the better sort of people." But even at the turn of the eighteenth century, in 1702 when the population of Virginia was approaching sixty thousand, Daniel Defoe, English author of *Robinson Crusoe* and writer on political affairs, could still comment: "Virginia did not yield any plenty of wives."

Further north in New England, Mother England, which was in a state of anarchy and near civil war, reaped the benefits of a strong base on America's Atlantic coast. Completely on their own, English nonconformists crossed the ocean, invariably arriving in family groups between 1620 and 1640.

First came the Pilgrims, sailing aboard the *Mayflower,* September 6, 1620. Twenty-eight of the one hundred and two passengers were female—eighteen wives, six daughters, one kind of foster daughter, one young cousin, and two maidservants. The wives and daughters, plus eighteen husbands and eighteen sons (including two born aboard ship) accounted for sixty of the *Mayflower* Pilgrims, meaning that three out of every five passengers arrived as members of family groups.

Immortality has been bestowed on the men who sailed aboard the *Mayflower* and then debarked at Plymouth either to perish that first winter or to live long enough to help establish the colony. They deserve every honor. But women who did the same have been made invisible through neglect. For example, no future historian would ever fail to rhapsodize over the Mayflower Compact, the first tangible evidence that American society would be a government of equal justice under the law. "All the *responsible people* [italics added] appended their names to the agreement," opined Yale's great historian Charles M. Andrews, writing his four-volume classic *The Colonial Period of American History* in 1934. He then described the forty-one men who signed the document and carefully accounted for the omission of twenty adult males among the sixty-one "people" entitled to inscribe their names. Not a word about the women.

But the suffering on the endlessly brutal crossing had made no distinction as to sex. Each person aboard the approximately 100-foot-long *Mayflower* had a space of less than six feet by three feet, hardly enough for one modern single bed, or, in 1620, for one straw mattress set on the bare deck. The crowding was made worse by the cold sea wind, storms, water leaking everywhere—and the stench of human waste.[2] And two wives, in the final stages of pregnancy, somehow agreed to set sail, though four others, either because of pregnancy or very young children, remained behind till their husbands made a home and sent for them. Amid near deathly conditions, Elizabeth Hopkins bore a son on the high seas, aptly

[2] Throughout the colonial period, ship crossings were dehumanizing as well as hazardous. As late as 1710, 500 in a group of 3,000 had to be buried at sea, voyaging in a fleet that took five months instead of the usual six to ten weeks. And an epidemic took the lives of 105 out of 400 in a 1738 sailing. In addition to illness, there were always pirates, enemy ships, and murderous winds and storms.

named Oceanus, and Susanna White was delivered of a son, Peregrine, just as the *Mayflower* landed at Cape Cod.

Nor was the nine-week *Mayflower* ordeal at an end for the women when the ship anchored November 11, 1620. Wives and children remained aboard while husbands went ashore to scout the land and build houses; some women were forced to live on ship for as long as 131 days. During the early weeks most women were left completely alone, since only a few husbands were able to return at night.

At this point some less than earthshaking facts provide a bit of relief: (1) Fifteen-year-old Mary Chilton was the first female to go—some say, jump—ashore. (2) Another young girl, Mary Allerton, became the longest surviving passenger of the *Mayflower* voyage. Her mother died during the first winter, but Mary lived on to marry, to raise four children, and to see the establishment of twelve of the thirteen colonies (all but the very late-blooming Georgia, which was founded in 1732). (3) Before finding a suitable place for settlement, many women left ship for the day on Monday, November 24. There had been little extra water aboard ship to use for laundry, and so in effect the women inaugurated the institution of washday Monday. The men provided the equipment, leading an anonymous poet to explain later:

> *For the earliest act of the heroes*
> *Whose fame has a world-wide sway,*
> *Was—to fashion a crane for a kettle*
> *And order a washing day.*

William W. Fowler, in his 1878 book *Woman on the American Frontier,* became one of the first to celebrate what his subtitle described: "Heroism, Adventures, Privations, Captivities, Trials, and Noble Lives and Deaths of the 'Pioneer Mothers of the Republic.'" The wives who crossed the Atlantic on the *Mayflower,* he declared, should have their names engraved in gold on the pillars of United States history. As the next best substitute he had them inscribed in his book in the blackest, most formal type available:

| | |
|---|---|
| Mrs. Catherine Carver | Mrs. Elizabeth Hopkins |
| Mrs. Dorothy Bradford | Mrs. Ann Tilley |
| Mrs. Elizabeth Winslow | Mrs. —— Tillery |
| Mrs. Mary Brewster | Mrs. —— Tinker |
| Mrs. Mary Allerton | Mrs. Alice Rigsdale |
| Mrs. Rose Standish | Mrs. Sarah Eaton |
| Mrs. —— Martin | Mrs. —— Chilton |
| Mrs. —— Mullins | Mrs. —— Fuller |
| Mrs. Susanna White | Mrs. Ellen Billington |

The Mrs. Mullins on William Fowler's list was mother of the most famous of the Pilgrim women, Priscilla Mullins Alden, whom Henry Wadsworth Longfellow made legendary in his 1858 poem, "The Courtship of Miles Standish." Retelling an anecdote first published by descendant Timothy Alden in 1814—and probably a figment of a lively imagination—the poet made her a strong-minded woman who viewed with amusement Miles Standish's attempt to use John Alden as his agent in courtship: "Why don't you speak for yourself, John?"

But this light, frothy poem bears little resemblance to the reality of the first years at Plymouth. It includes no mention of the recent deaths of Priscilla Mullins's father, mother, brother, and family servant, nor of the fact that Miles Standish was looking for a wife to replace Rose Standish, whom Governor William Bradford recorded in his journal as having "died in the first sickness."

More than half the passengers perished during the death-laden first year in Plymouth colony, including fourteen of the eighteen adult women and four of the ten younger females. Still, human reinforcements kept arriving in family groups, the Indians proved most helpful in teaching the Pilgrims how to coax food from the forbiddingly rocky soil (and sometimes, uninvited, the settlers entered Indian lodges and helped themselves to food), and eventually the colony set itself on a firm footing by the mid 1620s.

At about the same time, with no apparent reference to Pilgrim practice, philosopher-statesman Sir Francis Bacon in England theorized: "When the plantation grows to strength, then it is time to plant with women as well as men; that the plantation may spread into generations."

But lending weight to the contention that England's success in colonizing by family was bumblingly accidental, a group of Dorchester, England, Puritans attempted to establish a colony on Cape Anne, Massachusetts in 1623. Despite the Pilgrim experience and Bacon's advice, they sent out men alone. The effort failed, as did several other trial colonies in the 1620s. Then the would-be colonists reeled to the opposite extreme, and Salem in 1629 granted "maid lots"—until stern old Governor John Endecott put a stop to what he called the great evil of "granting lots unto single maidens not disposed of in marriage."

The wholesale transfer of population from old to New England began with the arrival of one thousand Puritans in Massachusetts Bay on June 12, 1630; and the population reached a total of some twenty thousand just ten years later. From the very beginning of this great Puritan migration, contemporary journals indicate the presence of wives and children as well as husbands, though lists of passengers sailing to New England (except for that of the *Mayflower* in 1620) have been lost forever for the years before 1634.

Puritan men who founded Massachusetts Bay under the leadership of John Winthrop have long been credited with a high degree of intellectualism and purposeful idealism as they attempted to establish New England as a modern utopia. Credit their wives as well.

The tyranny and anarchy of early seventeenth-century England trampled Puritan women as well as Puritan men. On the most basic level, as wives and mothers they saw a bleak future for their families and for themselves when their politically heretical husbands were slapped into prison or forbidden to pursue lifelong careers. In addition, they were in the discouragingly powerless position described in a treatise written when Elizabeth was queen but published in 1632, a generation after the death of the great female monarch:

> Women have no voice in Parliament. They make no laws, they consent to none, they abrogate none. All of them are understood either married or about to be married, and their desires are subject to their husband.

(This tract, titled "The Lawes Resolutions of Womens Rights: Or, the Lawes Provision for Women," occasionally finds its way into political studies of Tudor or Stuart England, but the sex and name of the author are uncertain.)

Thus, Puritan women watched helplessly when James I, a Scotsman and a foreigner who ascended the throne of England in 1603, demonstrated no feelings for England's sacred traditions of parliamentary government. Instead he proclaimed himself as God on earth, with nobody and nothing able to restrain his actions. His son, Charles I, succeeded him in 1625, and by 1629 plunged England into anarchy and to the brink of civil war, dissolving Parliament permanently and imprisoning its (Puritan) leaders.

The depression in the cloth industry, hitting the areas where Puritans lived and worked, again affected wives as well as husbands. John Winthrop, for example, was forced to live a good part of the year in London, fifty miles away from his large family in Groton, so that he could eke out extra income as a lawyer (until June 1629, when for some unknown reason he found it necessary to quit his job). His wife Margaret, living in not so splendid isolation, with no husband to share the cares of child-raising, was of course politically helpless as she faced a gloomy future.

Added to England's political unrest and economic crisis were two severe outbreaks of the plague. One occurred in 1603, and killed one out of every five people in London alone. Another, only slightly less severe, occurred in 1625. In the 1630s, the time of the great migration, continuing and fatal epidemics struck hard at the areas from which the Puritans departed for the New World: Devon, Dorset, East Anglia, Essex, and Sussex. From the point of view of the wife-mother charged with caring for her family, castastrophe struck when contagious disease felled even one member of the household. Immediately the entire house was quarantined, so that all contact with the outside world was cut off—meaning no way of earning money for necessities, and no means of purchasing or obtaining food. And even when the entire family escaped the plague or serious epidemic, members might suffer from starvation, especially in areas where, during a scourge, markets and fairs were closed to prevent further spread of the disease.

Nor was there safety in the streets. Robbers and murderers prowled about, day and night, preying on children, women, and men in towns, while notorious highwaymen laid low the countryside. In addition, stealing freshly washed laundry, which was usually spread to dry in the yard or hung on the hedges, was so common that the thief had a special name, a "prygman."

So much for some of the hard facts of English society up to the Puritan migration. Records tend to indicate that, unlike the impressed young maidens who went to Virginia, Puritan women were strong-minded, highly intelligent, idealistic individuals. They were nonconformists by personal choice, outside the mainstream of English society. Some remained in England to participate in the civil war, and even succeeded in having women's suffrage proposed, though not implemented. Others set sail for America of their own free will, on the basis of a decision taken jointly with their husbands. And those who migrated tended to be—like any self-selected group embarking on or experimenting with the unknown—above average in intelligence and physical stamina.

Margaret Winthrop was one of these women. Her whole-hearted acceptance of emigration appears over and over again in the voluminous correspondence she carried on with her husband John, the result of their frequent separations. For example, on June 22, 1629—in a letter that implies Margaret's previous agreement to abandon England (either her letter has been lost or the conversation occurred orally on one of his visits home)—John acknowledged: "My comfort is that *thou are willing* to be my companion in what place or condition severe, in weale or in woe." [Italics added.] Later, in her own hand Margaret wrote: "My thoughts are now on our great change and alteration of our course here, which I beseech the Lord to bless us in, and my good husband, cheer up thy heart in the expectation of God's goodness to us, and let nothing dismay or discourage thee; if the Lord be with us who can be against us?"

In the end, pregnancy forced Margaret to remain behind in the care of stepson, John Jr., over a year after her husband's departure. While still in England, impatiently marking time till the birth, she added more evidence pointing to the Puritan wife's making up her own mind. She wrote: "Mr. Wilson [Boston minister] cannot yet persuade his wife to go, for all he hath taken pains to come and fetch her. I marvel what mettle she is made of. Sure she will yield at last."

After the birth of her daughter, Margaret Winthrop urged John Jr. to make arrangements so that she could "go for New England as speedily as I can with any convenience." As for the marvelous Mrs. Wilson, it took four years and two trips back across the ocean to England by her husband before she decided to migrate. On April 1, 1631, Reverend Wilson had gone to England to persuade his wife to join him in New England. She stubbornly refused, agreeing to leave for the New World only after his second trip in 1635.

Another strong-minded Puritan woman had been among the thousand Puritans sailing from England at the end of March 1630. Eighteen-year-old Anne Bradstreet, mixing dismay with determination, wrote that on arrival with her parents and her new husband, "I found a new world and new manners, at which my heart rose. But after *I was convinced* [emphasis supplied] it was the way of God, I submitted to it and joined to the church at Boston."

Lady Arbella Johnson also traveled with the first group of Puritan migrants. In England her home had been a castle at Sherwood Forest; in Massachusetts she lived the one month that remained of her life in a one-room, thatched-roof cabin, leading a contemporary to observe that she had come "from a paradise of plenty and pleasure which she enjoyed in the family of a noble earldom to a wilderness of wants." She had been so strongly Puritan that she participated actively in the Massachusetts Bay Company of which her husband was a member. Both Johnsons gave enthusiasm and money to the venture, making John Winthrop decide to change the name of the lead ship of the fleet from *The Eagle* to *Arbella*. (Isaac Johnson's death followed that of his wife Arbella by one month.)

A fifth early Massachusetts Bay colonist, Anne Hutchinson, arrived in Boston on September 18, 1634, and left behind thousands of words spoken by and about her (as her intense intelligence led her to reinterpret Puritanism in a way that the leaders of the colony found threatening to both church and state). If in other cases the decision to emigrate was made by both husband and wife but by the man first and the woman second, the opposite order was followed by Anne and William Hutchinson. "A woman of ready wit and bold spirit," John Winthrop sneered in the privacy of his journal, where he pitied her husband as "a man of very weak parts and wholly guided by his wife." Indeed, the whole idea of the emigration of Anne and William Hutchinson and thirteen of their children originated in the wife's desire to follow her idol John

Cotton to the New World. He had been minister of the church she attended back in Boston, England, and when he fled the authorities there, she decided to leave, too.

Similarly, Reverend Thomas Shepard, who had been forbidden to preach in England, credited his wife with suggesting the move to the New World. In the course of listing all the reasons for his decision, he wrote: "My dear wife did much long to see me settled there in peace, and so put me on to it."

Still another Puritan woman showed her purposefulness by her very presence in New England. Anne Eliot married her husband John (missionary among the Massachusetts Indians) in October 1632. But what makes her appear more than usually independent in her decision to migrate was that she had become engaged to him the previous year in England, shortly before his departure for America. Then on her own she had sailed for the New World many months later, and became his wife shortly after her arrival.

In contrast, Lucy Winthrop Downing held off leaving with her husband Emmanuel for New England until 1638. She explained earlier in letters to her brother John Winthrop that she had many reservations about living conditions there ("if you were not supplied of incomes from hence your lives would be very miserable") and about the lack of a college where her son George could continue his education. Sounding positively feminist, she remarked at one point: "But now you may say I take too much upon me. I am but a wife and therefore it is sufficient for me to follow my husband; for that let me answer you that what I say to you by way of caveat I have objected to him; that I will not deny, for I thought it my duty."

Also proving the hypothesis about independent-minded Puritan women, there is Elizabeth Poole. She probably was unmarried and came over as a single settler, member of no family, and with no intention of changing her spinster status. She had long taken an interest in American colonization and, in fact, had been a member of the Dorchester Adventurers, who in 1623 had subsidized and sent forth others for the unsuccessful colony at Cape Ann. Sometime after her own arrival in New England, she led a group from Dorchester to Taunton, in Plymouth colony, where she purchased land in 1639 and became the continent's first female "mayor."

The great Puritan migration came to an end in 1641 with the eruption of civil war in old England. New England was no longer needed as a refuge, but the area now boasted twenty thousand colonists and firm roots. Massachusetts had spawned several daughter colonies: Connecticut, Rhode Island, and New Haven (plus four towns in New Hampshire, the nucleus of the future royal colony chartered in 1679). The population ratio became slightly less favorable to women: three males to every two females (instead of three to one as at the very beginning).

In colonies outside New England, women were less numerous but definitely present. They are sometimes bypassed completely, or given less space than their New England sisters, because their literacy rate was far lower, meaning no firsthand records of thoughts and actions for posterity to ponder.

Next door to New England was the Dutch colony of New Netherland, established in 1623 with the first shipment of colonists from Holland sent over by the West India Company. Initially, thirty families had sailed, and by August 19, 1626, contemporary Dutch historian Nicholas Jean de Wassenaer reported a population of "270 souls, including men, women and children." Other evidence of the presence of women as well as men was the 1636 building program of the chief town, New Amsterdam: a church, bakehouse, brick kiln, lime kiln, and houses for the minister and the colony's first midwife, Lysbert Dircken.

Maryland, a refuge for persecuted English Catholics, was settled in March 1634 by 220 men, a few of whom came with their wives. Four years later, in 1638, two unmarried sisters,

Margaret and Mary Brent, as independent as the Puritan women of New England, brought nine settlers across the ocean with them (four women and five men), bought land, and established their own feudal manor. They were joined as owners of large estates by at least three other single or widowed women: Elizabeth Beach, Winifred Seaborne, and Mary Tranton. At the other end of the economic scale, poor women arriving as maidservants increased the number of female colonists. Additional women came when the proprietor of the colony, Cecil Calvert, Lord Baltimore, offered to grant each man who paid his own expenses in migrating to Maryland one hundred acres of land forever, his wife one hundred acres, and each child fifty acres. Moreover, "any woman that shall transport herself or any children, under the age of six years, shall have the like conditions as aforesaid. . . . [And] any woman that shall carry over any women servants, under the age of 40 years, shall have for and in respect of every such woman servant, 50 acres. . . ."

Further south, and almost thirty years later in 1663, Charles II granted a charter for Carolina to eight of his court cronies. The new colony, consisting at first of population overflow from Virginia rather than migration from England, was established for protection against Spanish encroachment. Long before actual settlement, a report to Parliament submitted in 1650 encouraged colonization of "South Virginia" (modern North Carolina), extolling the potential riches of silk production, in which labor "women or children are as proper as men." In the same report the publicist notes that in the labor of clearing the land and growing crops, if a man brings his family, "his wife and children will be able to bear part in that labor, and many others." And to encourage emigration by family, the husband, wife, children, and menservants were to receive one hundred acres each for themselves and heirs forever in return for a modest sum. Woman servants and slaves would receive fifty acres. In 1666, three years after the charter had been granted, another publicist appealed for women as well as men colonists, writing on behalf of the Lords Proprietor of the colony in England: "If any maid or single woman have a desire to go over, they will think themselves in the Golden Age, when men paid a dowry for their wives; for if they be but civil and under fifty years of age, some honest man or other will purchase them for their wives."

South Carolina became a separate settlement in 1670, and two years later listed 268 men as able to bear arms, and 69 adult women. Using a similar but less generous system to encourage immigration by family, South Carolina granted fifty acres to each member of the family, man, woman, and child. And indentured servants "whether man or woman" were to receive fifty acres of land free of rent for ten years after completing their period of service to the master.

Sometimes called super-Puritans, the Quakers founded two colonies, New Jersey in 1677 and Pennsylvania in 1682. In addition, they eventually controlled Delaware, which England had captured from the Dutch in 1664 along with New Netherland. Like the Puritans they encouraged colonization by family. In a tract written one year before founding Pennsylvania, William Penn, still recruiting in London, noted: "Such as could not only not marry here, but hardly live and allow themselves clothes, do marry there and bestow thrice more in all necessaries and conveniences (and not a little in ornamental things too) for themselves, their wives, and children, both as to apparel and household stuff."

The last of the thirteen colonies, Georgia, settled in 1732, appealed for settlement to England's poorer, debt-ridden classes. According to the official narrative of Georgia settlement, published in 1741, leader of the colony James Ogelthorpe arrived with "114 persons, men, women and children . . . in decayed circumstances and thereby disabled from following any business in England." But back in London the men who called themselves the Trustees of Georgia were ambivalent about enticing women to the colony. They desperately needed the strength and stability of family settlement for protection against Spain at the border in Florida and against local Indians. On the other hand, they liked the feudal system of land grants to men only because this provided them with a good supply of soldiers. In any case, the official population figures published at the end of the first eight years of settlement on June 9, 1740, revealed a total of 1,521, specifically including 687 men. By deduction, therefore, there were 834 others, some of whom, based on Ogelthorpe's frequent references to families in his reports, had to be women.

Of course, the arrival of English colonists and their success in establishing strong, stable settlements had by no means signaled the end of Spanish and French efforts to colonize North America. Spain remained an active colonizer of North America until the early nineteenth century. She held fast to sixteenth-century settlements in Florida and New Mexico, colonized Texas in the seventeenth century, and in the eighteenth century planted modern California. However, she placed major emphasis on maintaining strongholds in Mexico, the Caribbean, and South America.

France, the other major European power in North America, founded New France in modern-day Quebec, Canada, in 1608. Most French immigrants were unmarried peasants or soldiers whose wives were subsequently supplied to them from northwestern French villages, slums, and foundling asylums. Even so, population growth was slow, as many returned to France.

The French government had somewhat more success when it gave bounties of three hundred *livres* per year for living families of ten and four hundred *livres* for families of twelve or more. Families of six to ten children became common, and there were frequently larger ones, despite the high infant mortality rate. In addition, France bestowed dowries of twenty *livres* on girls who married before sixteen and on boys who married before twenty.

Far away in the Gulf of Mexico region, Frenchmen also established colonies, in this case to keep out both Spain and England. In 1704 a colony was started near present-day Mobile, Alabama, with a population of 101: 75 soldiers, a priest, and 2 Grey Nuns chaperoning 23 girls sent over as wives and breeders.

By the 1720s the colony was larger and needed women. So eighty women from Paris houses of correction came to New Orleans with three accompanying nuns. Older settlers bitterly criticized the arrival of these female refugees from prison, so in 1728 the famous casket girls, *filles à la cassette* (their caskets or trunks full of clothing and linens for the new home) began arriving, twenty-three in the first shipment, and a constant trickle periodically until 1751. Subsequently in Louisiana, it was a matter of pride to be descended from the casket girls, so much so that the prison girls seem to have left no descendants.

The largely random arrivals of non-English women and men—Germans, Irish, Italians, Jews, Scandinavians, and Scots —made little impact. These settlers were few in number and too widely scattered to dislodge the language and customs England so indelibly imprinted on the Atlantic coast. And as for the estimated five hundred thousand blacks (one-third female) in the thirteen colonies by 1776, though they were second in number to the English, they were almost always slaves, with all that that implied and denied in rights, status, and influence. They were first brought to Virginia, where in 1625 there were twelve men and eleven women slaves, and to New Netherland, where there were four males in 1625 or 1626, joined by three females in 1628.

As time went on, all thirteen Atlantic colonies achieved permanence. And from arrival to survival to ultimate independence, women made the decisive difference—as they assumed many roles and responsibilities unknown back home in England.

# CHAPTER TWO

# *Home and Hearth*

The moment women boarded ship for the New World they left marital servitude behind. New England officials frowned on the old European practice of wife-beating—unless the wife struck the husband first. And in Virginia men were limited to using a stick no bigger than the thumb to inflict wifely punishment, and then only if they could prove justifiable provocation.

In contrast, Europe had a long tradition of subordinating women. A thirteenth-century Dominican, Nicholas Byard, reflected the thinking of his time: "A man may chastise his wife and beat her for correction, for she is of his household, therefore the lord may chastise his own." And canon law proclaimed: "It is plain that wives should be subject to their husbands and should almost be servants."

America had no cities, no feudalism assigning everyone to a particular place, and, completely unlike England, no aristocracy handing down orders from above. Instead, the recurring need for women to make on-the-spot decisions about life or death in wild, danger-infested lands led to a complete sharing of responsibility between early colonial husbands and wives— and a respect, enforced when necessary by the law. Thus in March 1682 the Essex, Massachusetts, court fined Daniel Ola forty shillings for telling his wife, according to the neighbors: "She was none of his wife, she was but his servant."

Some of the communal spirit that bred such regulation comes through in the writing of Edward Johnson, New England's ebullient eyewitness historian. He described several Puritan men, "their wives and little ones," who in 1635 trekked the nineteen miles inland from Boston to purchase land from the Indians and to found Concord:

> With many difficulties, traveling through unknown woods and through watery swamps, they discover the fitness of the place, sometimes passing through the thickets, where their hands are forced to make way for their bodies' passage, and their feet clambering over the crossed trees, which when they missed they sunk into an uncertain bottom in water, and wade up to the knees, tumbling sometimes higher and sometimes lower. Wearied with this toil, they at the end of this, meet with a scorching plain, yet not so plain but that the ragged bushes scratch their legs foully, even to wearing their stockings to their bare skin in two or three hours. If they be not otherwise well defended with boots or buskins their flesh will be torn . . . [and] the blood trickle down at every step . . . and this not to be endured for one day but for many.

Neither occasional nightlong rains nor driving snow could stop them, he concluded, and when they located suitable areas for building homes they would construct temporary shelters consisting of earth thrown over timber.

All along the Atlantic coast, each section had drawbacks and compensations. For example, though the climate made life difficult in the North, the threat of hostile Indians was minimal there compared to Virginia, where natives frequently massacred whole settlements of Europeans. A plague epidemic in 1616–1617, three years before the arrival of the Pilgrims, had reduced the native population in Massachusetts from perhaps as many as thirty thousand to around seven thousand, according to contemporary reports. Thus the North had a further advantage at the fatal expense of the natives—large areas of abandoned land, long cleared for agriculture and hunting by the Indians, and available just for the taking.

On just such land the Puritans who arrived in Salem built themselves a whole village of one-room shelters. Men constructed the fireplace—indispensable for heat and cooking—almost outside one end of the wigwam, using fieldstones set in mortar of "fish-shell lime," a substitute for the conventional and essential lime. Women made this lime substitute by pounding clam and oyster shells to powder.

Homelife was the special province and responsibility of women. Early permanent homes, both North and South, con-

Authentic reconstruction of a Salem house, c. 1630. Photographed at Pioneer Village, Salem, Massachusetts. *Courtesy of the Board of Park Commissioners, Salem, Mass.*

sisted of one tiny main room called the hall, where the whole family lived, loved, and worked on indoor, as opposed to outdoor, tasks—with no privacy. The hall served as the kitchen, dining room, and sleeping and storage area. And the low ceiling, and one or two windows covered with oiled paper, made the interior generally gloomy. Happily, some relief came with the light and warmth of spring and summer, which created a different emotional climate and the possibility of working outdoors to a greater extent.

With progress and prosperity, houses increased to two still very small rooms on either side of the chimney. Still later, lean-tos would be added to the rear of the house, making three additional rooms on the ground floor surrounding the central kitchen. The earlier kitchen—or hall—would then become that almost unheard of luxury, a living or sitting room, equipped with furniture reserved to wealthy European classes: wooden chairs and tables.[1] However, exactly as in England, the most valued piece of furniture, the bed, would be prominently displayed in every room, with the possible exception of the kitchen.

In the north, Plymouth experience and helpfulness made life considerably easier in the Massachusetts Bay colony. Furthermore, the new Puritan colonists brought over wealth in the form of supplies, and had access to money back in England from Puritans anxious to establish a personal escape hatch in the New World should the king carry out his worst threats against them. Thus it comes as no surprise that the Boston house of Governor John Winthrop and his wife Margaret in the mid 1630s had six small rooms with lofts and garrets. (The house stood until the Revolution when British soldiers tore it down to burn for firewood.)

---

[1] At first, chairs were such a rarity that only the head of the household could expect to be seated in one when dining at the table, or board. Hence the expression "chairman of the board."

Another glimpse into the lives of early Puritans comes from the will of John Dillingham. He had arrived with the Winthrop fleet in Boston in 1630, together with his wife and daughter, but by November 1634 he petitioned for and was granted a large tract of land in Ipswich, thirty miles out, to build his home. He died during the winter of 1635, and his wife succumbed almost eighteen months later in July 1636.

The will describes the house as having two rooms and numerous outbuildings, situated on huge acreage planted with corn and filled with thriving apple and other fruit trees. Live-stock consisted of four calves, three cows, two heifers, a mare, four pigs, and two steers. There were two indentured servants —Thomas Downs, who helped care for the stock and cultivate the land, and Ann Towle, who assisted Mrs. Dillingham in housework and also worked in the fields.

The house was small and simple, with the parlor or sitting room also used as bedroom, following common seventeenth-century practice. Furniture included two bedsteads (the word *bed* originally referred to the mattress only, placed directly on the floor), one cupboard, two chairs, a desk, and a round table. For sleeping comfort there were feather mattresses, bolsters, pillows, and coverlets, as well as flaxen sheets for Mrs. Dillingham and coarse sheets for the indentured servants. The warming pan is wordless testimony to winter temperature and ice-cold beds. During the day it hung by the kitchen fireplace. At bedtime it was filled with hot coals and, in a tricky proce-dure, used to warm the upper sheet, moving the pan quickly back and forth over the material to produce heat while avoid-ing burning.[2]

---

[2] At the end of the eighteenth century, diarists were still com-menting on freezing cold bedrooms where the pitcher or bucket of water to be poured into the basin on a table beside the bed for washing hands and face would seldom flow freely on a winter morning. First the ice on the top had to be broken, and even then the water would be icy enough to provide a rude awakening.

There is no mention in the Dillingham will of an upper floor. Two-story living was all but impossible on a year-round basis in the North, where the additional labor required to keep a second fire going upstairs, for about six or seven months, was too time-consuming and expensive. And with no companion fireplaces active in surrounding rooms, the single fire provided little winter warmth. Sap forced out of burning wood would turn to ice at the edges of logs, and the main hall would be warm only within three feet of the fireplace.

Nevertheless, maintaining a fire in just this main room was a twenty-four-hour task—and the logs were sometimes so huge that a horse and long chain had to be used for dragging them in. Each night the housewife herself, or her helper, had to cover very carefully with ashes any remaining fire to keep it alive till morning for rekindling. During the day she had to make sure of enough flame to last through the night. At times when the fire failed, someone, usually a small boy, had to take a fire pan or shovel to a neighbor and actually borrow some fire in the form of burning coals.

Frontier families who lived in isolated areas, with no neighbors, had to resort to use of a tinderbox, filled with tinder made of scorched linen obtained from worn-out handkerchiefs, underwear, or bed sheets. The tinder was ignited by a spark struck by rubbing together flint and steel.

Once started, the fire too often went out of control. Fireplaces had highly inflammable "catted" chimneys, consisting of logs plastered with clay inside and out. In addition, chimney sparks easily set fire to the ubiquitous thatched roof, frequently burning the entire house to the ground—and with it all possessions, memories, and deep family roots. This happened to poet Anne Bradstreet on July 10, 1660, when her Andover home of twenty years was completely incinerated.

> *When by the ruins oft I past*
> *My sorrowing eyes aside did cast,*

*And here and there the places spy*
*Where oft I sat and long did lie:*
*Here stood that trunk, and there that chest,*
*There lay that store I counted best.*
*My pleasant things in ashes lie,*
*And them behold no more shall I.*
*Under thy roof no guest shall sit,*
*Nor at thy table eat a bit.*
*No pleasant tale shall e'er be told,*
*Nor things recounted done of old.*
*No candle e'er shall shine in thee,*
*Nor bridegroom's voice e'er heard shall be.*
*In silence ever shall thou lie,*
*Adieu, Adieu, All's vanity.*

Fortunately, brick soon supplanted wood as material for making chimneys, though thatched roofs remained, replaced only when fire struck. Toward the end of the seventeenth century towns began passing laws forbidding construction with wooden chimneys and thatched roofs.

But in the early days the success of transplanting English life to the New World was far from certain. Amongst other difficulties, European newcomers, torn between maintaining their Old World culture and insuring sheer survival in America, were forced to imitate the creature habits of Indians while disdaining what they considered to be a pagan society. Anne Bradstreet's poetic epitaph for her mother, Mrs. Dorothy Dudley, who died at age sixty-one on December 27, 1643, gives an indication of what was considered the proper role for the early New England woman. Socially prominent as the wife of Thomas Dudley, permanent magistrate and sometime governor of Massachusetts Bay, Dorothy Dudley's life can be taken as the purely English ideal to which others should aspire:

*A worthy matron of unspotted life,*
*A loving mother and obedient wife,*
*A friendly neighbor, pitiful to poor,*
*Whom oft she fed, and clothed with her store;*
*To servants wisely awful, but yet kind,*
*And as they did, so their reward did find:*
*A true instructor of her family,*
*The which she ordered with dexterity.*
*The public meetings ever did frequent,*
*And in her closet constant hours she spent;*
*Religious in all her words and ways,*
*Preparing still for death, till end of days;*
*Of all her children, children, lived to see,*
*Then dying, left a blessed memory.*

Yet there had been no way for white women to avoid almost total dependence on their Indian sisters in learning to feed their families. At the outset, Indian women had demonstrated how to vary a diet of mere subsistence with a degree of sophistication. As a result, women colonists were soon baking beans in earthen dishes buried among the hot ashes and making sugar—in the form of bars, not granules—from maple tree sap. Like the natives, they pounded corn in a hollow stone to produce cornmeal, mixing grain with water and using a flat stone on which to bake a cake before the fire. The famous hoecake was an improvisation of the original Indian method. Early settlers used a mortar and pestle on the grain, and then baked the dough on the broad blade of a shovel or hoe.

For dessert, native women contributed one of the world's culinary delights, Indian pudding. This consisted of cornmeal, milk scalded in an iron kettle, molasses, and such spices as cinnamon or ginger. Ingredients were beaten smooth, poured into a stone pudding dish, and baked all night in a brick oven.

With his usual enthusiasm, Edward Johnson described

Puritan women using the Indian method of gathering food. He succeeded in finding Puritan virtue everywhere, and in this particular instance mixed pathos, high drama, and near starvation to write what should someday be produced as a great morality play. (Sense and words could be left unchanged, though slight editing would be needed: capital letters, frequent paragraphing, and two stage directions added):

[SETTING]: The women once a day, as the tide gave way, resorted to the mussels and clambanks, which are a fish as big as horsemussels, where they daily gathered their families' food with much heavenly discourse of the provisions Christ had formerly made for many thousands of his followers in the wilderness.

QUOTH ONE: "My husband hath traveled as far as Plymouth" [which is near forty miles] "and hath with great toil brought a little corn home with him, and before that is spent the Lord will assuredly provide."

QUOTH THE OTHER: "Our last peck of meal is now in the oven at home a-baking and many of our godly neighbors have quite spent all, and we owe one loaf of that little we have."

THEN SPAKE A THIRD: "My husband hath ventured himself among the Indians for corn, and can get none, as also our honored governor hath distributed his so far, that a day or two more will put an end to his store, and all the rest, and yet methinks our children are as cheerful, fat and lusty with feeding upon those mussels, clambanks, and other fish as they were in England, with their fill of bread, which makes me cheerful in the Lord's providing for us, being further confirmed by the exhortation of our pastor to trust the Lord with providing for us whose is the earth and the fulness thereof."

[THE HAPPY, MORAL ENDING]: And as they were encouraging one another in Christ's careful providing for them, they lifted up their eyes and saw two ships coming in, and presently this news came to their ears that they were come from Ireland full of victuals. Now their poor hearts were not so much refreshed in regard of the food they saw they were like to have, as their souls rejoiced in that Christ would now manifest himself to be the commissary general of this his army, and that he should honor them so far as to be poor sutlers for his camp. They soon up with their mussels and hied them home to stay their hungry stomachs.

Before too long, the average colonial diet consisted of boiled meats or fish, cornmeal, vegetables, and stews—with baked or stewed beans several times a week. Water, milk, and beer were the usual beverages. Tea was prohibitively expensive, even in England, and coffee was just appearing on the

Early colonists ate the same food, and in the same manner, as the natives. An engraving from a watercolor by John White, 1587. *Courtesy of the Fogg Art Museum, Bequest of Francis Calley Gray.*

world market. In this connection, prices of food in seventeenth-century Boston, while not identical with those in all early colonial towns, were at least in the same general range: butter, six cents, and cheese, five cents per pound; eggs, three cents a dozen; and milk, one cent per quart.

Cooking, which was exclusively woman's work, involved a great deal of heavy lifting and reaching in the use of massive cauldrons and pots (often weighing forty pounds each) and kettles (containing as much as fifteen gallons), mortars and pestles to pound corn and other foods, and utensils for moving meat and bread in and out of the oven. In addition, the housewife had to carry or push into a working position the butter churns and salt barrels, which were usually left in an out-of-the-way space in the hall. All cooking equipment was extremely expensive—kettles often cost three pounds each—and was sturdy enough to last several generations.

All women followed the same cooking methods, no matter the size or location of their houses. The brick oven, which was part of every chimney, opened into the kitchen fireplace. The wife would reach it by stooping below the oaken lintel and actually standing inside the fireplace, all the while watching that the flames remained a good distance from her woolen skirt. To preheat the oven for use in baking she would build a fire inside, using specially seasoned birch or pine wood kept in the house to insure dryness. When she was ready to bake, she raked the fire out and put her brown bread, Indian pudding, peas, pies, and rye drop cakes directly on the hot bricks at the bottom of the oven. Ingredients used included eggs, milk, cornmeal, and rye meal. Most women did their baking only on Saturday. An oven heated daily was a good indication that the family was wealthy.

Dining was one step above the habits of forest animals. The main dish used for eating was a plain wooden trencher, ten to twelve inches square by three to four inches deep—from which two people, husband and wife, or children, ate sitting side by side. There were no individual drinking cups. Instead, family and guests all used the same tankard. Fingers were used as often as knives and spoons of tin or pewter, and even at the end of the seventeenth century only a rare and wealthy family owned as much as a single fork. At most, the family ate two meals a day, breakfast early in the morning and the main meal in the middle of the afternoon. (This was still true at the end of the eighteenth century. A letter from Abigail Adams to her sister on May 24, 1797, casually describes her regular routine of rising at 5:00 A.M., breakfasting at 8:00 A.M., dining at 3:00 P.M., and then retiring for the night after several more hours of varied activities.)

Other housewifely responsibilities included distilling herbs, laundering, dyeing cloths and yarns, cleaning wooden and iron utensils, braiding mats or rushes, sweeping and sanding floors, weaving, sewing, and spinning. With no umbrellas or boots to protect clothes and shoes, the mother dried storm-soaked footwear by placing hot oats inside them, and put wet clothes on glowing logs. The children she cared for and taught were her own offspring, children from her or her husband's previous marriages, orphaned relatives, and/or apprentices.

All of these tasks were quite familiar back in England. The colonial housewife's one minor but distinct advantage over English homemakers would have been wooden floors instead of the dirt floors common in the mother country. And eventually the plentiful timber found everywhere made life more comfortable, as men built additional furniture and roomier houses.

The difficulty of making soap and its harsh quality go far to explain the personal filth and frequent illness so often cited in accounts of life in the seventeenth century. Soap was a mixture of animal fat and lye, which women boiled together in a huge kettle for many hours—after first making the lye themselves by pouring water over a hopper filled with ashes from various hardwoods. The water would then drip through an opening into the small wooden pail below, finally producing lye strong enough to pass the test of floating an egg. Six bushels of ashes were needed to make enough lye for a barrel of soap. Strong-acting, though quite soft in texture, such soap was used mainly for washing clothes, almost never for bathing.

Similarly, clean teeth were for the future. Toothbrushes, tooth powder and paste were unknown—though eventually wooden false teeth were present in many upper-class mouths.

In general, provisioning an early colonial household was one long labor of improvisation using local resources—first following the lead of the Indians and then later coming up with original solutions. For example, in all colonies women boiled down locally grown bayberries to make wax they could use for tallow. As a matter of fact, for 150 years they supplemented imports of English tallow by gathering vast quantities of bayberries from which they could extract wax. They hardened this wax into pale green candles, whose flame gave forth a spicy fragrance. Also, from the plentiful milkweed they gathered a silvery down, which they substituted for English feathers in stuffing pillows. Mattresses were made of pieces of scraps of wool, and poorer wives substituted cattails, tall-stemmed plants with long leaves found growing wild in the marshes. For maintaining health, they learned from the Indians to grow herbs that would cure minor illness and make major sickness bearable.

Homemade clothing replaced imported garments even in well-to-do households during England's civil war and the Cromwellian Interregnum from 1640 to 1660. Again labor was divided and shared, with men shearing, washing, and further preparing farm-raised wool, and women spinning and weaving the flax and wool, which would be used in making family clothes. Aiming directly at women, the Massachusetts General Court passed a compulsory spinning law in 1656, complete with weekly quotas of cotton, linen, or woolen yarn, and a hefty fine for not meeting the assessed quota.

The clothing produced for Sunday was slightly more ornate than that worn on weekdays. Sometimes ruffles appeared at the neck and wrists, though the color was generally black. On weekdays clothes tended to be ragged in appearance, but with an occasional outburst of color. Shoes were commonly made of leather, and frequently women wore clogs, a kind of Dutch half-slipper, which they used over their shoes for protection against mud. Plymouth and Massachusetts Bay women never wore wedding rings, reflecting strong Puritan disapproval of jewelry.

Life in the colonies south of New England showed similarities amid distinctly individual differences. Virginia, first settled in 1607, finally became stabilized in 1625, with most colonists living in small farming communities along the James River, plus one salt-making and fishing outpost on the eastern shore. By March 1628 the population was three thousand, and the Indians had been pushed further into the wilderness and their fields appropriated.

Far removed from the picture of the gracious plantation lady, the first generation of Virginia women were too stricken with disease, poverty, and Indian massacres to dress ornately. Proportionately, Virginia had just a few more members of the gentry than did New England at the beginning.

The second generation brought increased wealth and so more spacious and comfortable homes to some Virginia settlers. In 1656, John Hammond, back in London, described himself as having been a resident for nineteen years in Virginia and two years in Maryland. In a promotional pamphlet, *Leah and Rachel,* he wrote that in 1650 the homes were "pleasant in their building, which although for most part they are but one story besides the loft and built of wood, yet contrived so delightful that your ordinary houses in England are not so handsome for usually the rooms are large, daubed, and whitelimed, glazed and flowered, and if not glazed windows, shutters which are made very pretty and convenient." (Nowhere in the colonies were there movable shades. Shutters were the substitute for providing privacy.)

For women he had special words of encouragement: "The women are not (as is reported) put into the ground to work, but occupy such domestic employments and housewifery as in England, that is, dressing victuals, righting up the house, milking, employed about dairies, washing, sewing, etc., and both men and women have times of recreations, as much or more than in any part of the world besides. . . ." And for those women willing to pay their own way across the ocean in hopes of marrying well, he advised that they should "sojourn in a house of honest repute, for by their good carriage, they may advance themselves in marriage, by their ill, overthrow their fortunes; and although loose persons seldom live long unmarried if free, yet they match with as desolate as themselves and never live handsomely or are ever respected."

The warmer climate of Maryland and Virginia, compared to New England, made winter less formidable, but houses had fewer fireplaces, and so cold snaps spelled trouble. Another difference for women in Southern colonies was the relatively great distance between houses compared to the North, where people gathered in towns built around church meetinghouses. As a result women were cut off from relatives, or in fact from any human contact outside the immediate family. To visit as close as three miles away, a woman would have to get a horse from pasture, form some kind of halter, ride bareback, and somehow cross or swim a river bounding the property. There were few roads during the first few generations, and bad weather often made even well-worn paths impassable. (Carriage travel developed much later, well into the eighteenth century.)

The Dutch women of New Netherland in the 1620s and 1630s worked alongside their husbands building log huts thatched with straw. They also cultivated grain, harvested crops, and quickly learned to use a rifle against attacking animals or Indians. This was the setting for the birth of the colony's first female child, Sarah Rapaelje, daughter of Joris Jansen Rapaelje, who was probably a French-speaking Walloon, and his wife, a Parisian, Catalina Trico, who had sailed with the first group of immigrants on the ship *New Netherland.* When young Sarah reached womanhood she petitioned for a grant of land describing herself as "the first-born Christian daughter in New Netherland." (A boy, Jan Vinje, son of Walloon parents, Guleyn Vinje and Adrienne Cuville, was the first white child born in the colony.)

Catalina Trico, who could not sign her name on the birth register—she and her husband both used an X at the proper spot—had her brief moment in history's spotlight some sixty years after her arrival. Her deposition, taken to settle the future of counties on the Delaware River claimed by New York, Pennsylvania, and Maryland, serves as an excellent description of the first settlement by Dutch families. She recalled:

> As soon as they came to Manhattan now called New York they sent two families and six men to Hartford River, two families and eight men to Delaware River, and eight men they left at New York to take possession, and the rest of the passengers went with the ship up as far as Albany which they then called Fort Orange. When as the ship came as far as Sopus which is halfway to Albany, they lightened the ship with some boats that were left there by the Dutch that had been there the year before trading with the Indians upon their own accounts and gone back again to Holland and so brought the vessel up. There were about eighteen families aboard who settled themselves at Albany and made a small fort. . . .

Jaspar Danckers, sent over by Holland in 1679–1680 to find a place to plant a colony in the New York area (England had conquered the Dutch New Netherland in 1664 and ruled it as New York) described Catalina Trico, then eighty-three: "She is wordly-minded, living with her whole heart as well as body among her progeny, which now number 145 and will soon reach 150. Nevertheless, she lived alone by herself, a little apart from the others, having her little garden and other conveniences, with which she helped herself."

In a very real sense later colonies profited from the experiences of New Englanders and Virginians in eking out survival. Thus William Penn, who in 1681 had never visited the New World but planned to lead a colony there the following year, wrote in a tract recruiting familes: "America is another thing than it was at the first plantation of Virginia and New England. For there is better accommodation and English provisions are to be had at easier rates."

Yet, women who went far away to frontier settlements found life no easier in the 1680s than had their sisters in the 1620s and 1630s, as the story of the strong-minded Huguenot Judith Giton illustrates. She had escaped from France with friends, leaving all her possessions behind. After a brutal, nine-month voyage she arrived in South Carolina in 1685, married a fellow Huguenot, weaver Noe Royer, and worked side by side with him clearing the land. Almost starved for lack of food, she bemoaned in a letter to her brother: "Everything went wrong. Our elder brother died of the fever. We bore every kind of affliction, illness, plague, hunger, poverty, and hard work. I have had no bread to eat for six months and have tilled the soil like a slave. . . ."

Her husband soon died, and she married another Huguenot refugee, Pierre Manigault. And then life took a turn for the better. Her husband had escaped from France with enough money to purchase a house. Judith took in boarders while Pierre ran a distillery and cooperage. And somehow their joint earnings resulted in enough money to form the basis of a large fortune passed on to their son Gabriel and his heirs.

This is a happy ending to a hard life—the kind of story that glorified America as the land of opportunity. But for many others, forced into servitude or slavery, the New World proved to be the scene of perpetual torment.

# CHAPTER THREE

# White Servants,
# Black Slaves

Many came to America reluctantly, others unwillingly. In fact, south of New England, most colonial immigrants were servants and slaves. And at least one-third of both groups was female.

The servants, white, arrived first, and in another of history's accidents—no conscious design, no grand plan—paved the way for instituting black slavery. The long horror story began with servant-workers imported to provide the principal supply of labor from New York south to South Carolina. In the seventeenth century they accounted for around three out of every five immigrants in these colonies.

The thought of leaving Europe for the New World never seemed to originate with the servants. Quite the contrary. Slippery slick agents, acting on behalf of profit-mad shipowners or merchants, would use every imaginable trick or promise to herd the largest possible human cargo aboard ship, or, even worse, would resort to outright kidnapping. Still others marked for service would be literally hurled out of overcrowded prisons all the way across the Atlantic.

In return for ocean transportation, food, shelter, and clothing, servants were indentured for periods of from four to fourteen years. During this time they were forbidden to marry without the master's consent, or to earn extra money during spare time, or to vote. Also, they were considered the private property of their owner. After completing the agreed service, they were to receive awards in the form of money or land, as well as freedom.

A popular ballad in seventeenth-century England sang of the miseries of a female indentured servant who was trappanned, or tricked, into going to America:

THE TRAPPAN'D MAIDEN:
OR, THE DISTRESSED DAMSEL

This girl was cunningly trappan'd, sent to Virginny from
    England,
Where she doth hardship undergo, there is no cure it
    must be so:
But if she lives to cross the main, she vows she'll ne'er
    go there again.


(Tune of Virginny, or, *When that I was weary, weary, O.*)

Give ear unto a maid, that lately was betray'd,
    And sent into Virginny, O:
In brief I shall declare, what I have suffer'd there,
    *When that I was weary, weary, weary, weary, O.*

.  .  .  .  .  .  .  .  .  .  .  .  .  .  .  .  .

Five years served I, under Master Guy,
    In the land of Virginny, O,
Which made me for to know sorrow, grief and woe,
    *When that I was weary, weary, weary, weary, O.*

When my Dame says "Go" Then I must do so,
    In the land of Virginny, O;
When she sits at meat, then I have none to eat,
    *When that I am weary, weary, weary, weary, O.*

The clothes that I brought in, they are worn very thin,
    In the land of Virginny, O,
Which makes me for to say, "Alas, and well-a-day!"
    *When that I am weary, weary, weary, weary, O.*

.  .  .  .  .  .  .  .  .  .  .  .

So soon as it is day, to work I must away,
    In the land of Virginny, O;
Then my dame she knocks, with her tinder-box,
    *When that I am weary, weary, weary, weary, O.*

I have play'd my part both at plow and cart,
    In the land of Virginny, O;
Billets from the wood upon my back they load,
    *When that I am weary, weary, weary, weary, O.*

.  .  .  .  .  .  .  .  .  .  .  .

If my dame says "Go!" I dare not say no
    In the land of Virginny, O;
The water from the spring, upon my head I bring,
    *When that I am weary, weary, weary, weary, O.*

When the mill doth stand, I'm ready at command,
    In the land of Virginny, O;
The mortar for to make, which makes my heart to ache,
    *When that I am weary, weary, weary, weary, O.*

.  .  .  .  .  .  .  .  .  .  .  .

A thousand woes beside, that I do here abide,
    In the land of Virginny, O;
In misery I spend my time that hath no end,
    *When that I am weary, weary, weary, weary, O.*

Then let maids beware, all by my ill-fare,
    In the land of Virginny, O;

Be sure to stay at home, for if you do here come,
    *You all will be weary, weary, weary, weary, O.*

But if it be my chance, homewards to advance,
    from the land of Virginny, O;
If that I, once more, land on English shore,
    *I'll no more be weary, weary, weary, weary, O.*

A profit-making institution, pure and simple, indentured servitude gave consideration to all parties involved—the shipowners, the middleman, the master purchasing the contract—with the notable exception of the servants themselves. Servants never negotiated their own indenture contracts which, cutting out the middleman, could have been done by incurring a minimal debt to be worked off on arrival. And the contract invariably was set at a much higher figure than would have been required simply to repay the cost of ocean passage.

Most voyages took twelve weeks, and toward the end meat spoiled, water stank, and butter turned rancid. Provisions were sometimes long on quantity but so short on quality that they had to be dumped overboard for sanitary reasons. And sometimes captains would make extra profits by starving passengers in direct contradiction to requirements of the signed contract. Even when food was adequate and sleeping space provided, there were still the insoluble problems of storms, wind, and merciless sun—combined with the inevitable seasickness for which there was no preventive medicine. Close quarters also meant the easy spread of fatal diseases such as dysentery, smallpox, typhus, or yellow fever. Vinegar was commonly used to sweeten the ship, but the problem of lack of ventilation compounded by the stench of human waste remained.

As the ship neared port, passengers were ordered to wash faces, clean clothes as best as possible, and tidy the hair. On arrival in America, the human cargo would be displayed, inspected, picked over, and sold to the highest bidder. Thus immigration became a regular routine of trade and commerce, with profits to be made by shipowners who carried servants and by plantation owners who had a continuing source of cheap labor. In the process the way was prepared for handling even more crudely and cruelly the class of laborers who would come to replace white indentured servants—perpetual black slaves. Prospective buyers came aboard, pawed bodies from head to toe, ordered prospective servants to walk and to talk in order to judge physical stamina, morality, intelligence, and submissiveness.

Indentured servitude was a New World phenomenon with Old World roots. The practice was a refinement of apprenticeship—which had evolved in answer to the burgeoning industrialization of the seventeenth century—superimposed on feudal bondage, all but obsolete in England by 1550. In Europe an apprentice would be bound by legal contract to work without wages, during a set period, for a master who would teach an art or trade.

The fading of the old medieval order in England had a direct effect on the supply of labor available for shipment to the New World. The transition from feudalism to commerce to industry undermined the pillars of tradition in the mother country and created thousands of rootless vagabonds and people living with starvation and without hope. Significant numbers of the poor were turned away from manorial occupations and set adrift in a society that had no particular place for or concern about them. Some 250,000—including more than 80,000 females—migrated to America as indentured servants.

In addition to contributing much in the way of field labor and domestic service, female servants frequently became the wives or mistresses of woman-starved settlers. Perhaps the most famous example is the maternal grandmother of Benjamin Franklin, Mary Morrils, an indentured maidservant whom Peter Folger purchased for twenty pounds and later married.

The overall situation in the colonies regarding indentured servitude reflected deep differences between various regions. New England needed labor desperately but refused to import many servants.[1] Indentured servants had accompanied the Puritans during the period of the great migration in the 1630s, but after 1645 their numbers were negligible. Authorities preferred to keep qualifications high for land ownership (meaning that there could be no easy award of property on completion of indenture), and expansion was tightly controlled. Very early in the colonial period, New Englanders began selling their services for regular wages in the rapidly developing business economy. In contrast, land was granted much more freely in order to extend settled areas as quickly as possible from New York southward. And the tobacco-growing South set up the greatest demand of all for indentured servants, especially those with the skill necessary to produce the all-important cash crop.

Statistics, though scattered, seem to bear out these generalizations. For example, in the years between 1654 and 1786, when New England received 143 men and 22 women as indentured servants, Virginia imported 3,718 men and 1,206 women. In the years between 1718 and 1759 when New England took in a total of 17 indentured servants, the southern colonies received at least 1,225, or perhaps more, since some records indicate uncertain destinations, such as "New York or Carolina, 4," "Maryland or Pennsylvania, 40."

The quality of indentured servants varied, but as one might expect, most probably did no more than necessary. Mary Dudley, daughter of one Massachusetts Bay governor, John

[1] However, the typical family included several single adult women, who, not having yet achieved honorable refuge in marriage, remained with the family as virtual servants. All too often they were unwanted in a crowded household, but were kept on and supported financially out of moral obligation and colonial custom. They were then expected to contribute free labor—making clothes, for example.

Winthrop, and daughter-in-law of another, Thomas Dudley, in a letter to her mother grumbled about encountering "great affliction" from her maidservant:

> If I bid her do a thing she will bid me to do it myself, and she says how she can give content as well as any servant but she will not. . . . If I should write to you all the reviling speeches and filthy language she hath used towards me I should but grieve you.

Usually, males were bound as servants till the age of twenty-one, females till sixteen, eighteen, or sometimes till marriage, for which only the master could grant permission. The earliest law found on the subject is a Maryland statute of 1639 decreeing that males over eighteen were to serve for four years, under eighteen till reaching the age of twenty-four. Females over twelve would be bound for four years, under age twelve for seven years. The law was supplemented in 1654 by a requirement that servants under eighteen be registered at a court and in case of vagueness as to age the magistrates would decide.

Abbot Smith, author of the classic study, *Colonists in Bondage,* cites the case of one maidservant, Catherine Douglas of Lancaster, Virginia, who took her master to court in 1700 for trying to hold her to seven years' service instead of freeing her at the end of four. The master, Mottrom Wright, produced an assignment from one John Gilchrist, selling her for a seven-year period. Catherine Douglas argued through her attorney that she had had a four-year indenture contract, but that the documents had been destroyed without consent of the court. Three witnesses testified on her behalf, swearing that they had seen the contract and that she was telling the truth about the requirement of four years only. The court took jurisdiction in her case, found in her favor, and ordered her freed immediately. This kind of case shows a definite intention on the part of colonial courts to attain justice without regard to the servant's menial status. However, the courts were only partially effective in prohibiting masters from using cruelty or providing poor subsistence—because not all such cases reached the courts, and because an ignorant, inarticulate servant was less able to communicate with educated magistrates than would be masters, who were of the same class and background as the judges.

The worst problem masters contended with was runaway servants. Especially in the early years, there was great fear that servants would join with Indians and Negroes to kill the much smaller master class. Punishments for runaways were extremely strict. They might be branded with "R," or have their hair clipped for easy identification should they try again, or be put to death. In order to retrieve runaways, rewards were often given and servants kept in jail until claimed by the master. Frequently servants were required to carry certificates and passes each time they left the house for any reason, and were subject to heavy fines for disobeying the regulation. Similarly, anyone harboring a runaway was subject to a heavy fine. Newspapers advertising runaways sometimes described them as wearing permanent iron collars.

A runaway maidservant in Anne Arundel County, Maryland, was brought to court in March 1719 by her master, who claimed she had absented herself 133 days according to his records of her short absences over the years. She was approaching the end of her five-year contract of indenture, but the court awarded the master 1,330 days of extra service. In such a case, if she were as restless and unhappy as her absences would indicate, and if the courts continued to take her master's word for her absences, she may never have attained freedom.

Maidservants who despite their master's orders became pregnant were punished with at least an extra year of service to make up for the time lost in childbearing. If the master gave any assistance in the form of hiring a midwife or extra time off, he was entitled to claim—and receive—a longer period of extra service.

Many servant couples lived together without marriage. First of all, marriage between servants was strictly forbidden unless the master consented. Penalties for disobedience were heavy. For example, in 1768 a Chester County, Pennsylvania, court heard the case of James Hall and Margaret Ryan who had run away for thirteen days, gotten married, and were finally returned to their master at a cost of nine pounds. The court decided that each would have to serve thirty days for running away, five months to compensate for the nine pounds cost, and an additional year for marrying. Secret marriages between servants commonly meant an extra year's service in all thirteen colonies. The end result, of course, was a large number of so-called illegitimate children, usually unclaimed by any father. Particularly in the South, other reasons for couples living together were the informality and excessive freedom of the frontier, long distances from the minister or justice of the peace, and lack of churches in which to publish banns.

Education was included in the indenture contract, with boys being taught reading, writing, and, later on, arithmetic. Girls sometimes learned reading, and even less frequently were taught writing. Though provision for education appeared in almost all indenture contracts, many ignored the requirement.

More than thirty thousand, or approximately one out of every eight of the total number of indentured servants, were former convicts. These were men and women whose ignorance and early starvation had long since condemned them to weak physical stamina, continual disease, and a life of repeated thieving and crime. They would be released from prison on condition that they migrate to America as servants, deliberately sought out because they could be bound to longer terms of service than free men and women and because no one ever complained against masters who used the severest forms of discipline on ex-convicts. Usually their contracts called for a doubly long period of service, from seven to fourteen years, depending on the seriousness of the offense committed.

By the end of the seventeenth century, however, colonial masters were learning to refuse prisoners as servants because of their troublemaking tendencies. Still, throughout the colonial period, some masters continued to demand ex-convicts who, everything else being equal, cost half the price of other indentured servants. Female convicts were the best buy of all, selling for eight or nine pounds apiece, whereas male convicts who could work at useful trades brought in anywhere from fifteen to twenty-five pounds. Abbot Emerson Smith found evidence of ship captains visiting English prisons around 1750, plying female inmates with drink, and cajoling them into boarding ship for the New World. Even so, Smith concluded, if these women were not already too far gone in age and health, and if they could survive the voyage and the first few weeks of living in a new environment and strange climate, they would then have a better life than what they could have expected in prison or in London's slums. At the very minimum they would work in the fresh open air—as former convicts they would probably be assigned to field labor instead of to work inside the house—and would also have plenty of food at their disposal.

While many unmarried women arrived in the colonies as indentured servants, others, mostly from Germany and Switzerland, came already married to still another class of white servants, redemptioners whose prime purpose was to set up a new home for the family in America. Since they came of their own accord and tended to have more money than indentured servants—but not quite enough to transport themselves and family without borrowing extra money—they would sell themselves into indenture for a limited period of time, just long enough to pay off the indenture. Sometimes a wife or a daughter would join the head of the family in service in order to get the debt behind them more quickly.

The redemptionist system was first put into effect in the 1720s and widely used by the Germans and Swiss. German redemptioners were anxious to escape from their homeland, which had been ravaged till 1715 by Louis XIV of France and his invading armies and, after Louis's death, oppressed by petty local princelings trying to emulate the Sun King's absolute rule over all subjects. Thus, German migrants left for the New World in whole communities, with movable goods and families intact.

Throughout the colonial period, indentured servants, former convicts, and redemptioners continued to arrive, but they became less and less important as a source of labor by the eighteenth century. As early as 1670, relatively more emphasis and effort were devoted to importation of black slaves, so that by the time of the Revolution, blacks formed the second largest group in America, next only to the English in number. In a total population of 2.5 million when independence was declared in 1776, 500,000 were blacks—of whom more than 150,000 were female.

Black slavery made its appearance in the English colonies in 1619, twelve years after the settlement of Jamestown, when the Dutch sold twenty Negroes to Virginians. By 1625 there were twenty-three, classified by contemporaries as twelve men and eleven women.

From the beginning, Negroes were treated as nonhumans and set apart from white Christian society in general, white indentured servants in particular. (English masters saw indentured servants as humans, sometimes incorrigible but still part of the human race.) Furthermore, slaves were viewed as an even lower form of being than the "savage" natives. Significantly, however, little effort was made to enslave those natives although they were considered heathen and inferior—and were already here. Indians, after all, belonged to tribes and nations powerful enough to conduct murderous revenge—unlike the Negroes who had been captured on a distant conti-

From a 1775 engraving. *Courtesy of the British Library.*

nent, herded aboard ship, and sold one by one as members of no group that might offer either resistance or support.

As with indentured servitude, slavery was an Old World practice, adapted to New World conditions. Since the mid-fifteenth century Europeans had been enslaving Negroes (the Spanish term the English eventually incorporated into their language, replacing their own word *black*). And by at least 1550 the Spanish and Portuguese had made slavery part of the American scene. An accelerating trickle of Negroes into the English colonies after 1670 reached flood proportions in the 1700s.

Blacks were relegated to the status of chattel slavery. From birth to death blacks were the property of their masters. Thus, in eighteenth-century Virginia a wife had dower rights in one-third of the slaves in her husband's estate. And her own slaves would become the absolute property of her new husband should she remarry.

New England tended to be more casual in its laws, less harsh in treatment of slaves than the south. As early as 1638 Samuel Maverick of Boston had three black slaves, including one who claimed to be "a queen in her own country," according to John Josselyn who toured the area in the 1660s. By 1641, just three years after the arrival of these first blacks, John Winthrop reported to his journal the admittance of a Negro woman (possibly the same one Josselyn later noted) as a full member of the all-important First Church of Boston.[2] Two generations later, in 1705, Sarah Kemble Knight, setting down observations on a round trip from Boston to New York, described masters' allowing slaves to eat at the same table with the family. In Connecticut she is amazed when a dispute

[2] However, church seating was very much affected by class. Just as white men and women were separated, sitting on either side of the pastor according to social standing, blacks were assigned sections even further away, marked *B. M.* (Black Men) and *B. W.* (Black Women).

between a master and a slave goes to arbitration and the arbitrators find against the master, making him pay the slave and apologize. With the major exception that Negro servants were slaves for life and by heredity, New England blacks were treated in much the same way as whites bound to service. In fact, some Negroes found their status changed to free servants, the best known example being Revolutionary war poet Phillis Wheatley of Boston (discussed at length in Chapter Eleven, "Arts and Letters").

Slavery took firmest root in the South. New England had a couple of hundred slaves around 1680, but the total slave population never reached more than three percent in the eighteenth century (though the largest city, Boston, had a total of eight percent). New York, the Northern colony with the greatest number of slaves in the eighteenth century, had fourteen percent (fifteen percent in New York City), and in New Jersey and Pennsylvania slaves numbered about eight percent. Five southern colonies—Maryland, Virginia, North Carolina, South Carolina, and Georgia—had some 350,000 slaves (at least one-third female) in a total population of one million by 1760. In his scholarly study, *White over Black,* Professor Winthrop D. Jordan found that there were distinct variations even between neighboring colonies. For example, while twenty-five percent of the population of North Carolina consisted of black slaves, South Carolina had more than sixty percent. Within a five-mile radius of a South Carolina rice plantation it would have been quite usual to have ten slaves for each white man, woman, and child.

As early as 1640, Virginia county court records began mentioning the sale of female Negroes, including their offspring. For example, one Francis Pott in 1646 sold a black woman and boy (presumably her son) to Stephen Charlton "forever." And in 1652 it was recorded that William Whittington deeded to John Pott "one Negro girl named Joan, aged about ten years and with her issue and produce during her (or either

of them) for their life time, and their successors forever."
Similarly, in neighboring Maryland a man in 1649 sold two
Negro men and a woman "and all their issue both male and
female." Significantly, the will of Rowland Burnham of Rappahannock, Virginia, in 1657 clearly differentiated between
the status of his white servants and Negroes, specifying that
the whites should serve their "full term of time" and the
blacks "forever."

The price at which blacks were sold depended on their
health and the number of years of life remaining to them.
Healthy young women could be sold for high sums, on the
assumption that they would produce children who could also
be held forever.

However, the large number of mulatto children, so frequently noted by European travelers in their letters and
diaries, was distinctly frowned on. Marriage and sexual intercourse between whites and blacks brought severe punishment,
with laws against miscegenation appearing on the statute
books of Virginia and Maryland as early as the 1660s. Even
so, there was a great deal of miscegenation in all colonies by
the eighteenth century, mostly between lower-class whites and
Negroes but also between white men of all classes and Negro
women.

Very much related to the whole question of miscegenation
was the near-nudity of slaves. Both men and women wore few
clothes, partly out of long habit acquired in their native
tropics and partly because of the stinginess of masters who
refused to provide them with clothes. Whites often used this
nudity as an excuse for satisfying uncontrolled libidos.

But sexual relations between whites and blacks must have
been common even in the cold North, judging from the law
Massachusetts passed prohibiting miscegenation in 1705. Not
long after, such statutes were enacted in North Carolina,
1715; South Carolina, 1717; Pennsylvania, 1726, and
Georgia, 1750. Thus twenty-five years before independence,

all the plantation colonies of the South, plus two Northern colonies, had passed antimiscegenation legislation.

As for marriage between slaves, there was almost never a formal ceremony. Philip Fithian, tutor at Robert Carter's Nomini Hall, one of Virginia's grandest plantations, exclaimed in his diary for Wednesday, January 26, 1774:

> At supper from the conversation I learned that the slaves in this colony never are married, their lords thinking them improper subjects for so valuable an institution!

However, slave couples invariably referred to themselves as man and wife and remained faithful to each other, though all too frequently they were separated, one sold to a different master. As a result, newspaper advertisements often appeared stating that a runaway slave would probably be found visiting his wife at a faraway plantation.

In most cases, slave parents and their children lived in huts and ate food provided by the master. Since both mother and father worked, young children would be left in the care of an older woman at a common nursery. Parents worked from dawn to dusk, with nights, Sundays, and a few holidays such as Christmas and Easter to themselves—though they sometimes had to spend this free time cultivating land the master had allowed them, in order to supplement the meager amounts of food the master provided for the family.

A painful picture of how one master treated his slaves is available in the early eighteenth-century writings of William Byrd. He frequently mentioned quite casually in his diary his beating female slaves for negligible offenses: "August 6, 1709: Jenny was whipped for abundance of faults."

Another time, June 24, 1710, he returned home to find "all well except that a Negro woman and seven cattle were gone away." The next day she was still missing and he wrote of his own ugly humor that made him so out of sorts that he even

Female slave being whipped. From a 1775 engraving. *Courtesy of the Widener Library, Harvard University.*

chanced not saying his daily prayers. But four days later he could write more cheerfully that she was found again and duly punished by having a bit put on her mouth. She kept running away and being forcibly returned and harshly punished. Then for almost two months she stayed put, till on November 6 she again ran off, only to be found a week later—dead.

Outrageously, still another time slaves were whipped only for being physically present during a quarrel between Byrd and his wife:

> My wife caused Prue to be whipped violently, notwithstanding I desired not, which provoked me to have Anaka whipped likewise who had deserved it much more, on which my wife flew into such a passion that she hoped she would be revenged of me.

Documenting the contention that many slaves—particularly females—went raving mad on being captured, there is testimony before Parliament in 1788. Based on his own participation in slave trade, Alexander Falconbridge recalled:

> A young female Negro, falling into a desponding way, it was judged necessary in order to attempt her recovery to send her on shore to the hut of one of the black traders. Elated at the prospect of regaining her liberty she soon recovered her usual cheerfulness, but hearing, by accident, that it was intended to take her on board the ship again, the young woman hung herself.
>
> It frequently happens that Negroes on being purchased by Europeans, become raving mad and many of them die in that state, particularly the women. One day at Bonny, I saw a middle-aged, stout woman, who had been brought down from a fair the preceding day, chained to the post of a black trader's door in a state of furious insanity. On board the ship was a young Negro woman chained to the deck, who had lost her senses soon after she was purchased and taken on board.

In a former voyage we were obliged to confine a female Negro of about twenty-three years of age, on her becoming a lunatic. She was afterwards sold during one of her lucid intervals.

In the South, every aspect of life came to depend on the services of black slaves. For instance, a special assignment delegated to slave women was wet nursing, giving their own breast milk to white infants. Negro women suckled white babies till they were old enough for weaning, then turned them over to the care of Negro nurses, until a white tutor or governess took charge. Slaves or servants replaced women of the landed aristocracy in every phase of motherhood, except in the actual process of birth.

Slavery also affected white women who had no other means to support themselves and so found themselves in competition with slaves who received no wages. Julia Cherry Spruill in her book *Women's Life and Work in the Southern Colonies* quotes five newspaper ads inserted by women offering to do all sorts of plantation work. One appeared in the *South Carolina Gazette* for November 5, 1764: "A single woman, with a child, would be glad of a place on a plantation, to take charge of a dairy, raise poultry, etc." Still another woman advertised on January 24, 1775, for a position that would include work as housekeeper, nursing sick Negroes, or managing a dairy and raising poultry.

Slavery ended formally in New England after the Revolution, and in the South almost a century later following the Civil War. Unhappily, the last chapter in the story of its effects may not be written for another century.

# · *Part II* ·

## THE FAMILY

Anne Bradstreet. *From a stained glass window, St. Botolph's Church, Boston, England.*

*I had eight birds hatched in one nest,*
*Four cocks there were, and hens the rest.*

# CHAPTER FOUR

# Law and Marriage

Until modern times marriage was always more practical than romantic. In ancient days the purpose was to produce fieldworkers, the source of all wealth. Child labor was considered both natural and good, so that woman's most honorable distinction was to be mother of a large family. Strong sons were preferred, but daughters were needed, too, for help in the household beginning at about age six—and eventually to mother children themselves.

In labor-short America, woman's function as a breeder was similarly emphasized. New England's eyewitness historian Edward Johnson enthused over Mrs. Sarah Simmes, who was "endowed by Christ with graces fit for a wilderness condition, her courage exceeding her stature, . . . nurturing up her young children . . . their number being ten, both sons and daughters, a certain sign of the Lord's intent to people this vast wilderness."

But fortunately for colonial women, history let itself be pushed, shoved, and pulled till it went in two contrary directions simultaneously. On the one hand, American wives bore even more children than did their sisters in the Old World. On the other hand, in the setting of the New World women won all kinds of concessions, giving them new status.

Marriage traditions were the first to go. In a sharp break with English precedent, the wedding ceremony was changed from religious to civil. Governor William Bradford of Plymouth colony explained, shortly after landing at Provincetown:

> May 12, 1621, was the first marriage in this place which according to the laudable custom of the Low Countries, in which they had lived, was thought most requisite to be performed by the magistrate, as being a civil thing, upon which many questions about inheritances do depend . . . and nowhere in the Gospel to be laid on the ministers as a part of their office.

And in 1647 Governor John Winthrop of Massachusetts Bay reported his colony's attitude when a Hingham bridegroom invited his pastor to officiate at the Boston wedding. Refusing the request, Governor Winthrop explained: "We were not willing to bring in the English custom of ministers performing the solemnity of marriage."

In effect, the civil ceremony meant marriage by mutual contract, an agreement between two indviduals, involving not a holy sacrament but questions of ownership, residence, and inheritance. Under these circumstances complete male dominance was difficult to maintain.

Further emphasizing the civil and contractual aspects of marriage, New Englanders required that sometime within one month after the ceremony the bridegroom had to report the marriage to the town clerk or face a fine. This held true until 1691 when the king of England imposed the established Anglican church on New England, pushing the Puritans off center stage. Even after this date, however, well into the eighteenth century, many weddings were solemnized by civil magistrates, or in fact by any socially prominent man. Ministers were sometimes invited to be present, but told to stay on the sidelines without participating. (The recording of all marriages in civil records dates from the Puritan period and practice. Today, a religious minister performing the ceremony in effect acts as an agent of the state.)

New England courtship marked still another departure from Old World customs. Chaperons were rarely required, on grounds that everyone knew everyone else in the neighborhood, and that leaving the area was impractical, if not impossible. And girls—in demand because of their scarcity—shared with boys the initiative in choosing a mate, unless two sets of parents had worked out a match first. This was one more case of the Puritans bringing with them from old England the latest in radical innovations, and turning an avant-garde procedure into common practice. As a matter of fact, when Thomas Heywood, popular playwright and actor in early seventeenth-century England, wanted to surprise his audience he made a female character say:

> This is the fashion that's but late come up
> For maids to court their husbands.

Similarly, in the South as early as 1632, Virginia enacted legislation allowing freedom of choice in marriage without parental consent—an especially striking departure from English custom in an area which, unlike New England, tended to mimic closely the laws and traditions of the mother country. There were several reasons for this particular shift—the frontier with its shared dangers and easy informality, as well as the acute shortage of women of childbearing age.

In both North and South, however, there were parents who would have nothing to do with newfangled ideas of letting children choose marriage mates. Almost always they were a tiny minority, maybe five or ten percent of the population who saw the wedding of a son or daughter as the classic way to preserve and increase power and wealth. Thus, highly placed Massachusetts Puritans practiced a kind of inbreeding to strengthen the position of the elected few, the so-called saints in their group. One of the first examples was the wedding in 1633 of Mary Winthrop and Samuel Dudley, children of the

Bay colony's governor and deputy governor respectively. And this at a time when John Winthrop and Thomas Dudley were quarreling publicly over Winthrop's administrative practices, and one year before Dudley defeated Winthrop for governor at the annual election. Still, the children's marriage seemed to reconcile the fathers personally if not politically, since they remained good friends for the rest of their lives.

Another instance came as the result of the mid-seventeenth-century marriage of Dorchester minister Richard Mather to the widow of Boston minister John Cotton. To the marriage each brought a child, Increase Mather and Mary Cotton, who were raised as brother and sister but later married each other and produced Cotton Mather, distinguished as minister, historian, and diarist.[1]

Virginia took longer than New England to achieve stability and wealth. But by the eighteenth century a small wealthy class of plantation owners was very much in evidence. And like those in the North who were prosperous and powerful, they intermarried, restricting relationships to a tiny group, who consequently acquired great influence serving in the Governor's Council or House of Burgesses and holding other high offices almost as a matter of right.

Back in Boston, at the very end of the seventeenth century there was at least one case where a strong-willed, socially prominent daughter rejected three different partners chosen for her by her father. "If you find in yourself an unmovable, incurable aversion from him," Judge Samuel Sewall wrote to his daughter Betty, referring to selected suitor number three, "and cannot love and obey him, I shall say no more, nor give you any further trouble in this matter." Postscript: Betty

---

[1] Bernard Bailyn in his study *The New England Merchants of the Seventeenth Century* devotes four pages to naming and describing the descendants of several generations of intermarriage among the powerful and the prosperous, pp. 135 ff.

Sewall took her time, but reconsidered a full year later and so married the persistent Grove Hirst in October 1700.

Whether children or parents did the selecting, it was the parents' right and duty to grant permission before courtship could even begin. But after they gave approval, parents were forbidden to withdraw consent for any arbitrary reason. For their part, children who found their parents' choice of a marriage mate unacceptable could veto the selection.

Once set in motion, courtship was a wild mixture of romance and finance. The young couple would retire to a corner somewhere getting better acquainted while the parents haggled over business details. Among the well-to-do, the dowry or bride's portion would be discussed openly with the understanding that if the girl's father failed to live up to his part of the bargain he was liable to lawsuit, fine, and punishment. Among all classes there would have to be agreement on buying or building a separate dwelling for the new couple (no problem in land-rich America where even the poorest family could expect to receive several acres, a situation unknown in crowded England). The nuclear family (husband, wife, and children), rather than extended families (including grandparents, aunts, uncles) dominated the American scene, though sometimes a widowed parent or unmarried sister lived in the household.

As time went on, the dowry requirement receded further into the background, easily ignored or minimized by those who could not afford it. This was in conspicuous contrast with English practice. The bride's portion was so important in the motherland that destitute daughters of peasants and artisans sometimes received dowries from charitable institutions.

No doubt the male-female ratio also favored women on this score. At the same time that Boston had three men to every two women, London had ten men to every thirteen women. In fact, among the English nobility the average dowry paid out on a daughter's marriage doubled between 1550 and

1700, probably because of the increasing surplus of women to eligible men. A contemporary scholar, Gregory King, studying England's population in 1694 found that fourteen boys were born to every thirteen girls, but by adulthood a goodly number of men had been carried off "by wars, the sea, and *the plantations,* in which articles females are very little concerned." (Purposely italics have been added to "the plantations," meaning colonies in this context.) King minimized the number of women who died in childbirth, concluding that males were far more exposed to death from the age of three or four than were their sisters.

A popular mid-seventeenth-century ballad by Martin Parker supports the figures on the shortage of men in London:

*The Wiving Age*
or
*A great complaint of the maidens of London,*
*Who for lack of good husbands are undone.*

England's dispatch of men to the colonies was, as Gregory King remarked, partially responsible for the relative shortage of males in the mother country. This demographic disparity between the Old and New Worlds, plus the dire need to produce more babies in order to expand the population in the labor-short colonies, made the age of marriage lower in the colonies than in England. In early seventeenth-century England, upper-class women married at around twenty-one to twenty-two, lower classes at twenty-four to twenty-five. By the end of the century, when poverty and a labor surplus overtook the English lower classes, many women held off marriage until their early thirties. In New England in the first half of the seventeenth century (when the sex ratio definitely favored women), females married at around twenty to twenty-one, and slightly older in the second half of the century—twenty-one to twenty-three, for all classes as the sex ratio evened out.

Husbands would vary in age by about three to four years older in England, five to seven years in New England. In the South, where men outnumbered women by the ratio of four to six males to one female, girls married at an even younger age, before reaching twenty. According to genealogical records and contemporary observers, teen-age brides were quite usual, some only fourteen or fifteen years old. In fact, when William Byrd's daughter Evelyn reached the age of twenty, the father despaired, calling her the most "antique virgin" of his acquaintance.

Not surprisingly, the shortage of women produced a mad male scramble to secure a wife before she was promised to someone else. One man in Virginia even tried to bind his fiancée—unsuccessfully, it turned out—by making her sign a solemn-sounding contract:

> These are to certify to all persons in the world that I, Sarah Harrison, daughter of Mr. Benjamin Harrison, do and am fully resolved, and by these presents, do oblige myself, (and cordially promise) to William Roscoe, never to marry, or contract marriage with any man during his life, only himself. To confirm these presents, I, the abovementioned Sarah Harrison, do call the Almighty God to witness, and so help me God. Amen. To these said presents I set my hand. Sarah Harrison. Test April 28, 1687.

But Sarah Harrison must have had her fingers crossed, because just two months after her "cordial promise" to marry William Roscoe she married James Blair instead.

Marriage was considered so vital in the colonies that there was special legislation on the subject. In Massachusetts Bay, for example, colonists were not even allowed to remain if they had left their mates behind. This applied equally to men and women, and was strictly enforced by fines or deportation. Additional early laws protecting New England wives included forbidding a man to desert his wife or to keep her in distant or dangerous areas. He was required "to bring her in, else the town will pull his house down." Furthermore, a man could not leave his wife for long periods of time, could not marry more than one wife who was living, and could not use "hard words" to her. For her part, the wife was forbidden to use a "cursed and shrewish tongue" to her husband. Punishment for verbal abuse was the stocks or pillory.

As early as 1646, Massachusetts protected orphan girls from having to marry for money, or even for mere subsistence, by requiring that their marriages be approved by a majority of the selectmen of their towns. Previously the guardian had been responsible for protecting his orphaned ward. And not all guardians were as conscientious as John Endecott, a chief magistrate of Massachusetts. Governor Winthrop's sister Lucy and her husband Emmanuel Downing wrote proposing a marriage between their son James and Endecott's ward Rebecca Cooper, whom Downing considered "a very good match" with "an inheritance much to be desired." Mrs. Downing added some prodding of her own, finding the child "tolerable" and her "estate very convenient."

Endecott reacted indignantly, emphasizing the girl's wishes and well-being: "First, the girl desires not to marry as yet. Secondly, she confesses (which is the truth) herself to be altogether yet unfit for such a condition, she being a very girl and but fifteen years of age. Thirdly, where the man was moved to her she said she could not like him. Fourthly, you know it would be of ill report that a girl because she hath some estate should be disposed of so young, especially not having any parents to choose for her. Fifthly, I have some hopes of the child coming on to the best things. If this is not satisfactory, let the court take her from me."

In cases where parents and children agreed on betrothal, the next step was to publish the intention to marry three times. (These banns, it was thought, would counteract any tendency toward secret marriages.) After that, the sooner the ceremony took place the better. The Puritans preferred to prevent rather than punish illicit sexual intercourse. Such behavior was always a temptation, especially in the cold winters of the Northern colonies where overcrowded dwellings and lack of heat made bundling—courtship in bed, fully dressed— both acceptable and respectable until after the Revolution.

For more than 150 years the New England colonies, New York, and Pennsylvania practiced the custom of bundling, brought over from the wintry climes of Holland (where it was called queesting), Scotland, and Wales. The custom proved a perfect solution for a courting couple, too exhausted from the day's labors to frolic at parties, too cold in winter to find leaving the house exciting or practical. A board placed along the length of the bed prevented temptation should the watchful but weary parents fall asleep.

The Puritans seem to have covered every aspect of courtship and marriage in either their formal laws or their personal writings. But it is impossible to discover the exact words used in their marriage ceremony.[2] "There was no established form of the marriage covenant . . . in the new plantations," wrote Massachusetts Bay historian Thomas Hutchinson in 1764. The closest—though far from satisfactory—approach to a recorded Puritan ceremony can be found among the Quakers, the English sect who shared with the Puritans a strong opposition to the Established Anglican Church, but whose forward-looking ideas and actions the Puritans had rejected and punished with death up to 1660. The Quakers in 1661 prevailed on Massachusetts to allow their special marriage ceremony. Bride and groom took each other in the presence of the

---

[2] Judge Sewall's letter to his daughter discussed her indecision as to whether she could "love and honor and *obey*" [italics added] her suitor. This would seem to indicate inclusion of this vow in the marriage ceremony. On the other hand, Judge Sewall was writing some thirteen years after the imposition on New England of Anglicanism, which did include the promise to obey.

Quaker meeting. There was no promise to obey on the part of the woman—or of the man, for that matter—and all present signed the marriage certificate. As with the Puritans, there was no minister officiating and no ring to symbolize the union.

Fortunately for posterity, the 1684 Quaker marriage of John Pemberton and Margaret Matthews was recorded:

JOHN PEMBERTON: Friends, you are here witness, in the presence of God and this assembly of His people, I take this maid, Margaret Matthews to be my loving and lawful wife, promising to be a true and faithful husband unto her till death shall us part.

MARGARET MATTHEWS, IN THE SAME MEETING: Friends, before God and you His people, I take John Pemberton to be my husband, promising to be a loving and faithful wife until death shall us part.

At least the fragments of another wedding ceremony have survived—this time in Virginia during the summer of 1687 and involving the same Sarah Harrison who had so defiantly broken her signed and solemn promise to marry only William Roscoe. "No obey," she repeated three times at her wedding to Dr. James Blair, future founder of the College of William and Mary, until finally Reverend Smith, with the apparent consent of the bridegroom, yielded and proceeded with the rest of the ceremony.

Side by side with courtship and marriage, law played an equal role in affecting the status of women. In 1636 Plymouth wrote into law the provision that land set aside for the wife and children was inviolate, could not be touched even to satisfy the creditors of a deceased husband. Later, in 1664, Plymouth went so far as to insist that the wife consent formally to the sale of houses or lands.

The legislature of Massachusetts Bay gave its citizenry a tradition-shattering Body of Laws in 1641. In several clauses the legislature specifically dealt with women, and did quite well by them. Clause 79, in a section titled "Liberties of Women," reads: "If any man at his death shall not leave his wife a competent portion of his estate, upon just complaint made to the General Court she shall be relieved." In other words, the Bay colony wrote into law the traditional English allowance of one-third—or more if American circumstances made it necessary—of the husband's estate to the widow for use as a dowry in case of remarriage.

Then follows clause 80, putting into writing the early proscription against a man's following the old European custom of beating his wife, "unless it be in his own defense upon her own assault"—i.e., unless she struck first. One of the first to be hauled into court for disregarding this clause was Jacob Pudeator who was fined for striking and kicking his wife. Later he succeeded in having the sentence moderated on proof of his claim that she was a woman "of great provocation."

Two other clauses were directed not toward married women but to females in general. Conceding that sons had the first rights of inheritance when parents died without a will, clause 82 specifically named daughters as heirs when there were no sons. Brothers, uncles, cousins would not take precedence just because they were male, as was the case under the English feudal system of primogeniture—practiced in the southern colonies up to the time of the Revolution.

Climate and topography made the South turn backward to this kind of feudal law—to the detriment of women. Thus the rich soil and long growing season of the South produced "brown gold" or tobacco, resulting in an insatiable desire for more and more land and a plantation-based economy. Land ownership and control became so all-important that every effort was made—using the old feudal practice of entail—to keep an estate from being broken up after the owner's death. The most that daughters could expect to inherit was a legacy of a far smaller portion than the sons. The usual custom in dividing southern property was to leave the home place to the oldest son, and to give back-county lands to the younger sons. For daughters there might be a few Negroes and some money, as well as a few personal belongings of the father.

In contrast, the rocky terrain, deep harbors, and icy winters of the North made the population turn early to trade and commerce and to living closely together around the meeting-house. Land was mainly viewed as a place to construct a dwelling and, in the early days, to raise a garden or graze a few animals for family subsistence. And wealth was more easily earned than inherited.

Yet colonial law treated women—both North and South—better than the common law of England. Back in the mother country, the common law merged the wife into the identity of the husband. A married couple acted as one person, and spoke with one voice—that of the husband.

America pierced huge gaps into the common-law unity of husband and wife. From time to time colonial wives acted as agents for their busy or temporarily absent husbands—or supervised a business for a friend. For example, there was Elizabeth Davenport, wife of the minister and co-founder of New Haven (a separate colony until 1664). Around the middle of the seventeenth century, when Governor John Winthrop Jr. of neighboring Connecticut was frequently out of the colony or the country on official business, she would manage his ironworks business—ordering and paying for supplies, employing workers, and keeping his books in order. And in a North Carolina court in 1695, Frances Kitching responded to a suit against her husband, Robert. Similarly, two unforgettably named women appeared in Maryland courts, acting as attorneys for their husbands: Restituta Hallowes and Ann Dandy.

Some married women even made contracts, unheard of in England for all but men and—occasionally—single women. Ability to own property affected by contracts made the difference. In England, where the wife was not allowed to own property, she could make no contracts, even with her husband's consent, or even when he was a joint contractor with her. But in the colonies where she could own property—and this was true particularly in colonial trading centers—she could make contracts. On the other side of the coin, the fact that she owned property and was thus allowed to make contracts meant that she lost the advantage of pleading her common-law incapacity to agree to binding contracts. She had won acceptance as a responsible adult, and the law treated her as such.

Allowing women to convey land was one of America's chief contributions to elevating the legal status of women. In contrast to English procedure, in the colonies the husband and wife each joined in executing the deed by which title was passed. Afterward, the deed had to be acnowledged by both marriage partners. In the husband's absence, the wife would be examined by the court to ascertain that her signature was voluntary, no undue pressure by the husband one way or the other. In addition, court records, in New England at least, reveal land grants to wives whose husbands were still alive.

Under English common law, husband and wife having identical interests could not testify on behalf of or against each other. Although this was true also in some of the middle and southern colonies (and by the eighteenth century was true in most colonial courts), the legal unity of husband and wife did not achieve a firm foothold in such seventeenth-century jurisdictions as Massachusetts Bay, Plymouth, New Haven, and New Netherland. In these colonies there were frequent cases of married women testifying under oath on behalf of husbands who were either defending themselves in contract or tort actions, or bringing suits. In this way, evidence otherwise unobtainable was gathered. Significantly, factual testimony by wives showed close familiarity with their husbands' activities. Typical of such lawsuits was that brought by Margaret Pastree of Massachusetts in 1702 in her own name, though her husband was still alive. On appeal she won the case against one Sanders, a creditor of her husband, who had demanded the return of some silk.

Sometimes, too, colonial wives took the stand to testify against their husband's civil actions. One example of this occurred in New Haven in 1651. William Bunnell sued to have his son and daughter released from apprenticeship indentures. He claimed that his wife and father had apprenticed the children without his consent when he had gone to England. But Goodwife Bunnell testified for the defendant, claiming that her husband had provided little or nothing with which to feed or shelter the children and when "she asked him what she should do with them, he said they were hers as well as his and he left them with her." Her son confirmed the conversation, and the court sustained the indentures, thus ruling against the husband.

In general, seventeenth-century American courts resorted to "equitable jurisdiction"—i.e., taking into consideration the special conditions faced in America, compared to deeply rooted, ancient England. In the motherland, the husband under common law was required to support his wife. Thus, one-third of the husband's estate went to the wife on the husband's death, an inviolate portion, which creditors could not attach. On the negative side, each man controlled his wife's possessions—including her earnings and her very clothes—acted as sole administrator of her property, had use of any profit, and was not accountable to explain. The only mitigating factor for English women was the antenuptial contract made between the engaged man and woman before marriage, legally recognized as protecting the property of the woman as well as the man forever after.

In general, America treated wives less harshly. And the colonies encouraged widespread use of the one English practice that protected women, the antenuptial contract. As a result, the wife could retain her own property in her own name and dispose of it "at her own free will from time to time and at any time as she shall see cause." The quote is from the antenuptial contract of 1667 between John Phillips of Marshfield and Faith Dotey of Plymouth.

The record of Faith Dotey's life shows the actual working of this contract. Her first husband, a widower, Edward Dotey, was a servant on the *Mayflower* voyage, one of the signers of the Mayflower Compact. The couple had seven children after their marriage on January 6, 1634. Upon his death, August 23, 1655, he left his estate to his wife and eldest son Edward. The antenuptial contract before her second marriage allowed Faith Dotey to retain the estate left her by her first husband. Thus, despite her remarriage she could on her own death, on December 21, 1675, leave her goods and property to her daughters by her first marriage, Mary, Elizabeth, and Desire, making no provision for giving anything to husband number two. She had no children with John Phillips.

A great deal of attention was devoted to antenuptial contracts in colonial days. They were used particularly by widows, and it was a rare widow who remained unmarried for any length of time—except among the Quakers, who frowned on remarriage for a year after the death of a spouse to show respect for the memory of the loved one. The validity of antenuptial contracts was upheld in court decisions in Maryland (1654), Plymouth (1667), Connecticut (1673), and New York (1683). And when challenged in Massachusetts as late as 1762, the practice was again approved.

On the subject of remarriage, it has been estimated that almost every living male and female colonist had three, four, and five different spouses. That sprightly old Puritan governor of Massachusetts, John Winthrop, lost his beloved third wife Margaret, to whom he had been devotedly married for more than nineteen years, on June 14, 1647. Just six months later, one month short of age sixty, he married Charlestown widow

Martha Coytmore.[3] He died the following year, on March 29, 1649, father of a five-month-old son. The child Joshua died three years later, shortly before his widowed mother married her third husband, himself a widower, John Coggan of Boston. Significantly, Martha Coytmore had inventoried all her property after the death of her first husband. As a result, when she married John Winthrop her property was entirely her own.

Similarly, remarriage was frequent in Virginia. Julia Cherry Spruill, in *Women's Life and Work in the Southern Colonies,* writes of "one Elizabeth whose maiden name is unknown," but married successively five prominent gentlemen and probably a sixth to make her "the woman having the most husbands to her credit." Mrs. Spruill then names six other brides of multiple marriages, concluding with Dame Frances Berkeley, whose distinction was to have married three governors of Virginia.

Contrary to legend, divorces were granted in the colonies—definitely if not frequently. There were six in Plymouth during its existence as a separate colony, from 1620 to 1691. Five were granted for adultery, one for desertion, though the colony had no divorce law. Likewise, Massachusetts had no divorce statutes but granted a minimum of twenty-seven divorces in the years between 1639 and 1692, when England imposed Anglicanism on the colony. Grounds for divorce in New Haven were adultery and desertion.

Pennsylvania and New Jersey granted legislative divorces. However, Southern colonies, adhering as they did to the Church of England, granted no divorces. These would have

[3] Martha Coytmore Winthrop is another good example of colonial inbreeding. She was the daughter of Captain William Rainsborough of Charlestown, brother-in-law of Stephen Winthrop, son of John and Margaret Tyndal Winthrop. Thus, Stephen Winthrop was an uncle of Margaret Coytmore, who then became for a time his stepmother.

required consent by church courts, which were nonexistent in the South.

But even in the South the proscription against divorce was not so hard and fast as it first seemed. The lack of ecclesiastical courts to enforce this policy meant that lay officials operated more or less on the Puritan concept of marriage as a civil contract enforced by civil laws. Though they never went so far as to allow divorce, southern officials were far more liberal in their concessions to unhappy wives than were the Anglican ecclesiastical courts.

Where divorce was granted, there were at least three practical reasons. First, many men had left their reluctant wives back in the old country, found life impossible without a helpmate, and wanted to be free to remarry. Second, there was the desperate need to increase the population with frequent births by remarrying compatibly. Thirdly—and pointedly—unhappy wives, forced to stay married, frequently ran away anyway.

Postmarital contracts went hand in hand with divorces and legal separations. One example occurred in Plymouth in 1686. The court had refused to grant a divorce but allowed a legal separation, including a postmarital contract between both partners as to the division of the estate. There was no clear precedent for this approach to equality between husband and wife in contemporary English law. Quite the contrary, common law in the mother country, by decreeing the absolute oneness of husband and wife, made the idea of two equal contracting parties to a marriage impossible.

Colonial courts were more open-minded on separation agreements than courts after the Revolution. Seventeenth- and eighteenth-century courts in all colonies often allowed protection of financial interests of the wife and children without forcing recourse to divorce, which entailed unpleasant publicity. Nineteenth-century courts, in contrast, disliked separation agreements, on grounds that private judgment was replacing judicial supervision of marriage dissolution.

In some colonies, wives who had been deserted controlled disposition of their own personal property. And such property could not be attached to pay the debts of the husband who had deserted.

Admirers of the early colonists would like to think of them as humane and advanced in their attitude toward women. But more probably they were simply being practical. With future success uncertain, and the need to insure life from minute to minute, each family—headed jointly by husband and wife— was charged with maintaining health, law and order, and good government. The theory in early years was that with every family policing and taking care of itself (in the beginning there were no hospitals, old-age homes, orphanages, or poor-houses), there should be almost no corruption or expense for social services. God would be pleased and utopia would arrive early.

In practice the idea worked minimally well only when a colony was tiny and the population dispersed. Growth and outside threats to security led to increasingly formalized politics on every level—town, colonial, and eventually supracolonial. However, for women, the early years of involvement in politics through governing the family and sharing equal responsibility with the husband over children and servants made a lasting imprint, forever raising female expectations. In fact, as late in the colonial period as October 10, 1713, Judge Samuel Sewall, wealthy and a social and political leader in Boston, could write in his diary this anecdote reflecting the great power at least one woman had assumed within her household:

> Sam and his wife dine here, go home together in the calash. William Ilsly rode and passed by them. My son warned him not to lodge at his house; daughter said she had as much to do with the house as he. Ilsly lodged there.

# CHAPTER FIVE

# Childhood and Education

Toys, musical instruments, and education separated the boys from the girls in colonial days.

In Puritan Massachusetts, for example, young males played with kites, whistles, slingshots, balls, small boats, miniature soldiers, and articles they or their fathers fashioned from birch bark. And for further amusement they would walk around on stilts, jump rope, or play leapfrog. In contrast, their sisters would spend their free time inside the house making cat's cradles, mothering homemade dolls, and pretending to cook or bake with temporarily unused kitchen utensils. Outside, girls would fashion daisy chains from the wild flowers they found everywhere, weave garlands of oak leaves, split dandelion stems, and whistle through blades of grass.

As the colonies became prosperous enough to provide music lessons, each sex was directed to particular instruments. The spinet, harpsichord, and (in the eighteenth century) piano were reserved for females. And the flute, violin, and French and German horns were played by males only.

Up to about the age of six, boys and girls were dressed identically, educated similarly—and treated like easily ignored household objects. Child mortality was so high during the first few years of life—half those who survived birth would die before age three—that parents consciously restrained themselves from investing too much attention or affection on their offspring.

At most, each new baby would be the center of attention for two years—at which time the mother would again give birth in order to insure a family of any size or permanence. And early in life children stood a very good chance of losing their mothers, since every fifth woman died of pregnancy-related causes. In a poem addressed to her husband and titled "Before the Birth of One of Her Children," young Anne Bradstreet describes this death-infested atmosphere:

> *How soon, my dear, death may my steps attend.*
> *How soon't may be thy lot to lose thy friend.*

Rickets was a childhood disease affecting all colonies and treated with an extract from snails. Preventive medicine often consisted of draping necklaces of amber or wolf's fangs around children's necks to ward off various illnesses. And popular medicines were made from snakes, roses, or licorice. Thus, those who survived their childhood had some hope of living to old age.

Statistics on living through childhood and then on to a ripe old age are very unreliable, but at the same time fascinating. (Either they have had to be based on admittedly scanty official records and grave markers, or on contemporary writings.) For example, there is the poem by Anne Bradstreet who had eight children, seven of whom survived her.

> *I had eight birds hatched in one nest,*
> *Four cocks there were, and hens the rest,*
> *I nursed them up with pain and care,*
> *Nor cost, nor labor did I spare,*
> *Till at the last they felt their wing,*
> *Mounted the trees and learned to sing.*

A generation later, at the beginning of the eighteenth century, families with eight to fourteen living children supposedly became increasingly common (and half the population was under the age of sixteen). The reasons generally given were that experience taught colonists how to cope with the strange New World, and prosperity brought abundant food and comfortable living space. But exceptions to the rule are all too easy to find—for example, the comfortably placed children of the powerful Cotton Mather. Of fifteen sons and daughters produced by two wives, six survived childhood: Increase, Samuel, Elizabeth, Abigail, Katharine, and Hannah. Only Samuel and Hannah lived on after their father's death.

Maybe no more acceptable, but surely provocative, are statistics on longevity. Thus, daughters getting past the first few years of childhood faced the prospect of a life some seven years shorter than that of their brothers. Because of the wear and tear of frequent childbirth, females would go to their graves by age sixty-three. Males, on the other hand, once they reached the age of twenty-one, could look forward to reaching age seventy. (Today the situation is exactly reversed.)

Eventually, the healthier New World climate, together with greater prosperity, led to a conspicuously greater survival rate. Less and less did mothers have to hold themselves back from showing or receiving affection. Even so, the Old World conviction remained that young children had to be disciplined strictly and kept at a distance because they were incapable of reasoning. Invariably, children were forbidden to open their mouths in the presence of adults, except to admit food at mealtime. If ever they were called on to answer a question they were expected to address their parents as "Honored Sir" or "Honored Madam," or alternatively as "Esteemed Parent." Happily, however, there is no proof that seventeenth-century parents used the rod any more frequently than modern parents, despite Cotton Mather's aphorism "Better whipped than damned." They considered the rod a last resort only. In fact, for his own children Cotton Mather wrote in his diary that he disapproved of corporal punishment, preferring instead to take away privileges for a limited time—for example, confining the child to the house for several hours.

Simply living up to the names bestowed on them must have kept some children in their place. Biblical names were used frequently, with the Puritans adding their own particular stamp. Thus Roger Clap, who arrived with the Winthrop company in 1630 as an indentured servant, wrote his memoirs for his thirteen children: Desire, Elizabeth, Experience, Hope-still, Preserved, Samuel, Supply, Thanks, Thomas, Unite, Wait, Waitstill, and William. Other names heard in Puritan communities were Believe, Hoped For, More Mercy, Reform, Return, and Tremble.

Whatever their name or condition, offspring were not left to be children long. This is shown by their dress. After the sixth year—though sometimes as early as age four for girls, as late as age eight for boys—adult clothing was bestowed on children, a change that admitted them to adulthood, as completely as modern graduation ceremonies. In the years when they dressed alike and were being introduced to domestication, both boys and girls wore a kind of long robe, opening down the front, with a pair of (never explained) ribbons dangling from the back of the shoulders. Where winters were cold, they would have bulky clothes for warmth, including homemade blankets or shawls attached with pins. The switch to adult-differentiated clothing was a giant, traumatic step. Afterward, boys looked like small models of their fathers, girls of their mothers. Their childhood was behind them.

In Massachusetts, six-year-old girls with poor parents were set to work spinning flax, combing wool, and weaving—whenever they were not otherwise occupied on the farm or the kitchen. Their brothers did the heavy farm work, chopped wood, and helped with home manufacture of such articles as shoes or brooms. Boston established a workhouse in 1682 to employ children (of both sexes) "who shamefully spend their time on the street."

Similarly in the South, lower-class children were bound out for service. North Carolina in November 1702 noted in its official records: "Martha Plato binds her daughter Hester Plato to Capt. James Coles and Mary his wife till she comes of age or marries, she now being six years of age." Just prior to the Revolution, on November 19, 1772, Virginia records contained the announcement: "Timothy Ryan being runaway, his children, viz.: Mary aged eight, Martha, aged five, and Jeremiah, aged two, to be bound out."

This custom of binding out children was not much different from the system of apprenticeship known as "putting out," a practice adopted from sixteenth- and seventeenth-century England. Boys were to learn a trade while living, away from their own family, at the master's house. The master then became a substitute father, in charge of imparting technical skills and maintaining strict discipline. The natural parents were allowed Sunday visits, but only if they did not distract or detain the child from his work—in which case they were subject to payment of damages to the master. Girls were often "put out" to learn housework. Especially in the North, even wealthy parents put their children out, with the thought that they would learn better manners if brought up in someone else's home. At the same time, children of the financially destitute or mentally incompetent would be sold outright to masters who would pledge to care for them completely and to teach them a trade before the age of twenty-one—another practice imported directly from England.

From birth to early entry into adulthood, children received an informal but stern education at home. The family—especially the mother and older siblings—was responsible for introducing the child to the world outside, to the prevailing manners, morals, and civilization of the group. Thus, discipline by the family prepared small boys and girls for living up to the rules of society and of the state.

A New England primer, c. 1725. Used for teaching the alphabet—and morality. *By permission of the Houghton Library, Harvard University.*

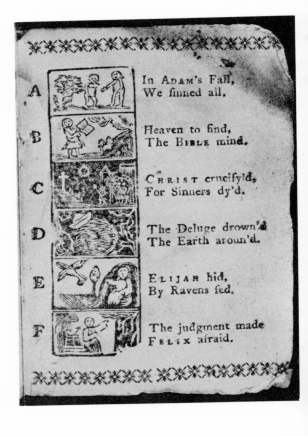

In ADAM'S Fall,
We finned all.

Heaven to find,
The BIBLE mind.

CHRIST crucify'd,
For Sinners dy'd.

The Deluge drown'd
The Earth aroun'd.

ELIJAH hid,
By Ravens fed.

The judgment made
FELIX afraid.

If the mother was herself literate, she would instruct her young children in religion and teach them to recognize letters. Next, they would attend "dame schools"—an institution brought over from old England. As the name indicated, women were in charge of teaching both boys and girls the elements of the three Rs (reading, 'riting, and 'rithmetic). These schools were for children of both sexes up to the age of six, though sometimes up to the age of ten for boys, or for even older girls. They were conducted in the schoolmistress's kitchen, so that she could tend simultaneously to her other household chores and her babies. Although the amount of

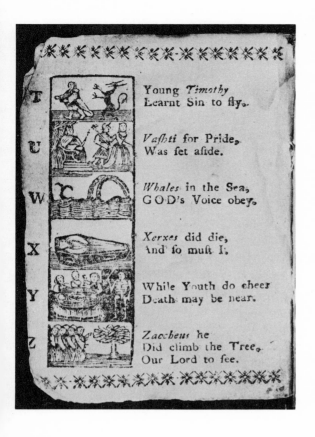

Young *Timothy*
Learnt Sin to fly.

*Vaſhti* for Pride,
Was ſet aſide.

*Whales* in the Sea,
GOD's Voice obey.

*Xerxes* did die,
And ſo muſt I.

While Youth do cheer
Death may be near.

*Zaccheus* he
Did climb the Tree,
Our Lord to ſee.

learning derived was sometimes questionable, dame schools at least kept children out of mischief and prepared them to get along with each other by following social rules and regulations. These dame schools lasted throughout the colonial period—the first ones recorded were taught in New England in 1635 by Bridget Fuller, a former teacher in England, and in Rappahannock county, Virginia, by a Mrs. Peacock—and continued in existence as late as 1840.

The greatest emphasis in dame school was on reading. There was a definite progression whereby a child had to master reading before going on to writing, and writing before going on to arithmetic. In other words, the three skills were not taught simultaneously, and, particularly for girls, only reading was considered necessary.

For those boys and girls who went on after dame school, the next level was called writing school. Finally, and this time for boys only, there followed a study of classics in grammar (Latin) school. Just five years after their arrival in Massachusetts, in 1635, the Puritans hired Philemon Pormont as schoolmaster of what would eventually become Boston Latin School, supported by wealthy families, to be used exclusively by their own sons.

Ignoring education for females had a strong religious base. Among Protestants, upper-class men could hope for salvation only by learning to read the Scriptures. The Puritans wrote this idea right into the preamble to the Massachusetts law of 1647 establishing a school for every town of fifty families: "It being one chief project of that old deluder Satan to keep men from the knowledge of the Scriptures . . ."

New England's neighbor, the Dutch colony of New Netherland, also stressed the close relationship between education and religion—though the settlers there may have been slightly more liberal in their attitude toward schooling for girls. In the largest town, New Amsterdam, the schoolteacher, who was also the chorister, reader, and sexton of the church, was a living embodiment of church and state. Moreover, his classroom work was supervised by the political magistrate as well as the parish domine and wardens. The teacher would hold classes in his own home every day beginning at 8:00 A.M., except Sundays and five holidays. He taught reading and writing to girls as well as boys, and when there was enough local commerce to warrant the subject, he added arithmetic to the curriculum. Occasionally, he also lectured on contemporary history. But the main stress was on knowing and fearing the Lord, since children were considered the only hope to replace widespread depravity among adults. For his various services the teacher received a minimal salary, supplemented by tuition paid in beaver or bear skins. Children who were too poor to contribute to his salary were allowed to remain in school "for God's sake." In 1665, when England took over control from the Dutch and renamed the colony New York, new laws were passed compelling parents to educate their children or have them taken away by county officials.

In Quaker colonies, the schoolhouse quickly followed the erection of the meetinghouse. And if funds were lacking, the schoolhouse and meetinghouse were combined in one building. Here, education was not entirely religiously oriented, since Quakers believed that each person's own inner light and inspiration were the basis for faith. Therefore, education also had practical, secular purposes, and was for girls as well as for boys. In 1685, at the urging of proprietor William Penn, Pennsylvania passed a law requiring a basic elementary education for both girls and boys "so that they may be able to read the Scriptures and to write by the time they attain twelve years of age, and that then they be taught some useful trade or skill, and the rich if they become poor may not want: of which every county should take care." However, as time went on in Pennsylvania, with its liberal immigration policy, the influx of such heterogeneous sects as the Mennonites, who began arriving at the very beginning in 1683, and the Moravians, who came around 1740 (both groups strove to maintain separate identities and struggled against assimilation), central control of education dissipated. As a result, not every Pennsylvania boy, let alone every girl, was assured of receiving an education.

Further south for almost all of the seventeenth century, education faced near-fatal difficulties compared to the North. There was far less community and church reinforcement. And homes were too far apart to give each other support in molding the young for entry into society.

When the plantation economy took hold in the eighteenth

century, the South grew radically different from the North. Under the twin feudal practices of primogeniture and entail, the son, whose position in the family made him sole heir, would be educated to fit him for taking over plantation proprietorship, profits, and problems. Younger sons would be trained to go into the ministry or the military. And daughters would be prepared to get along by snaring eldest sons of the wealthy. Along these lines, John Baptista Ashe, an eighteenth-century gentleman of North Carolina, expressed in his last will and testament the general attitude of his upper-class compatriots toward education. First he gave detailed instructions for his sons' education in Latin, Greek, French, and mathematics. Then, for the education of his only daughter, he instructed: "I will that my daughter be taught to write and read and some feminine accomplishments, which may render her agreeable; and that she be not kept ignorant as to what appertains to a good housewife in the management of household affairs."

Generally speaking, the southern colonies, unlike those in the north, had few public schools, substituting instead mostly private schools, home tutoring, or "old field schools," centrally located for better accessibility to every child in a far-flung area. If the father had wealth to protect and a son to whom he could bequeath it, he might himself train the boy in agriculture, business management, horsemanship, and socially approved manners. Later he might send his oldest son abroad to exclusive schools. Sisters or brothers too far down the family roster to have any chance of inheriting property would receive leftover crumbs of attention from the mother—or, if he had extra time and energy, from the father. When, occasionally, public schools existed, they were funded by private contributions (in contrast to community taxation in New England). Education for girls was more limited than that for boys, but not totally neglected. For example, differing education for boys and girls is spelled out in the indenture contracts of

Susanna and Isaac Atkins. Her education would consist of reading the Bible, learning sewing, and absorbing the necessary skills for household work. He would learn reading, writing, and arithmetic—including multiplication and division up to the threes table—and be taught the trade of carpentry.

In all colonies, north and south, for the boy who had intelligence and a rich father, college followed. The fourteen- or fifteen-year-old student would enroll first in a liberal arts program, and then, if he chose, would study theology, looking to enter the ministry. The fact that the first colleges established in the colonies were for men only and were church-sponsored tells a great deal about the prime purpose of education: Harvard, 1636, Puritan; William and Mary, 1694, Anglican; Yale, 1701, Puritan; Princeton, 1746, Presbyterian. Not until 1755 did the University of Pennsylvania open to pioneer in secular education, followed in 1769 by similarly secular Dartmouth, which grew out of Moor's Indian Charity School.

Meanwhile, the attitude about education for women remained unchanged: They needed to know nothing more than how to accomplish household tasks and to take care of the problems of family well-being. This required no Latin, only training by their mothers beginning at the age of four, six at the latest. Enough geography to get around the house, and enough chemistry to boil, cook, and clean up afterward—that would be more than adequate schooling for girls, a colonial wit assured his audience. And the joke had an uncomfortable degree of truth in the colonial setting where the family division of labor gave the running of the household to the woman only.

In fact, education was a field where the male–female ratio actually worked against girls. The dire shortage of labor meant that it was all but impossible to release young females from needed chores. Some of this comes through in the memoirs of Anne Grant. Looking back to her mid-eighteenth-century years in New York, she wrote that girls learned domestic skills from their mothers and were "constantly employed in knitting stockings, and making clothes for the family and slaves; they even made all the boys' clothes. This was the more necessary as all articles of clothing were extremely dear." (The casual reference to having girls sew clothes for slaves—a task designed to save, not make, money—must mean that slave labor was carefully confined to work that would produce profits for the owner.)

Of course, denying an education to females had all sorts of insidious effects. Women were treated as intellectual inferiors, a status that their lack of schooling perpetuated even when they were the mental peers—or sometimes the superiors—of men. Furthermore, refusing to allow girls a thorough education in Latin resulted in a lifelong ignorance of ancient societies, cultures, and practices—and also insured their exclusion from college, where Latin was the language used in instruction and in many textbooks. In turn this meant they could never talk as equals with the educated gentry, clergymen, lawyers, or political leaders. After marriage, they could not even share their husbands' interests, the rationale being that these intellectually inferior creatures would be out of their depth, and besides could never be expected to keep secrets. Some women broke out of this mold, against all odds, throughout the colonial period. But they had more hindrance than help all along the way.

In the very years that Massachusetts was setting noble precedents for community-supported education, no provisions whatever were made to allow girls to share in this New World bonus. Even the fact that an anonymous woman was credited with giving the land for the first town school in Massachusetts did nothing to alter the situation—until someone figured out that keeping the schools open in the summer, by permitting females to attend while males did their fishing or heavy harvesting, was a good way to use empty buildings and give teachers a year-round income. These fortunate females studied basic reading, writing, and arithmetic, but seldom grammar, languages, or other subjects available to young males. However, even this practice was far from universal: at least one town in Connecticut voted against "wasting" any of its money educating girls. The few girls who did learn to read the classics did so independently—or by listening through keyholes to their brothers' tutorial sessions—or by inveigling older brothers into sharing their lessons learned at college—or by cajoling doting fathers to impart at least some of their knowledge.

One such woman, Anne Bradstreet, had received extensive tutoring from her learned father, Governor Thomas Dudley—and had had available to her from earliest childhood his excellent collection of books. Also, she was wise enough to make use of the growing legend of Elizabeth, England's queen from 1558 to 1603, a great monarch in her own right who assumed goddess proportions in comparison to her Stuart successors. About Good Queen Bess, Anne Bradstreet wrote:

> *She hath wiped off the aspersion of her sex,*
> *That women wisdom lack to play the Rex.*
>
> . . . . . . . . . . . . . . . .
>
> *Now say, have women worth? or have they none?*
> *Or had they some, but with our queen is't gone?*
> *Nay masculines, you have thus taxed us long,*
> *But she, though dead, will vindicate our wrong.*
> *Let such as say our sex is void of reason,*
> *Know 'tis a slander now, but once was treason.*

Elizabeth had demonstrated to the world that women could have great intellect and could use knowledge wisely and well. Among her other accomplishments she was expert in such traditionally masculine studies as Latin and Greek, spoke fluently four modern languages—English, French, German, and Italian—and wrote eloquently literate speeches in her own clear hand. During her reign, Richard Mulcaster in England, headmaster of the Merchant Taylors' and St. Paul's schools, wrote: "That young maidens can learn, nature doth give them, and that they have learned, our experience doth teach us. . . . What foreign example can more assure the world than our diamond [Elizabeth] at home?"

Though Elizabeth remained a heroine to women colonists, the men were apparently too preoccupied with the foul deeds of her male successors to make the connection between the queen's femaleness and her ability to use education to great advantage. Similarly, Anne Bradstreet, acclaimed both at home and abroad as America's great poet, was looked on as the exception who could never be the rule. And this despite lavish praise by nine highly respected men, printed in the preface to her published poems. In Massachusetts her most surprising devotee was Nathaniel Ward, who so completely disdained women as to make them the butt of one of his poetic jokes and to include them in the Massachusetts Body of Laws along with "idiots and other distracted persons." This learned lawyer and minister, who had once been a neighbor of Anne and Simon Bradstreet when they lived in Ipswich, wrote humorously, but with deference:

> . . . *I muse whither at length these girls will go;*
> *It half revives my chill frost-bitten blood,*
> *To see a woman once do aught that's good;*
> *And shod by Chaucer's boots and Homer's furs*
> *Let men look to't, lest women wear the spurs.*

This poem was followed in the same preface by rhymed praise from her brother-in-law John Woodbridge, who had himself taken the collection to England, where it was published in 1650 under the whimsical title *The Tenth Muse Lately Sprung up in America*. Included in his seventy-four lines were these:

*. . . If women are with wit and sense inspired,*
*Yet when your works shall come to public view,*
*'Twill be affirmed, 'twill be confirmed by you. . . .*

Then followed rhymes of praise by seven other men. And in both old and New England *The Tenth Muse* became a best seller. In fact, within seven years of publication, bookseller William London of Newcastle-on-Tyne listed Anne Bradstreet in his catalog. Her name appeared under the category of poetry, along with John Donne, Michael Drayton, John Milton, and William Shakespeare.

Still more praise came later from Cotton Mather, New England's famous historian and minister, and from Edward Phillips, nephew of John Milton, who wrote and edited early encyclopedias and dictionaries. In addition, Mrs. Bathsua Makin, known in England as the learned woman who had tutored the daughters of the martyred King Charles, wrote: "How excellent a poet Mrs. Bradstreet (now in America) is her works do testify."

It is more than likely that Cotton Mather's expressed admiration for Anne Bradstreet led him to educate his own daughters. Her poems, he had written in his *Magnalia,* history of New England, in 1702, "have afforded a grateful entertainment unto the ingenious, and a monument for her memory beyond the stateliest marbles." And he included her in a small select category of "learned women."[1] Using italics to share his excitement with the reader, he bestowed sky-high praise on Anne Bradstreet:

[1] Currently being rediscovered by the twentieth century, Anne Bradstreet is the subject of a superlative biography published in 1971, *The Tenth Muse* by Elizabeth Wade White. The author remarks that the poet's writings were "varied in subject and so filled with materials of learning . . . Among the few English women writers before her none had displayed so encyclopedic a mind."

If the rare learning of a *daughter* was not the least of those bright things that adorned no less a judge of *England* than Sir *Thomas More*, it must now be said that a judge of *New England*, namely Thomas Dudley, Esq., had a daughter (besides other children) to be a *crown* unto him.

In his *Ornaments for the Daughters of Zion*, Cotton Mather wrote that a woman in his social circle would need to learn housewifery, needlework, arithmetic, accountancy, and surgery. Then he added practically, "and such other arts relating to business, as may enable her to do the man whom she may hereafter have, good and not evil, all the days of her life." If she had any spare time left over after following this regimen, she should learn music and language—but not brag of these particular accomplishments. Significantly, he followed his own suggestions when it came to educating his small daughters, to whom he showed himself to be a thoughtful and attentive father. Unhappily, only one of his four daughters survived him, but his granddaughter Hannah Mather Crocker (1752–1829), daughter of his son Samuel, became one of America's first feminists and a distinguished author.

Overall, female education showed occasional spurts of progress during the colonial period, but by and large the outlook must have been discouraging. In New England, despite the area's boast of superior enlightenment compared to old England, education for girls seemed to go further downhill in the second generation of settlement. For example, a survey of Essex county, Massachusetts, wills made in the years around 1650 shows that the fewer than one-third of the women who were able to write their own names had mostly, judging from their ages, been educated in England rather than in America. Even in the 1700s the situation showed far less improvement for females than for males. By the time George Washington took his oath of office as first President of the newly independent United States in 1789, almost every New England man was literate, but female literacy stood at less than forty-five percent (according to a recently published study, *Literacy in Colonial New England,* by Kenneth A. Lockridge). In other words, men had gone from fifty percent literacy in the seventeenth century to near-universal literacy by 1789, while women went only from about one-third to still less than half in the same period.[2]

In the rural areas and backcountry, both men and women tended to have far less opportunity for education than residents of towns and cities. Even so, men of the frontier and farms improved from around fifty percent in the seventeenth century to something like sixty-five percent at the time of the Revolution, while women in these same areas remained at a stagnant one-third. And in highly cosmopolitan Boston, economic status had less effect on literacy than did sexual discrimination. Thus, men of low income were eighty percent literate, whereas similarly poor women had the same rate as all Boston women, rich or poor—forty-five percent.

Certainly, all these figures make woman's lot appear hopeless. But new impulses began stirring around 1700. In 1694 Mary Astell of England had written two widely circulated tracts, *Reflections on Marriage* and *A Serious Proposal to the Ladies.* She contended that men refused equal educational opportunities to women in order to subjugate them permanently. Her fellow countryman Daniel Defoe shared her opinions. Like her, he was convinced that better education for women would make them more companionable and capable wives, though in marriage they would, of course, be ruled by their husbands. This was very advanced thinking for the time.

[2] For purposes of this study Professor Lockwood defined literacy as the ability to sign one's name, a skill that runs parallel though slightly below reading proficiency, and likewise runs parallel though slightly above the ability to write. Thus, a person who signs his or her own name probably has the ability to read but may be slightly less likely to possess the skill to write a whole sentence or paragraph.

Mademoiselle Marie de Gournay of France, a scholar and protégée of Montaigne, had written an essay on the status of women in 1622, which was cited by Cotton Mather in one of his letters in 1716. She mentioned Socrates, Plato, and Plutarch as believing in the equal ability of women. Most men, she asserted, wished to keep women in a state of permanent subjugation, thus destroying half the world. She turned around the story of Genesis so that instead of showing Eve (woman) as second in creation, Adam (man) was created both male and female. Thus, one sex was not superior to the other. St. Paul, who refused to allow women to become ministers, she disposed of easily. She attributed his attitude to a fear that women preaching in public might place themselves in too favorable a light, thereby diminishing the stature of men.

Not surprisingly, a best seller from England crossed the ocean in 1744 to find runaway success in Boston bookstores. *Pamela* by Samuel Richardson said some of the things women longed to hear through the medium of one of the first English novels. Richardson told the story of a poor servant girl loved madly by her master. She, of course, refused his advances, finally making him agree to marriage, after which he had to educate her to fit her exalted station in life.

Women found quite agreeable the idea that their sex could profit from extensive education. But Richardson, being an eighteenth-century man, refused to go any further in raising the status of women. Instead he merely advocated a combination of intellectual and domestic attainments, with men retaining superior authority. One adverse reaction to Richardson appeared in the journal of Esther Edwards, who before her death in 1756 accused the novelist of degrading her sex through a mistaken moral code. The wife of the second president of Princeton, and the daughter of Jonathan Edwards, prominent Puritan preacher, she had strong convictions on female ability. She disliked *Pamela,* she wrote, for its overemphasis on riches and honor, though the book was helpful in raising discussion.

For all of this, women were not totally without educational opportunities in America. In Boston, two private schools established in the 1680s welcomed both girls and boys of any age to learn English and that most recondite of subjects, Latin. In contrast, the two public schools of the town accepted only boys who were at least seven and could already read. In the next decade, Harvard graduate Peter Burr noted in his account book that "Faith Savage and Abigail Gillam began to learn Latin, September 7, 1696."

Also, in his study, *The Evening School in Colonial America,* Robert Francis Seybolt found that young women frequently attended evening school, sometimes joining classes for boys, sometimes segregated by sex. This occurred mostly in seacoast towns such as Boston and Salem, Massachusetts; Newport, Rhode Island; New York City; Philadelphia; and Charles Town, South Carolina. In such schools, girls were free to choose exactly the same vocational and liberal arts curricula selected by boys.

These evening schools met usually for six months, from October to April, six evenings each week for two to three hours, six to eight or nine o'clock. The buildings used were the same as for day school. However, day school was community-supported, whereas a fee was charged for evening classes.

Definitely, then, there were glimmerings of progress and ferment—probably more than the few that were recorded. All the same, a father in pridefully intellectual Boston was undoubtedly closer to the norm. *The Evening Post* for December 10, 1744, described him as advising his wife how to educate their daughter:

> *Teach her what's useful, how to shun deluding;*
> *To roast, to toast, to boil and mix a pudding;*
> *To knit, to spin, to sew, to make or mend;*
> *To scrub, to rub, to earn and not to spend.*

A Quaker woman of the early 1700s. Artist Francis Place painted this rare portrait of a female Quaker. She was Hannah Callowhill Penn, who was the wife of the founder of Pennsylvania and who resided in America for twenty-three months, 1699–1701. *Courtesy of the Historical Society of Pennsylvania.*

## · *Part III* ·

## THE WORLD OUTSIDE

# CHAPTER SIX

# Political Stirrings

The surprise is not that so few women were involved in seventeenth-century politics, but that so many participated actively—and in so many different ways. Best known is Anne Hutchinson, whose deviant religious stand almost toppled the entire political establishment of early New England.

There was no separation between religion and politics in the early seventeenth century. Both were the same side of the same coin, as the Puritans had learned to their horror and terror in England, where Charles I repeatedly called the Established Church "the chiefest support of royal authority."

But to the Puritans the lesson learned was not the need for separation of church and state. Instead all that they ever asked, first in England and subsequently in their New England utopia, was that the single established religion be purified to meet their own high, exacting standards. Toleration of other religious beliefs would make living together in harmony impossible. Let those who disagree "have free liberty to stay away from us, and such as will come to be gone as fast as they can, the sooner the better," proclaimed Nathaniel Ward, Puritan preacher, lawyer, and author of the Massachusetts Body of Liberties.

In fact, the first charge John Winthrop brought against Anne Hutchinson was of having "troubled the peace of the commonwealth and the churches here." How far she had gone in this direction, as she attempted to reinterpret Puritanism, emerges in a letter written at the height of the Hutchinsonian controversy by Margaret Winthrop, loyal wife of the governor. When John Winthrop was forced to move the General Court from hostile Boston—filled with friends and supporters of Anne Hutchinson—to more friendly Cambridge, even Margaret Winthrop was led to date her letter to him "Sad Boston" and to reveal some inner feelings:

> Sad thoughts possess my spirits, and I cannot repulse them; which makes me unfit for anything, wondering what the Lord means by all these troubles among us. Sure I am that all shall work to the best to them that love God, or rather are loved of him. I know He will bring light out of obscurity and make his righteousness shine forth as clear as the noonday. *Yet I find in myself an adverse spirit, and a trembling heart, not so willing to submit to the will of God as I desire.* [emphasis added]

Anne Hutchinson had begun innocently, using her intense intelligence, to interpret the only book available to her, the Bible. Noting that male members of Boston's church regularly met after the sermon to discuss the minister's ideas, she started to hold similar meetings for women in her own home, directly across the street from Governor and Mrs. Winthrop. She attracted an average of one hundred women—aided by her reputation as a skilled practitioner of medicine and midwifery, always smilingly and selflessly prepared to help any woman or family in need. Soon men, too, joined her discussion group. "Come along with me. . . . I'll bring you to a woman that preaches better gospel than any of your black coats that have been at the ninneversity," eyewitness Edward Johnson quotes one of her admirers (a man) as saying.

But she frightened the rulers of the colony with her complex theology, maintaining the radical concept that each person could experience his or her own salvation and then be "filled with God" after this unique experience. To her opponents, questioning the church meant also questioning the state. In fact, crossing the bounds from religion to politics, she rallied to her support all of Boston's merchants and residents, with the exception of John Winthrop and four others. Finally, her activities forced John Winthrop to move the emotionally heated election of 1637 from the usual locale, Boston, to Cambridge. And even in supposedly friendlier Cambridge, Winthrop noted there was violence, "some laid hands on others."

After winning the election, John Winthrop took the only course he knew—putting Anne Hutchinson on trial for heresy. At this trial she parried all questions so well that Edmund S. Morgan, an admiring recent biographer of John Winthrop, was led to comment that Anne Hutchinson was the governor's "intellectual superior in everything except political judgment, in everything except the sense of what was possible in this world."

Unfortunately for her, she was a woman born too soon. Sentenced at a parody of a trial to banishment from the colony "as being a woman not fit for our society," she protested, "I desire to know wherefore I am banished."

"Say no more," retorted Governor Winthrop. "The Court knows wherefore and is satisfied."

Governor Winthrop's words and demeanor triggered a centuries-long dispute. Either he was an out-and-out tyrant, in the same mold as the Stuarts from whom the Puritans had fled back in England. Or he was trying to salvage the fragile unity of the colony at a time when (1) another iconoclast, Roger Williams, had just finished battering it almost into oblivion with his radical ideas and had been similarly sent into exile—though treated far more gently and with deference by John Winthrop, who for the rest of his life corresponded with the exile and remained his friend, (2) the king was demanding the return of the precious charter that allowed the colony complete independence, and (3) the Pequot Indian War had just erupted and threatened to demolish a disunited colony.

In any case, far removed from this crisis atmosphere, some twentieth-century observers credit Anne Hutchinson with being the first American woman to lead the public fight for religious diversity and female equality. In fact, Joseph P. Lash in his 1971 biography, *Eleanor and Franklin,* reported that Eleanor Roosevelt began her list of America's greatest women with Anne Hutchinson.

Back in the late 1630s, however, Anne Hutchinson's life went from banishment to tragedy to murder. She left with her husband, thirteen children, and sixty followers for Rhode Island, where they purchased land from the Indians and established that colony's first civil government. In 1640 her husband William became a magistrate, but died just two years later in 1642. After his death she took her children, except for her eldest son and daughter, to modern-day Pelham Manor, Long Island. In 1643 Indians murdered her and all her children, except for one small daughter taken captive. A treaty signed between the Dutch and the Indians in 1645 made the Wechquaeskecks promise to return the child to the European colonists at New Amsterdam on payment of a ransom by the Dutch. From there the small girl returned to Boston.

Thomas Welde, Roxbury minister, had a typical reaction to news of her murder: "God's hand is the more apparently seen herein to pick out this woeful woman to make her and those belonging to her an unheard-of heavy example above others. . . ."

And definitely there were "others," prodded on by the strong sense of nonconformity embedded in Puritanism itself. Especially in a new land, free of tradition, all sorts of possibilities for defiance opened up. Slowly but surely, women even poked holes in the much vaunted Puritan patriarchy, which taught that men alone were fit to govern church and state.

Contemporary writings and records are full of allusions to the new role seized by women in community affairs. For example, John Winthrop, describing the unorthodox activities of Roger Williams, commented in his journal for January 1636: "He had so far prevailed at Salem as many there (especially of devout women) did embrace his opinions, and separated from the churches." Looking back, the twentieth century sees this kind of activity as a decisive political step in separating church and state.

In another aspect of working through religion to politics, there is John Winthrop's journal entry dated September 1637, two months before the final banishment of Anne Hutchinson. Governor Winthrop noted an assembly resolution allowing smaller groups of women to meet "to pray and edify one another" while at the same time denouncing a gathering of sixty or more led by one woman who "took upon her the whole exercise, was agreed to be disorderly, and without rule." In defeat, Anne Hutchinson had made inroads.

Edward Johnson, sounding more bitterly sarcastic than usual in his history of early New England, reported the further activities of the women who had accompanied Anne Hutchinson to her first place of exile in Rhode Island:

> Some of the female sex . . . (deeming the Apostle Paul to be too strict in not permitting a woman to preach in the public congregation) taught notwithstanding, they having their call to this office from an ardent desire of being famous. . . .

Undoubtedly, few women colonists noticed or took much comfort at the time, but Dedham, Massachusetts, dealt male dominance an early blow. Late in 1638 the town began the arduous, onerous task of assembling a church, first screening all male candidates for the Seven Pillars (founders) on the basis of wisdom, humility, and an honorable life. Joseph

Kingsbury donated land for the building, but his generosity brought him no concessions. He was rejected first as Pillar and then as member. His authority was undermined in the community and subsequently—worse still—in his own home, when his wife was selected for membership since she was a "tender-hearted soul full of fears and temptations but truly breathing after Christ." Ola Elizabeth Winslow, who first unearthed this story in her 1952 book *Meetinghouse Hill*, noted that it took four more years for the congregation to agree to accept Joseph Kingsbury as a member.

Poet Anne Bradstreet thought the unthinkable and doubted the undoubtable, but only in the privacy of her diary—perhaps because she had seen firsthand the public persecution visited on Anne Hutchinson. (As the daughter of one permanent magistrate and governor, Thomas Dudley, and wife of another similarly reelected throughout his life, Simon Bradstreet, she lived at the center of power, in a house teeming with politics.) She questioned the very existence of God and the Puritan teaching that theirs was the only true religion. Intellectually restive, she was challenging the whole basis of New England society:

> Many times hath Satan troubled me concerning the verity of the Scriptures, many times by atheism. How could I know whether there was a God; I never saw any miracles to confirm me, and those which I read of how did I know but they were feigned. . . . When I have got over this block, then have I another put in my way. That admit this be the true God whom we worship, and that be His word, yet why may not the Popish religion be the right? They have the same God, the same Christ, the same word. They interpret it one way, we another.

Surely, it was difficult to venerate masculine rule at a time when the Stuart kings had suffered a spectacular loss of power—and this may well have inspired Anne Bradstreet's poetic plea for recognition of female wit:

> *I am obnoxious to each carping tongue*
> *Who says my hand a needle better fits,*
> *A poet's pen all scorn I should thus wrong,*
> *For such despite they cast on female wits:*
> *If what I do prove well, it won't advance,*
> *They'll say it's stol'n, or else it was by chance.*

Another time, using her poetic pen she plunged into politics, creating 299 lines of rhymed "Dialogue between Old England and New; Concerning Their Present Troubles, Anno, 1642." Speaking through "daughter" New England and "mother" old England, she covered every pivotal event in England's long political history. And she used England's civil war to promote her own ideal society. Out of England's troubles she foresaw "much good fruits to be":

> *Then justice shall in all thy courts take place,*
> *Without respect of person or of case;*
> *Then bribes shall cease, and suits shall not stick long,*
> *Patience and purse of clients oft to wrong.*
>
> .   .   .   .   .   .   .   .   .   .   .   .   .   .
>
> *Then fullness of the nations in shall flow,*
> *And Jew and Gentile to one worship go;*
> *Then follow days of happiness and rest;*
> *Whose lot doth fall to live therein is blest.*

(In the second line quoted, did she purposely use the asexual word *person?*)

There are, of course, other indications of the Puritan woman's place in colonial Massachusetts that bolster this image of incipient independence. Some instances are admittedly isolated ones, but no less startling—and where research has unearthed a single example, there may well have been others, now forever lost. First there is Mary Dodge Woodberry, who early in the history of the North Beverly church actually cast the deciding vote, following a lengthy debate, in favor of calling Reverend John Chipman as minister. Then there is a Mrs. Oxenbridge, who arrived in Boston with her husband John early in 1670 and who certainly deserves promotion to legendary status based on the tantalizingly little information known about her. On March 20, 1670, both Oxenbridges were admitted to the First Church in Boston, long the leading congregation in Massachusetts Bay, and Reverend Oxenbridge was installed as pastor, until he died on December 28, 1674, aged sixty-six. No more was recorded about Mrs. Oxenbridge in America, but back in England before she migrated she had been referred to in glowingly Amazonian terms. In Eton College chapel, antiroyalist poet Andrew Marvell had erected a monument to her during the civil war period, 1640 to 1660, with an inscription describing her "as a scholar beyond what is usual in her sex, and of masculine judgment in the profound points of theology." Most significantly, her husband "loved commonly to have her opinion upon a text before he preached upon it." After the restoration of the monarchy in 1660, the royalists painted over the inscription, which they considered highly offensive, and Mrs. Oxenbridge eventually took off for America. The known facts end here, but the imagination has plenty of material to work on.

Still another woman, the wife of Colonel Foxcroft, warden of the Anglican King's Chapel in Boston, actually chose to belong to a different church, and so remained a Puritan Congregationalist. Also, by the turn of the eighteenth century, two staunchly Puritan men, Cotton Mather and Samuel Sewall, both leaders of Boston society, had made additional contributions to the emancipation of women by defending the religious equality of women and stating their belief in the possibility of salvation and religious achievement for women as well as men. Indeed, Cotton Mather, usually considered a hidebound Puritan, allowed his daughters Katy and Nibby to wait until adulthood before they made their own decision about joining a church.

If nothing else, the larger number of women church members showed that they stubbornly refused to follow their men into religious neglect or nonattendance. This was true from the very beginning, when 411 women joined the First Church at Boston compared to 379 men in the years 1630 to 1649, a time when men outnumbered women in the general population. Later, as the population ratio evened out in Boston, there were something like three women for every one man in church. As a result of belonging to church, women were allowed to participate in town meeting discussions of such local issues as roads, schools, and taxes—though they could not vote.

On the more discouraging side, women at both church and town meetings were expected to sit segregated from the men. Wives of clergymen and magistrates (in equal deference to church and state) were seated up front, on one side of the pulpit or moderator's lectern, as the case might be, while their husbands sat up front on the other side. Seating preference was so important that in case of disputes—involving either men or women—the Puritans passed a law empowering the selectmen of each town to assign seats according to wealth and position. Anyone who took someone else's location without due permission was fined.

Adding to this picture of sexual segregation, the Puritan founding fathers relegated women to the bottom of the church hierarchy when they produced the Cambridge Platform of

1648, the rules governing the churches of Massachusetts Bay. In order of declining importance, they decreed, there would be the pastor, teacher, ruling elder, deacon, and in addition:

> The Lord hath appointed ancient widows, where they may be had, to minister in the Church, in giving attendance to the sick, and to give succour unto them and others in the like necessities.

Still, as an unexpected result, Plymouth and Salem occasionally promoted widows, especially those close to sixty, to serve as church deacons, with the general responsibility of helping and comforting the poor and sick members of the congregation.

The Quakers went even further than the Puritans, finding scriptural justification for choosing women to preach and to participate actively in all community affairs. As early as the middle of the seventeenth century in England, Quakerism taught that though women had been put in a position of subjection after the fall of Eve, they had been redeemed by the restoration of holiness, and in Christ were the equals of men.

Quakerism arose during the English civil war, a fertile period of political innovation and calls for radical change, including at one point a demand for women's suffrage. Women were among the first in England to proclaim the Quaker message. And the sect arrived in the New World in the persons of two women, Ann Austin and Mary Fisher. In July 1656, they landed in Boston from Barbados, but were severely whipped and deported immediately—under provisions of a law passed in 1637 to deal with Anne Hutchinson and her followers. Eight more Quakers arrived just three weeks later in August 1656, four men and four women, including the sharp-tongued Mary Prince. Taken to the house of Governor John Endecott on September 8 for questioning, she denounced the two ministers in charge of the interrogation as "hirelings, Baals [false gods or idols] and seed of the serpent."

Like Anne Hutchinson, Quaker women roiled the political establishment through religion, refusing to take oaths of any kind, denouncing infant baptism, priesthood, and liturgy. In addition, they contended that sex was no determinant for gifts of prophecy and teaching and that women stood on equal footing with men in church worship and organization. Two who come close to qualifying as direct protégées of Anne Hutchinson were Lady Deborah Moody and Mary Dyer.

As a follower of Anne Hutchinson, Lady Deborah Dunch Moody (her un-American-sounding title came from marriage to Henry Moody, who became a baronet in 1632, just before leaving England) had been excommunicated by the Salem church in 1642 for her unorthodox views, including denunciation of infant baptism. But she escaped the further punishment of banishment from Massachusetts Bay. She owned four hundred acres of land in Salem and a farm, "Swampscott," in the area of present-day Lynn, both acquired in her own name from money inherited on her husband's death. There is suspicion that she averted forced exile because local officials liked the tax money on her property—a possible indication that religion was beginning to separate from and bow to politics, or at least to economics.

In any event, Lady Deborah decided on her own to leave Massachusetts for New Netherland, where she purchased land in Gravesend, Long Island (the southern part of modern Brooklyn, New York), and established a small colony in 1643, the first English settlement in the Dutch territory.[1] Then her rebelliousness burst out in all directions. She refused to have a minister in her jurisdiction, or to keep the Sabbath,

[1] Calling her "a wise and anciently religious woman," Governor Winthrop noted that "to avoid further trouble, etc. she removed to the Dutch against the advice of all her friends."

or to allow baptism of infants. Further, she freely admitted residents who were Quakers or Jews, instituted town meetings, and paid Indians for their lands. As one of the colonial patentees of New Netherland, she also exercised political power, being frequently consulted by the governor for nominations for various civil offices—and is recorded in the summer of 1655 as voting in a colony-wide election.

In 1657 she supposedly held the first Quaker meeting anywhere in America at her own house, which was also the site of the largest library in the Dutch colony. Dutch historian Gerard Croese wrote in 1695 that Lady Moody allowed the local residents "the liberty of meeting in her house, but she managed it with such prudence and observance of time and place that she gave no offense to any stranger or person or any other religion than her own, and so she and her people remained free from all molestation and disturbance." Her colony prospered, and she remained the leader until her death in 1659.

Mary Dyer, on the other hand, lived a life of tragedy and martyrdom for her Quakerism. She had left Massachusetts in the late 1630s along with Anne Hutchinson, but returned twenty years later to promote the Quaker cause.

Her reappearance was ill-timed. The Massachusetts General Court was in the midst of passing a series of laws—permitting banishing, whipping, and using corporal punishment (cutting off ears, boring holes in tongues)—to get rid of the Quaker menace. They explained that Quakers "write blasphemous opinions, despising government and the order of God in church and commonwealth, speaking evil of dignities, reproaching and reviling magistrates and ministers . . ." Finally, in 1658, the General Court, by a single vote during an emotionally stormy session, passed a further law ordering death by hanging for all Quakers who refused to leave the colony. The Puritans were hysterical and frightened. They had lost all their early great leaders to old age and death. And back in England the years 1658 to 1660 marked the end of the Cromwell Interregnum and the subsequent Restoration of the Stuart monarchy, so that it was uncertain whether Massachusetts had any future at all, let alone a future of independence and complete self-government.

Even on threat of death, however, Mary Dyer refused to recant her beliefs, to remain silent, or to leave the colony. So she was forced to watch three of her male Quaker companions hanged, while she herself had a noose around her neck. Her son's intercession saved her, but only temporarily. She was put on horseback and returned to Rhode Island, but she came again to Boston on May 21, 1660.

"Are you the same Mary Dyer that was here before?" demanded Governor Endecott.

"I am the same," Mary Dyer answered.

"You will own yourself a Quaker, will you not?"

"I own myself to be reproachfully so called."

Again she was condemned to hanging. From jail she made a moving plea to the General Court to repeal laws against the Quakers, "that the truth and servants of the Lord may have free passage among you . . ." Then adding eloquence to martyrdom she continued:

> I have no self-ends, the Lord knoweth, for if my life were freely granted by you, it would not avail me, nor could I expect it of you, so long as I should daily hear or see the sufferings of these people, my dear brethren and seed, with whom my life is bound up. . . . Were ever the like laws heard of among a people that profess Christ to come in the flesh . . . Woe is me for you! Of whom take you counsel? . . . In love and in the spirit of meekness I again beseech you, for I have no enmity to the persons of any; but you shall know that God will not be mocked, but what you sow, that shall ye reap from him, that will render to everyone accord-

ing to the deeds done in the body, whether good or evil, even so be it,

saith
Mary Dyer

On June 1, 1660, Mary Dyer was hanged in Boston. Humphrey Atherton, pointing to her lifeless body, remarked: "She hangs there as a flag." Some have reported his saying this

The statue of Mary Dyer at the Massachusetts State House.

in jest, while others find the statement symbolic of Mary Dyer's devotion to inner-perceived truth.[2]

New England persecution brought at least two other women to the verge of insanity. Lydia Wardel of Hampton watched in horror as her husband was tortured and several women were stripped and beaten. Driven to distraction, she ripped off her clothes and appeared in the congregation at Newbury as a "naked sign," for which act she and her husband suffered further beating.

Inhumane treatment was also the punishment for Deborah Wilson, who likewise walked as a "naked sign" through her town of Salem. Her punishment was to be tied to a cart, with her mother and sister alongside. All three were dragged and whipped through the town. Her husband, whose Quakerism was not as strongly felt as her own, tried as often as possible to soften the whiplashes by placing his hat between the whip and her back.

Thankfully, amid all these barbarous responses to Quakerism, there is one supremely happy story of a Quaker woman reaching the pinnacle of success and respect in early colonial politics—Mary Coffin Starbuck. Born in Haverhill, Massachusetts, February 20, 1645, just two years after her parents' arrival from Puritan Devonshire, England, she moved to Nantucket with her father, Tristram Coffin, who led the coloniza-

---

[2] Almost three hundred years later, on July 9, 1959, Massachusetts erected a statue of Mary Dyer on the terraced lawn of the State House in front of the east wing. Zenith Ellis of Fairhaven, Vermont, a descendant of Mary Dyer, gave money for the monument, sculpted by Sylvia Shaw Judson of Lake Forest, Illinois. Appropriately, at the opposite wing of the State House is a statue of Mary Dyer's good friend and mentor, Anne Hutchinson, who had been recognized a full generation earlier as hero material. The older statue is the work of Cyrus Dallin and was given by the Anne Hutchinson Memorial Association and State Federation of Women's Clubs on June 2, 1922. The statue was once bronze and possibly impressive, but is now heavily worked over by pigeons.

tion of the island in 1660–1661. Shortly afterward she married Nathaniel Starbuck, a prosperous farmer, local official, and partner with her father in purchasing the area from the Indians. Mother of ten children, of whom five daughters and three sons lived to maturity, she and her eldest son Nathaniel helped make Quakerism the leading religion on the island sometime after her own conversion from Puritanism.

"The islanders esteemed [Mary Starbuck] as a judge among them, for little was done without her, as I understood," wrote Englishman John Richardson, describing his 1701 visit. He bestowed on her the epithet "the great woman," and in the same journal entry deprecated her husband as "not a man of mean parts but she so far exceeded him in soundness of judgment, clearness of understanding, and an elegant way of expressing herself . . . that it tended to lessen the qualifications of her husband."

Throughout her long life, Mary Starbuck figured prominently in the political and religious affairs of Nantucket. Public business was often transacted at her home, which soon came to be dubbed "Parliament House." She died on November 13, 1717, aged seventy-two.

In addition to Mary Starbuck and her earlier Quaker predecessor, Lady Deborah Moody, there were groups of anonymous Quaker women who gained experience in politics—according to some dismayingly scanty information, at least. In Burlington, New Jersey, in the early 1680s these women held meetings among themselves. The purpose was to provide charity for the destitute or sick and to oversee the organizational problems of women's membership in the group. The conceivable result was that women learned techniques of group action. And for what it may or may not be worth, a Charles Town, South Carolina, doctor reported in 1707 that the local women had a club that met weekly and were turning themselves into politicians.

Before the arrival of the Quakers in America, the only

colony to make any move in the direction of religious toleration had been Maryland, founded as a refuge for upper-class
Catholics fleeing from England because of persecution. Like
the Quaker settlements, Maryland treated women with special
consideration. Thus, the oaths taken by all officeholders de-
claring allegiance to Cecil Calvert, Lord Baltimore, in this
feudal-like proprietary colony used the word *her* as well as
*his:*

> I do further swear I will not . . . trouble, molest, or
> discountenance any person whatsoever in the said province
> professing to believe in Jesus Christ, and in particular no
> Roman Catholic, for or in respect of *his or her* religion, nor
> *his or her* free exercise thereof within the said province, so
> that they be not unfaithful to his said Lordship or molest or
> conspire against the civil government established under
> him. . . . [emphasis added]

At least partially responsible for the wording of this oath
was a woman, Margaret Brent. Eleven words spoken by a
dying governor in the presence of witnesses made her a power
to be reckoned with in early Maryland. "I make you my sole
executrix; take all and pay all," instructed Leonard Calvert in
one of the shortest oral wills ever recorded.

Accordingly, she took charge of all the late governor's
rentals and income, paid his debts, and supervised planting
and harvesting on his estates. Then she made herself forever a
heroine to later feminists by taking charge of many of Maryland's political affairs. In addition to playing a major role in
the passage of Maryland's landmark Toleration Act and in
negotiating with the Indians to purchase land, she collected
and dispersed some of the colony's money.

Maybe her greatest claim to fame, however, was making
the first formal demand in America for female suffrage. Her
legal activities on behalf of the late Governor Calvert led her
to march right into the chambers of the Maryland legislature

on January 21, 1648, demanding not one but two votes—one for herself individually and one in her position as executrix for her deceased client. She had all but won over the legislators when Governor Calvert's personally appointed successor, Thomas Green, overcame his usual weakness and hesitation long enough to thunder "no" and break up the session in confusion.

Margaret Brent became the subject of reams of official records almost from the day of her arrival in Maryland. Together with her sister, Mary, she established a feudal manor in 1638 and exercised complete supervision, even holding judicial proceedings. In the eight years between 1642 and 1650 her name appears in Maryland court records as attorney 124 times. She acted as attorney for her sister Mary, her brother Fulke, and many neighbors—as well as serving as executrix for Governor Calvert. Because she never married, she could act with a great deal of freedom on behalf of her clients. She also carried on many real property actions in her own name. Here, for example, is a quote from the records of the Maryland Land Office:

At a court held at St. Mairies, 7 December, 1648, came Mistress Margaret Brent and required the opinion of the court. The court granted her the privilege of an opinion.

Around 1650, she apparently became a victim of Maryland's attempt to win the favor of the new Protestant Lord Protector of England, Oliver Cromwell, by denying further privileges to Catholics. She moved with her sister and brother to Westmoreland county, Virginia, where they began all over again with another plantation, inspirationally named "Peace." Her last days are as shrouded in mystery as the beginning of her life.

But for twelve memorable years she had battered political barriers, assuming a greater role in public affairs than at least ninety percent of her male contemporaries. Like other members of the colonial establishment—male and female—she combined financial wealth with intellectual energy and initiative to overcome the social and economic hurdles that kept most of the population—male and female—out of politics. For those who wonder whether only femaleness kept her from the pinnacle of power, there is William H. Browne's dry comment on Governor Green's defeat of her demand for two votes from the Maryland legislature:

> In view of subsequent occurrences one is tempted to think that if [Governor Calvert] had reversed his testamentary dispositions and made Green his executor and Mistress Brent governor, it would have been on the whole a better arrangement.

(Mr. Browne wrote the official history of early Maryland in 1904, when female suffrage was very much an issue, sixteen years before passage of the Nineteenth Amendment giving women the right to vote.)

# CHAPTER SEVEN

# *Witches and Women*

Most women were not witches. But everywhere and always, most accused witches were women.

The continent of Europe had begun to find witches in its midst in the 1300s, and by 1700 had put perhaps nine million to death.[1] Britain, isolated across the Channel, remained free of the scourge until the 1560s. Then, sparsely populated Scotland, affected and infected by its alliance with France, began to hunt witches, torturing and burning as many as two hundred a year, seven thousand in all. By 1580, toward the end of Elizabeth's reign, England joined the search.

Elizabeth's successor, King James, was a firm believer in witchcraft. While still king of Scotland, before ascending the English throne, he had written a scholarly treatise on witchcraft, *Daemonologie*. And in 1607, four years after his coronation as king of England, bracketing women and witches, he told poet Sir John Harrington of his constant wonder that the devil invariably chose hags as his agents.

Between 1580 and 1660, England hanged more than thirty thousand witches, mostly in the Puritan counties of Suffolk, Norfolk, and Essex. Unhappily, this was precisely the place

---

[1] Again, records are incomplete. But more and more historians use this startling figure.

and exactly the time to give future New England colonists at least one full generation of living with and witnessing the phenomenon firsthand. Even the fact of hanging witches, rather than following the Scottish or continental savagery of burning them, was considered a hallmark of English humanitarianism, carefully transmitted to America.

Thus, the Puritans came to the New World weighted with the heavy baggage of witchcraft. Between 1647 and 1700, there were one hundred trials, with thirty-eight people put to death as witches. And women accounted for something like seventy percent of those executed and around seventy-five percent of those accused.

Even so, the initial victim in the colonies was probably a man, about whom almost nothing is known except his asexual-sounding name, and the date, place, and cause of his death: Achsah Young of Windsor, Connecticut, hanged for witchcraft on May 26, 1647. The first to be tried and executed for witchcraft in Massachusetts, however, was definitely a woman, Margaret Jones of Charlestown, who went to the gallows on June 4, 1648, proclaiming her innocence.

John Winthrop, spewing out his fears and superstitions on the subject of witchcraft in general and witch Jones in particular, was no different from any of his contemporaries in the seventeenth-century world. Luridly and at length in his private journal he described the entire affair from accusation to execution:

> The evidence against her was, (1) that she was found to have such a malignant touch as many persons (men, women and children) who she stroked or touched with any affection or displeasure, or, etc., were taken with deafness, or vomiting, or other violent pains or sickness; (2) she practicing physic, and her medicines being such things as (by her own confession) were harmless, as aniseed, liquors, etc., yet had extraordinary violent effects, (3) she would use to tell such as would not make use of her physic that they would never

be healed, and accordingly their diseases and hurts continued, with relapse against the ordinary course, and beyond the apprehension of all physicians and surgeons; (4) some things which she foretold came to pass accordingly; other things she could tell of (as secret speeches, etc.) which she had not ordinary means to come to the knowledge of; (5) she had (upon search) an apparent teat in her secret parts as fresh as if it had been newly sucked and after it had been scanned, upon a forced search, that was withered, and another began on the opposite side; (6) in the prison, in the clear daylight, there was seen in her arms, sitting on the floor, and her clothes up, etc., a little child, which ran from her into another room, and the officer following it, it was vanished. The like child was seen in two other places, to which she had relation; and one maid that saw it, fell sick upon it, and was cured by the said Margaret, who used means to be employed to that end. Her behavior at her trial was very intemperate, lying notoriously, and railing upon the jury and witnesses, etc., and in the like distemper she died. The same day and hour she was executed, there was a very great tempest at Connecticut, which blew down many trees, etc.

As was his habit, Governor John Winthrop had shed all inhibitions in his private journal. Here, his fear and superstition are encased in unbridled, naked emotionalism. Unfortunately, this was no isolated confrontation.

The next witch to be executed in Massachusetts was Ann Hibbins of Boston in 1656. She was the aged widow of William Hibbins, a highly placed colony official and wealthy merchant, who toward the end of his life had suffered severe business losses. As a result, he left his wife only a small estate —a major problem for a woman too old to remarry unless she could offer a man great wealth. Her poor financial status meant a dismal future, with the prospect of some day being reduced to begging food or shelter. Looking back with horror and compassion more than one hundred years later, Massachusetts historian Thomas Hutchinson found that this situation "increased the natural crabbedness of [Ann Hibbins's] temper, which made her turbulent and quarrelsome, and brought her under church censures, and at length rendered her so odious to her neighbors as to cause some of them to accuse her of witchcraft." The jury found her guilty, but out of deference to her late husband, the magistrates at first refused to accept the verdict, and the case was heard in the General Court. (This was the first time that the Massachusetts legislature, the General Court, considered a case involving a life-or-death verdict.) Popular clamor caused her to be condemned and executed when, after seeing two of her accusers huddled in conversation, she accused them of talking about her. This accurate guesswork convinced her tormentors of her powers of clairvoyance. Bitterly, Reverend John Norton remarked that she was put to death "only for having more wit than her neighbors."

Spasmodically, witchcraft persecution occurred everywhere in New England. A generation before the Salem hysteria of 1692, New Haven and Connecticut recorded at least ten witches hanged—eight women and two men, husbands of two of the condemned women. One more woman in southern New England was possibly executed, and two women and four men were acquitted. In other cases involving one woman and two men, the jury divided and so made no finding of guilt. And when William Ayres and his wife submitted to ordeal by water, to see if they would float with the aid of Satan, they saved themselves only by fleeing and remaining out of sight forevermore.

Only two towns in Plymouth colony heard witchcraft accusations. Marshfield court tried the case of a young girl, Dinah Silvester, who accused the wife of William Holmes of being a witch who turned herself into the shape of a bear to cause trouble. But the court convicted the accusing Dinah of slander and demanded that she apologize publicly to Goodwife Holmes. Later, in 1677, the town of Scituate indicted Mary

Ingham for supposedly bewitching Mehitable Woodworth. However, after long jury deliberation she was acquitted.

Not so lucky was Mary Reeve Webster of Hadley, in Massachusetts Bay. She was tried for witchcraft and acquitted in 1683. But at one point in the proceeding she was dragged out of her house, hanged till near death, released, buried in the snow, and left to die. Unaccountably, she survived and lived on to old age.

In Puritan Boston, "Witch" (her only known first name) Glover was definitely an outsider. She was Irish, she was Catholic, and besides she spoke Gaelic. Her execution took place in 1685. Somehow the washerwoman was found responsible for the fits that seized the four previously well-behaved young children of John Goodwin, God-fearing laborer and member of Cotton Mather's congregation in Boston. Reverend Mather took the eldest child, thirteen-year-old Martha, into his home, where he performed a whole series of psychic experiments, prayed with her, and soothed her nerves. When she was cured to his satisfaction, he returned her to her home as a living and breathing example of socially acceptable behavior. Seeing her, the other children immediately reformed themselves, either out of awe for the Reverend, or from fear of being similarly locked up in his house for months.

On the basis of this proud achievement, Cotton Mather wrote his detailed book, *Memorable Providences Relating to Witchcraft and Possession,* published in 1689 and widely circulated throughout the colony. But if he had expected to rid Massachusetts of witchcraft, he was tragically disappointed. Within three years in Essex county, 165 men and women (twenty-six percent were males, seventy-four percent females) were accused as witches, and the court at Salem ordered twenty humans (six male, fourteen female) and two dogs (sex unknown) put to death in six frenzied months between March and September, 1692.

For one reason or another, many of the accused escaped

prosecution. (This partially accounts for the discrepancy in figures for accusations and actual trials. Imperfect records count for further inaccuracies.) But there was no way out for those who caused their supposed victims to fall into fits. Without any question they were witches who had to be removed from society immediately. They were placed in irons—which more often than not meant that they could not lie down to sleep or move any part of the body freely—thrown into a hole serving as a prison, further tortured to extract a confession, and then put on trial where they would be confronted with the most damaging evidence of all, their supposed victims playing out a hysterical routine. In addition, there would be supporting evidence given by a much larger group claiming to have suffered some misfortune such as illness, loss of domestic animals by death, or forfeit of personal property. Invariably, this second string of witnesses had also suffered failure in important daily activities such as farming, fishing, or hunting. Whereas the so-called victims of the supposed witches were mostly young, unmarried girls in their teens, the supporting witnesses were seventy-five percent men, usually married.

Most of those brought to trial as witches were married or widowed women, aged forty-one to sixty. When young people were accused, they usually turned out to be children of alleged witches. This follows the seventeenth-century assumption that witchcraft was transmitted through family lines or close relationship. Men accused of witchcraft were mostly husbands of supposed witches or were put on trial after denouncing the whole idea of witch-hunting.

Those accused of witchcraft came from every social and economic level—the aristocrat and the servant, the rich and the poor. However, all seemed to have had some personal eccentricity, or were nasty-tempted, or pursued dubious activities such as fortune-telling and folk healing. Some were wizened old women: pipe-smoking Sarah Good looked at least seventy but had to be younger since she was pregnant; Sarah

Osburne was bedridden and died; Rebecca Nurse was seventy-one and almost deaf; and Mary Esty, younger sister of Rebecca Nurse, was fifty-eight. The aptly named Martha Carrier was known as a smallpox carrier in Andover. Some were men: One such was John Proctor, husband of the pregnant Elizabeth Proctor whose execution was postponed until January 1693, because it would be wrong to kill her innocent unborn child. (Her husband died on the gallows, but she escaped the hysteria, which ended four months before her postponed execution was to take place.) Another was Giles Cory, who, preferring to die mute and thus pass his property on to his descendants, was pressed to death with huge boulders laid on his chest. Still another was John Willard, a former deputy constable who had brought in some of the first alleged witches in March and then turned against the proceedings. Another accused witch was Bridget Bishop, the town flirt, a flashy dresser and middle-aged tavern keeper. No less flirtatious, but trimly and primly dressed and forever attracting male glances, was Susanna Martin, a widow who had previously been found guilty of witchcraft in 1669, but escaped, only to be tried and executed in the Salem persecution. Public scolds, who were disliked generally, included George Burroughs and Sarah Wild. And lastly there was Dorcas Good, six-year-old daughter of Sarah Good, starved, imprisoned, and finally driven mad for the rest of her life.

Two women accused of witchcraft symbolize the excesses to which the Salem delusion went. Rebecca Nurse, seventy-one, bedridden, and almost deaf, was acquitted—only to have her case reopened when her young accusers pronounced themselves suffering new tortures as a result of the verdict. She was pronounced guilty as charged and hanged on Gallows Hills. Her own words were her undoing, the foreman of the jury, Thomas Fisk, explained in a certificate written to Goodwife Nurse's distraught family. He explained that when Deliverance Hobbs, a self-confessed witch, and her daughter had entered the courtroom to testify against the old woman, Mrs. Nurse had cried out: "What, do these persons give evidence against me now? They used to come among us." With no great difficulty the court had interpreted these words to mean that Rebecca Nurse used to associate with the Hobbses as witches. Unfortunately, deafness had caused the prisoner to miss the significance of the court's pronouncement and so she made no objection, leading the judges to assume her agreement with their interpretation. It was already too late when subsequently she protested that she had known her accusers as fellow prisoners, not as fellow witches. So she was hanged, though no one accused of witchcraft had so much said in her favor, or so little spoken against her.

The other representative case involved Elizabeth Cary. Her husband, a wealthy shipbuilder in Charlestown and a member of the General Court, decided to take matters into his own hands on hearing that Abigail Williams in Salem was denouncing his wife as a witch. The Carys arrived at the Salem court and sat in the same room as the young girls and her "afflicted" friends. Mrs. Cary's supposed victims gave no recognition that they were in the presence of their torturer. Hoping to put an end to the matter, Nathaniel and his wife arranged to meet one of the girls privately after court. But just hearing the name Cary was apparently enough to send the girl into her fits. Mrs. Cary was immediately whisked away to jail where she was kept in irons. Her husband, deciding that justice could never triumph with the free and easy admission of spectral evidence (in contrast to traditionally strict common-law procedures and rules of evidence), managed somehow to free her from prison. The two fled first to Rhode Island, and then to be entirely out of reach, went on to New York, where Governor Benjamin Fletcher gave them complete asylum.

Nobody—especially no woman—was immune to prosecution for witchcraft. Almost the only way to avoid accusation was to become an accuser. Still, several women defiantly fought in the age-old Anglo-Saxon political tradition of petition and affidavit. In one conspicuous instance, fifty-four Andover residents, including thirteen women, signed a long, detailed affidavit directed to the Salem court on behalf of five women accused as witches:

> We were surprised to hear that persons of known integrity and piety were accused of so horrid a crime, not considering, then, that the most innocent were liable to be so misrepresented and abused. When these women were accused by some afflicted persons of the neighborhood, their relations and others . . . took great pains to persuade them to own what they were, by the afflicted, charged with, and indeed, did unreasonably urge them to confess themselves guilty, as some of us who were then present can testify. But these good women did very much assert their innocency, yet some of them said they were not without fear lest Satan had some way ensnared them, because there was that evidence against them which then was by many thought to be a certain indication and discovery of witchcraft. . . . And it is probable, the fear of what the event might be, and the encouragement that it is said was suggested to them, that confessing was the only way to obtain favor, might be too powerful a temptation for timorous women to withstand. . . . Now, though we cannot but judge it a thing very sinful for innocent persons to own a crime they are not guilty of, yet, considering the well ordered conversation of these women while they lived among us, and what they now seriously and constantly affirm in a more composed frame, we cannot but in charity judge them innocent of the great transgression that hath been imputed to them. . . .

Lady Mary Phips, wife of the governor, is credited with having the courage to assume responsibility, in her husband's absence, for signing a warrant freeing an accused witch from prison. The jailer ultimately lost his job for obeying her order, but the prisoner was saved. Coincidentally, the six-month witchcraft craze came to an end with the crying out of highly placed people, including not only Lady Phips but also the governor himself.

Witchcraft made little headway in other colonies outside New England, but when it did appear it involved mostly women. In New York, shortly after the English conquered the colony from the Dutch in 1664, a man and his wife were accused of witchcraft. The husband was acquitted and set free after a trial, but the wife was released only on payment of a bond by her husband. In 1670, a Hartford woman, who had been found guilty of witchcraft at home but somehow escaped punishment, wandered to Westchester where she was ordered to stand trial. For no clear or recorded reason, she was released before the trial and allowed to take up residence wherever she chose.

In Pennsylvania, William Penn found a technical error in the proceedings against the one accused witch brought before him. He then dismissed the case without an accusative judgment.

Occasionally, witchcraft erupted in the southern colonies. As early as 1626 Goodwife Wright of Virginia was so accused before the General Court, but there is no record of any punishment. A generation later, three women were executed as witches on the seas beyond the shores of Maryland and Virginia: Mary Lee, 1654; Elizabeth Richardson, 1658; and Katherine Grady, 1659.

Father Francis Fitzherbert, a Jesuit and a passenger on the violently stormy voyage from England to Maryland, explained the need to murder Mary Lee. In his required yearly report to the general of the Society of Jesuits at Rome, he wrote:

> The tempest lasted two months in all, whence the opinion arose that it was not raised by the violence of the sea or atmosphere, but was occasioned by the malevolence of witches. Forthwith they seized a little old woman suspected

of sorcery; and after examining her with the strictest scrutiny, guilty or not guilty, they slayed her, suspected of this very heinous sin. The corpse, and whatever belonged to her, they cast into the sea. But the winds did not thus remit their violence, or the raging sea its threatenings.[2]

Why witchcraft? why Salem? why mostly women?

First, what caused witchcraft? The one hard fact involved seems to be that the cult is a holdover from pagan tradition, not entirely eradicated even in the twentieth century. The two most obvious manifestations today are of course Halloween and May Day. Halloween, the eve of All Saints' Day, in pagan times was winter eve when a fire was kindled to give hope for the rebirth of light after the darkness of the approaching winter. And the first of May, presently celebrated as May Day or sometimes as Law Day, was a fertility festival time in pagan centuries. Both festivals took place at night when, in the light of the full moon, witches were said to dance in the open meadow, seducing Satan.

Another avenue to explore looking for the cause of witchcraft is the effect of the uprooting of long-held beliefs. Repeatedly, there has been a revival of witchcraft following each such uprooting: paganism to Christianity in Europe, Catholicism to Anglicanism and Puritanism in England, independent Puritanism to royally imposed Anglicanism in Salem.

A possible answer to the second question—why Salem?— lies in comparing areas affected by witchcraft: Scotland and Salem Village, for example. Scotland, the first area in the British Isles to hunt witches, was the most primitive and isolated area in Great Britain. The Scots were great practitioners of magic, perhaps as an antidote to their unsettled political climate and internecine warfare.

---

[2] Despite ridding the ship of Mary Lee's supposed sorcery, almost everyone aboard became ill, and a few died before the ship reached Maryland.

Similarly, Salem Village (modern-day Danvers), which began the hunt and then supplied half of the twenty executed as witches, was a tiny farming community outside the main area of Salem. And Salem, in turn, was fifteen miles from the main commercial and cultural capital of the colony, Boston. Furthermore, Salem Village was a factious, quarreling community. In 1672 it had broken away from Salem to form its own parish. At the time of the witchcraft persecutions, in 1692, it had no school, was a community of poor farmers, and had no educated ministers. Its single preacher, Reverend Samuel Parris, had studied at Harvard, but never finished the requirements for a degree. He had tried to make a living from trade in Barbados, failed, and then decided to look for a call to the ministry.

Adding to the problems of the entire county, Indian raids, accompanied by very heavy fighting, occurred during the witch trials, and in neighboring Andover there had been an outbreak of smallpox. Nor was there any stability to be imbibed from the rest of the Massachusetts Bay colony, which had in 1691 lost its charter and so its independent status. Substituted for a locally elected governor was a royally imposed chief executive, and instead of their own Puritanism they now had to accept the king's Anglicanism.

There may never be a complete answer to the first two questions—why witchcraft? why Salem? But at least most writers on the subject take a stab at an explanation. However, there is almost nothing said about why the accused were overwhelmingly women. The whole subject is either ignored totally, or buried in a statement such as, "Twenty persons were executed as witches," repeated everywhere from Salem travel guidebooks to scholarly tomes.

The best way to answer that question—why mostly women?—is to concentrate on the moon, and then on the myriad superstitions, ideas, words, and phrases it has spawned. As obvious as it is significant is the idea that the moon shines

"Accusation of a Witch." *Courtesy of the Essex Institute, Salem, Mass.*

only at night when darkness and mystery hold sway—and in ancient mythology the moon was represented by a goddess, the sun by a god. Further, to the ancient pagan or (relatively modern) seventeenth-century mind, the moon as it went through its phases, from first quarter to full, represented the woman in pregnancy.

Another connection between the moon and woman as witch is the menstrual cycle, a woman's monthly period, occurring as regularly as each new moon, and sometimes also referred to as menstruation or menses—all three terms derived from the Latin word *mensis,* meaning "month." In fact, some have suggested that the whole idea of time derived from the regular recurrence of women's periods.

The relation of the words *lunatic* and *moonstruck* to both the moon and to witchcraft needs no elaboration, nor does Hecate, who was not only the ancient Greek goddess of the moon but also of the underworld, and later was additionally worshiped as the dark goddess of magic. Along the same line of thought, there is the official Catholic encyclopedia of witchcraft, *Malleus Malifacarum* ("Hammer of Witches"), published by two Dominican inquisitors, Heinrich Kramer and James Sprenger, in 1486, at the direction of Pope Innocent VIII in an effort to exterminate the scourge in Germany. More than once Kramer and Sprenger refer to women riding abroad at night with Diana, Roman goddess of fertility and the moon.

Men must have been as frightened by woman's connection to the moon's mysteriousness as they were awed by her ability to produce miniature human beings from inside her own body. Only slightly less frightening was the magic involved in midwifery and in using herbs to effect cures.

Again, John Winthrop's journal provides an uninhibited insight into a male reaction, this time to a stillborn child. When Mary Dyer, whom the Bay colony eventually put to death as a Quaker in 1660, first came to John Winthrop's attention, he wrote that she was "notoriously infected with Mrs. Hutchinson's errors, and very censorious and troublesome (she being of a very proud spirit and much addicted to revelations)." It came as no surprise to him, then, that she should give birth to a monster—which he felt compelled to describe in every gruesome detail:

It was a woman child, stillborn, about two months before the just time, having life a few hours before; it came hiplings [breach birth] till she turned it; it was of ordinary bigness; it had a face, but no head, and the ears stood upon the shoulders and were like an ape's; it had no forehead, but over the eyes four horns, hard and sharp, two of them were above one inch long, the other two shorter; the eyes standing out, and the mouth also; the nose hooked upward all over the breast and back, full of sharp pricks and scales, like a thornback; the navel and all the belly, with the distinction of the sex, were where the back should be; and the back and hips before, where the belly should have been; behind, between the shoulders, it had two mouths, and in each of them a piece of red flesh sticking out; it had arms and legs as other children; but, instead of toes, it had on each foot three claws, like a young fowl, with sharp talons.

Quite logically to Winthrop's seventeenth-century mind there was a strong probability that the midwife who delivered this freak was also a witch: "It was known that she used to give young women all the mandrakes and other stuff to cause conception; and she grew into great suspicion to be a witch, for it was credibly reported that, when she gave any medicines (for she practiced physic), she would ask the party if she did believe she could help her, etc." Women could not win. Instead of finding gratitude for their roles in medicine as midwives, doctors, and herbalists, they were instead viewed as performing black magic—which by definition made them witches.

There is another tangent worth investigating to find out the answer to the third question—why women? From the dawn of civilization, there seemed to be a close connection between society's suppression of women and witchcraft. For their part, women willingly joined witch cults as their best outlet for self-expression. On the other hand, especially in times of stress, men viewed witches as blameworthy and evil. Thus, removing them from the face of the earth was a way to preserve social order.[3] Sanction for this course of action came with the devel-

---

[3] Though different in pain and finality from being burned at the stake or hanged for witchcraft, attitudes of many men toward women's suffrage reveal the same belief in women's tendency to unsettle society.

opment of the written word when the Old Testament proclaimed, "Thou shalt not suffer a witch to live." (Exod. 22:18.) Further justification came with the New Testament, which exalted men, subordinated women.

Paganism as well as the Bible gave incontrovertible support to the prosecution of witches in Puritan New England. Colonists observed ceremonies and rituals of the Indians they considered pagan, half in fascination, half in frightened contempt. For example, in Massachusetts, Indian women could be seen performing a rite to protect newly planted corn in the spring. A woman would leave her wigwam quietly on the first dark (moonless) night, disrobe, and drag her main garment, a *matchecota,* all around the field, creating a charmed line to keep harm away. Then she would return to sleep, assured that she had protected her family's food supply for another year. The custom might be primitive, but it seemed to work. The Indians had an abundance of corn with which to feed themselves and to use in trade with the newcomers. This impressed the pragmatic Englishmen.

And, writing his *Decennium Luctuosum* the "Woeful Decade" New England suffered in the years 1689 to 1699, Cotton Mather opined:

> The story of the prodigious war made by the spirits of the invisible world upon the people of New England in the year 1692 hath entertained a great part of the English world with a just astonishment; and I have met with some strange things . . . which have made me often think that this inexplicable war might have some of its origin among the Indians whose chief sagamores are well known unto some of our captors to have been horrid sorcerers and hellish conjurers and such as conversed with demons.

Living amid one kind of paganism, then, some Puritans could make a short, easy jump to acceptance of another kind

—African. And this was, of course, the opening scene in the Salem witchcraft delusion. Tituba, a slave from Barbados, employed in the Salem Village home of the prime mover against witches, the Reverend Samuel Parrish, was a half-Indian, half-Negro who taught young Betty Parish and her circle of teen-age friends all her tricks and spells. And these were the girls who in their seizures paralyzed first Salem Village and then all of Essex county with their lurid tales and accusations of witchcraft.

Furthermore, seventeen-year-old Mercy Short, one of the accusers, had been taken by Indians from her home in Salmon Falls, New Hampshire, on the Maine border just two years before. She had seen what Cotton Mather in his account of her affliction described as the butchering of her father, mother, brother, sister, and other relatives. Then, with three surviving brothers and two sisters, she was carried off to Canada for a long period till ransomed from her Indian captors and returned to Boston where she became a household servant.

Called in by alarmed parishioners to minister to her after the conclusion of the Salem trials in the fall of 1692, Cotton Mather combined psychic research with prayer—as he had done in the Goodwin case—finally pronouncing her "deliverance" the following March 16, 1693. Again he wrote up the case, which he considered typical and therefore a valuable lesson, in a manuscript titled "A Brand Pluck'd out of the Burning." He described how the devil presented himself to Mercy Short as "a short and a black man . . . no taller than an ordinary walking-staff; he was not of a Negro but of a tawney or an Indian color."

Further on in this study he noted:

> One who was executed at Salem for witchcraft had confessed that at their chief witch meetings there had been present some French Canadians and some Indian sagamores

to concert the methods of ruining New England. Now though Mercy Short had never heard . . . of any such confession . . . she told us that at such times the spectres went away to their witch meetings . . . that there were French Canadians and Indian sagamores among them. . . .

The witchcraft trials of Salem were six months behind him when Cotton Mather finished his tract on Mercy Short, but he was as superstitious and frightened as ever. As March 1693 came to a close and he wrote *finis* to his latest research, his wife gave birth to a deformed, short-lived baby—the direct result, he contended, of her being "affrighted with an horrible spectre, in our porch, which fright caused her bowels to turn within her."

The young girls in their seizures and fits proceeded from overtones of paganism and, if Cotton Mather quoted Mercy Short accurately, a patent desire to assert independence from the older generation. She protested to what he called the "filthy witches":

What's that? Must the younger women, do you say, hearken to the elder? They must be another sort of elder women than you then! They must not be elder witches, I am sure. Pray, do you for once hearken to me. . . . What a dreadful sight are you. . . . You that should instruct such poor, young foolish creatures as I am to serve the Lord Jesus Christ, come and urge me to serve the devil.

On the other hand, the judges at the witchcraft trials based their decisions on the Bible. As early as 1641, Massachusetts Bay, in its first written code of laws, the Massachusetts Body of Liberties, had included under the heading "Capital Laws," the following: "If any man or woman be a witch, (that is, hath or consulteth with a familiar spirit,) they shall be put to death." As was their custom, Puritan leaders relied heavily on the Old

Testament in the formulation of their laws and included the biblical references in the margin—"Exodus 22-18, Leviticus 20-27, Deuteronomy 18-10."

The less-than-atoning final chapter in Massachusetts witchcraft began almost twenty years after the last trial in Salem court, and ended not so long ago in the late 1950s. In 1710 the legislature passed laws annulling all convictions, reversing attainders, and granting indemnities to heirs of the victims. But the governor at the time, Joseph Dudley, forgot to sign the act concerning attainders, and so reputations remained besmirched.

Finally, on August 28, 1957, the Massachusetts General Court passed a resolution giving the descendants of accused witches their relatives' good names, though no monetary compensation. In response to a TV play about executed Ann Pudeator, Massachusetts legislators voted approval of Chapter 145, Resolves of 1957:

> Whereas, One Ann Pudeator and certain other persons were indicted, tried, found guilty, sentenced to death and executed in the year sixteen hundred and ninety-two for "Witchcraft"; and
>
> Whereas, Said persons may have been illegally tried, convicted and sentenced by a possibly illegal court of oyer and terminer created by the then governor of the Province without authority under the Province Charter of Massachusetts Bay; and
>
> Whereas, Although there was a public repentance by Judge Sewall, one of the judges of the so-called "Witchcraft Court," and by all members of the "Witchcraft" jury, and a public Fast Day proclaimed and observed in repentance for the proceedings, but no other action taken in regard to them; and
>
> Whereas, the General Court of Massachusetts is informed that certain descendants of said Ann Pudeator and said other

persons are still distressed by the record of said proceedings; therefore be it

Resolved, That in order to alleviate such distress and although the facts of such proceedings cannot be obliterated, the General Court of Massachusetts declares its belief that such proceedings, even if lawful under the Province Charter and the law of Massachusetts as it then was, were and are shocking, and the result of a wave of popular hysterical fear of the Devil in the community, and further declares that, as all the laws under which said proceedings, even if then legally conducted, have been long since abandoned and superseded by our more civilized laws, no disgrace or cause for distress attaches to the said descendants or any of them by reason of said proceedings; and be it further

Resolved, That the passage of this resolve shall not bestow on the Commonwealth or any of its subdivisions, or on any person any right which did not exist prior to said passage, shall not authorize any suit or other proceedings nor deprive any party to a suit or other proceeding of any defense which he hiterto had, shall not affect in any way whatever the title to, or rights in any real or personal property, nor shall it require or permit the remission of any penalty, fine or forfeiture hitherto imposed or incurred.

This last paragraph becomes all the less contrite, and the entire resolution even more wishy-washy, when it is recalled that in addition to suffering torture and imprisonment, and in too many cases losing their lives through ill-treatment or hanging, those accused of witchcraft were required to pay the Commonwealth for their prison board and lodging.

# CHAPTER EIGHT

# Indian Retaliation

Increasingly, the Indians retaliated in blood against the land-hungry intruders. And often their targets were women left alone in the wilderness with infants and small children.

There is nothing remotely admirable in the colonial attitude toward, or treatment of, the Indians. Somewhat hypocritically, however, the twentieth-century United States, comfortably ensconced on land cleared and settled by white Europeans, has concentrated only on villains and heroes, all but ignoring a third category: victims.

Thus, in the Jamestown, Virginia, massacre of 1622, two women barely managed to escape capture. One was the widow Alice Proctor, who defended her home against Indian attacks for more than a month, defying orders of the local council to move to a safer area—until the authorities threatened to burn her home to the ground. The other was a Mrs. Nuice, who energetically nursed and fed her suffering neighbors, and later won special praise in the official records of the Virginia Company in London.

Less fortunate was Mary Rowlandson of Massachusetts, who got caught up in the Indian uprising of 1675–1678 known as King Philip's War (led by the son of Massasoit, Metacomet, who had been renamed King Philip by the colonists). The wholesale slaughter on all sides was the result of more than a full generation of accumulated grievances and abrasive culture conflict involving different attitudes toward land use, crime and punishment, and law and order. Thus, the Indians laid siege to the Rowlandson home in the early-morning hours of Thursday, February 10, 1676. Reverend Joseph Rowlandson, minister of the tiny frontier town of Lancaster—fifty houses, population less than three hundred—had gone to Boston, thirty-five miles to the east, seeking help against the impending attack.

At once, the war party killed twelve of the thirty-six women, children, and old people huddled together in the small dwelling, their own houses burned to the ground—including Mrs. Rowlandson's oldest sister and several relatives. Mary Rowlandson and her six-year-old daughter Sarah, who were both shot and wounded, were among the twenty-four taken prisoner for use as servants to replace dead or captured tribe members (a usual Indian practice). Also seized were the two other Rowlandson children, fourteen-year-old Joseph and eleven-year-old Mary, who both escaped injury but were separated from their mother.

For eleven weeks and five days Mary Rowlandson was forced to march some 150 miles through frozen, snow-filled northwestern Massachusetts, southern New Hampshire and present-day Vermont as the Indians fled the pursuing English. Twenty different times they had to abandon camp, Mrs. Rowlandson recalled later, "with those barbarous creatures, with our bodies wounded and bleeding, and our hearts no less than our bodies."

Helplessly she watched her injured child sink into death. And she poured her emotions into words that make the Indian–colonial confrontation uncomplicated only to the hard-hearted:

One of the Indians carried my poor wounded babe upon a horse; it went moaning all along, "I shall die, I shall die."

I went on foot after it, with sorrow that cannot be expressed. At length I took it off the horse and carried it in my arms till my strength failed and I fell down with it. Then they set me upon a horse with my wounded child in my lap, and there being no furniture upon the horse's back, as we went down a steep hill, we both fell over the horse's head, at which they like inhuman creatures laughed, and rejoiced to see it, though I thought we should there have ended our days, overcome with so many difficulties. . . .

After this it quickly began to snow and when night came on they stopped. And now I must sit down in the snow before a little fire, and a few boughs behind me, with my sick child in my lap, and calling much for water, being now (through the wound) fallen into a violent fever. My own wound also growing so stiff that I could scarce sit down or rise up; yet so it must be that I must sit all this cold winter night upon the cold snowy ground, with my sick child in my arms, looking that every hour would be the last of its life, and having no Christian friend near me, either to comfort or help me. . . .

Nine days I sat with my babe upon my lap, till my flesh was raw again. My child being even ready to depart this sorrowful world, they bade me to carry it out to another wigwam, (I suppose because they would not be troubled with such spectacles,) whither I went with a very heavy heart, and down I sat with the picture of death in my lap. About two hours in the night my sweet babe, like a lamb, departed this life, it being about six years and five months old. It was about nine days from the first wounding in this miserable condition, without any refreshing of one nature or another, except a little cold water. I cannot but take notice, how at another time I could not bear to be in the room where any dead person was, but now the case is changed. I must and could lie down with my dead babe all the night after. I have thought since of the wonderful goodness of God to me in preserving me so in the use of my reason and senses in that distressed time that I did not use wicked and violent means to end my own miserable life. . . . In the morning when they understood that my child was dead, they sent for me

home to my master's wigwam. I went to take up my dead
child in my arms to carry it with me, but they bid me let
it alone. There was no resisting, but go I must and leave it.
When I had been [awhile] at my master's wigwam, I took
the first opportunity I could get to go look after my dead
child. When I came I asked them what they had done with
it. Then they told me it was upon the hill, then they went and
showed me where it was, where I saw the ground was newly
digged, and there they told me they had buried it.

After almost three months of captivity and slavery, Mary
Rowlandson was ransomed for twenty pounds and returned
to her husband on May 2, 1676—through the efforts, she
noted, of several Boston gentlemen and "Mrs. Usher, whose
bounty and religious charity I would not forget to make mention of." (Mrs. Usher was the ancestor of Alice Morse Earle,
scholarly pioneer historian of colonial women, who wrote a
score of books at the end of the nineteenth century.) Several
weeks later her son was released on payment of seventeen
pounds, and her daughter without having to hand over any
money—in a kind of tribute to the respect the Indians had
begun to accord Mrs. Rowlandson for her dignity and courage,
as well as for her willingness to help out with her skill in
knitting and sewing. Toward the end of her ordeal, in fact, an
Indian had even presented her with a Bible he had found in
the course of a raid. Gratefully, she remarked that this Bible
"was my guide by day and my pillow at night."

Following the (naturally caused) death of her husband in
1678, Mary Rowlandson received an annual pension of thirty
pounds and settled down to write the story of her captivity for
her own children. First published at Cambridge, Massachusetts, and London, England, in 1682, the slender volume, *The
Narrative of the Captivity and Restoration of Mrs. Mary
Rowlandson,* became an instant best seller in the mother
country as well as in the colonies, and has since been reprinted
in more than thirty editions. Catharsis for the author, her

narrative of the drama of her captivity puts life—and death—into that near cliché, "Attacked and captured by Indians." A born storyteller, she divided her poignant, forty-nine page tract into twenty subsections—"First Remove," "Second Remove," etc.—thereby allowing the reader pauses to digest the full impact of her words.

Those who would promote peaceful coexistence and mutual respect between peoples and races can find support in Mary Rowlandson's narrative as she reveals dawning understanding for the captors she has previously labeled "barbarous creatures" or "pagans" or "merciless enemies." As early as the fifth remove, she began questioning the stance of her fellow colonists, so supremely self-assured of their own superiority. She noted that the English came close enough to give hope of rescue but let themselves be stopped by the river. Yet the Indians accompanying her, mostly squaws with papooses on their backs and carrying all their possessions, had previously crossed the same river.

Another time, commenting that she never once saw an Indian die of hunger (in decided contrast to the fate of so many colonists), though some of their food was hardly fit for "hog or dog," she describes some of the foods she can easily identify: ground nuts, acorns, artichokes, ground beans, lily roots, corn, wild birds, deer meat, horses' feet—which she herself finds tasty though tough—bear, beaver, squirrels, dogs, skunks, and rattlesnakes. Almost admiringly, she commends the Indians for their ability "with the help of the wonderful power of God" to find endless food in the wilderness.

At the very end of her captivity, when John Hoar of Concord came to take her home she observed, in words far removed from the usual colonial disdain or outright hostility toward Indians:

When there was such a great number of the Indians together and so greedy of a little good food, and no English there but Mr. Hoar and myself . . . they did not knock us in the head and take what we had, there being not only some provision but also trading-cloth, a part of the twenty pounds agreed upon.

And in an afterthought appended to her narrative, she came close to defending Indian retaliation against the colonists:

But now our perverse and evil carriages in the sight of the Lord have so offended Him that instead of turning His hand against them the Lord feeds and nourishes them up to be a scourge to the whole land.

Spellbinding and full of insights, Mary Rowlandson's little book is a classic in the fields of literature, history, and sociology. At the time, however, with her descriptions of mysterious rituals and devil-like creatures, Mrs. Rowlandson may well have fueled the Salem witchcraft hysteria—which followed publication of her narrative by ten years. For example, those who saw Indians as the black devil incarnate found added proof included in her story in the First Remove:

Oh the roaring, and singing and dancing, and yelling of those black creatures in the night, which made the place a lively resemblance of hell.

Again, in the course of the Fourth Remove, she watched as the Indians stripped naked a captured companion, Goodwife Joslin, pregnant and carrying her two-year-old in her arms. They "set her in the midst of them, and when they had sung and danced about her (in their hellish manner) as long as they pleased, they knocked her on the head, and the child in her arms with her. When they had done that, they made a fire and put them both into it." This is definitely reminiscent of witchcraft tales.

In all accounts of Indian retaliation, there emerges a further undeniable connection between Indian captivity and witch-craft: the inordinately large number of women as victims in both. And, in at least one case, the relationship was sharply pinpointed—Mercy Short, the seventeen-year-old former Indian captive who became an accuser of witches (discussed in Chapter Seven). Unhappily, however, there is no recorded contemporary observation of this tantalizing association, though Cotton Mather probably came closer than anyone else to linking the two ordeals. With his credentials as a witch expert already established, on the basis of his psychic research on the Goodwin children and Mercy Short, he wrote his *Decennium Luctuosum, The Woeful Decade of New England, 1689–1699,* seven years after the Salem hysteria of 1692. In the context of a litany, which included royal control over formerly independent New England, the Salem trials (for which he found Indian pagan practices highly blameworthy), and constant Indian warfare, he gave considerable attention to women captured by Indians.

Thus, he described the plight and heroism of the widow Elizabeth Heard. After barely escaping death during an Indian attack in which her young daughter was taken captive, she established her own military garrison, where for ten years she fended off marauding Indians. Admiringly, Mather commented:

> By her presence and courage it held out all the war. . . .
> The garrison had been deserted if she had accepted offers
> that were made her by her friends, of living in more
> safety at Portsmouth, which would have been a damage to
> the town and land. But by her encouragement this post was
> thus kept, and she is yet living in much esteem among her
> neighbors.

Another woman, Mary Ferguson, he reported, had to watch helplessly as a companion had her head cut off when she dared to complain to her captors. And Mrs. Sarah Gerrish, "a very beautiful and ingenious damsel, about seven years of age,"[1] was made to suffer the worst of tortures. For sixteen months she was threatened constantly with death by burning, by shooting, by starvation, and by freezing as she was forced to march to Canada. Eventually a rescuing party, in an exchange of prisoners, succeeded in returning her to her home. Other examples Cotton Mather uncovered of torture and killing by Indians were Mehetabel Goodwin, whose five-month-old infant was hanged from a tree when it annoyed one of the captors, and Mary Plaisted, whose three-week-old son was dashed against a tree and thrown into the river, after which the mother was told that "she was now eased of her burden and must walk faster than she did before!"

In the South, too, women were involved in colonial–Indian hostilities. Back in that same summer of 1676 when Mary Rowlandson returned home and "King" Philip was beheaded in New England, there was an eruption of warfare in Virginia. Known as Bacon's Rebellion, the conflict produced no clear-cut heroes, villains, or results—but promoted several women to the point of occasional mention in history books.

High-born Nathaniel Bacon led the rebellion against Governor William Berkeley, royally appointed and stiff-necked. Bacon was furious about special privileges granted to the governor's cronies, but his immediate cause of distress was official refusal to aid local settlers against constant Indian harassment and deadly attack. He marched with his followers to Jamestown, demanding authority and help in subduing the Indians. When the governor refused, Bacon and his men drove Berkeley out of Jamestown and burned the town to the ground. However, the entire rebellion collapsed a month later with the

[1] Custom dictated that young Sarah Gerrish, though unmarried, was entitled to be called Mistress, abbreviated to Mrs., because she belonged to a socially prominent family.

sudden death of Bacon, and the governor hanged some twenty rebels.

Women were among the most zealous activists in this rebellion—reacting fiercely against threats to home, hearth, and family. Mrs. No-First-Name Haviland traveled everywhere on the Virginia frontier, helping her husband round up supporters. Sarah Drummond made fiery speeches to convince the wavering. Shouting her contempt for England, she asserted that she feared its power no more than a piece of broken straw, and illustrated her words by breaking a stick of wood. Lydia Chiesman also spoke for the rebels. When her husband was condemned to death, she begged the governor to pardon him, saying that he would not have entered the fray if he had not been influenced by her. She went so far as to proclaim her own guilt and ask that her husband be pardoned and she hanged in his place. The governor ignored her plea, but before Chiesman could go to the gallows he died in prison.

As an eyewitness, Anne Cotton wrote one of the leading chronicles of the rebellion, "An Account of Our Late Troubles in Virginia." In her 3,500-word monograph, dated 1676, she described Bacon's using four women as a shield while their husbands built fortifications.

Bacon's wife and staunch supporter, the former Elizabeth Duke, had been a rebel—social rather than military—since girlhood. Her rebelliousness took the form of marrying without parental consent despite the fact that her father's will said specifically that she would inherit two thousand pounds, "but if she marry Bacon void." She had the audacity to sue in England, but without success. The Lord Chancellor publicly scolded her, saying that "such an example of presumptuous disobedience highly merited such a punishment."

Even after the rebellion, women carried the complaints against Governor Berkeley's high-handedness all the way across the ocean, appearing personally before the Lords of Trade and Plantations. Among other things, the governor had charged his opponents with treason (though not out of any particular love or sympathy for the Indians), confiscated their property, and hanged more than twenty. Vehemently protesting the unjust sentencing and execution of her husband, and the depriving of her and her five children of their means of subsistence, fiery Sarah Drummond caught the ear of the king, who ordered her property restored to her. In addition, he declared that her husband's death, under martial law, was contrary to the laws of England. Subsequently, King Charles II recalled Governor Berkeley, commenting: "This old fool has killed more people for a little mutiny in his naked country than I did for the murder of my father." (Charles I had been executed by the Cromwellians in 1649, during the course of England's civil war.)

Twenty-one years later, another woman, Hannah Dustin,[2] was captured by Indians in the course of the first war between the French and the English to be fought on New World soil. On March 15, 1697, just six days after giving birth to her twelfth child Martha, Hannah Dustin, her infant, and Mrs. Mary Neff who was acting as nursemaid, were taken prisoner.

Thomas Dustin, at work in a nearby field, had caught sight of the attacking Indians, but had been too late to warn his family. However, he succeeded in taking seven of the older children far enough away to escape to safety before their house burned to the ground.

As often happened, the Indians killed the infant by smashing it against a tree until dead. Newborns were a nuisance on forced march, and could serve no useful function once destination was reached.

The Indians and their captives—Hannah Dustin, the nurse Mary Neff, and some forty other residents of the town of

[2] Recounting the story in his monograph, *Decennium Luctuosum,* Cotton Mather titled the three-page section on Hannah Dustin "A Notable Exploit; Wherein Dux Foemina Facti" ("a woman as leader in the accomplishment").

Haverhill, Massachusetts—trudged over one hundred miles north to an Indian settlement near modern-day Concord, New Hampshire. There, Hannah and Mary were made servants to an Indian family of twelve, along with a previously captured boy Samuel Lennardson, taken some eighteen months before at Worcester, Massachusetts.

Threatened with a still more deathly trek of a hundred miles northward, where after arrival they would be forced to strip and run the gauntlet, the three servants concocted a bold plan of killing their captors. The young boy Samuel somehow got his master to show him how to murder and then scalp an enemy. Then, before daybreak on March 30, while the Indians were still sleeping, Hannah and Samuel attacked with hatchets. Samuel killed one, Hannah nine. They allowed one wounded squaw and a child to escape, and themselves set out to return to Haverhill.

However, the always practical Hannah, fearing that no one would believe her story without actual proof, raced back to the site, gathered the ten scalps, and only then made her way home.

Reunited with her husband and seven living children, Hannah petitioned the General Court a few days later for reparation. On presentation of the ten scalps, she was voted a bounty of twenty-five pounds for herself and another twenty-five pounds to be divided equally between Mary Neff and Samuel Lennardson. An instant heroine, she was glorified by Cotton Mather in his *Magnalia,* History of New England, and invited to dine at the home of one of Boston's most respected citizens, Judge Samuel Sewall.

She lived on uneventfully to her death in 1736. By the nineteenth century—during the frenzy to abrogate all former treaties made with the Indians and thereby seize most of their remaining land—she was promoted to folk hero. In 1874, Penacook or Dustin Island, the site of her exploit, erected a statue showing her wielding a hatchet. And in 1879, her hometown of Haverhill erected a similar monument to her memory.

Actually, the Hannah Dustin sage reveals every participant as victim—Hannah, her nurse, and infant; the ten dead Indians; and, in fact, all colonists and all Indians. They were all trampled in the bloodletting duel between England and France. The so-called French and Indian War, which ended in 1763, was simply the culmination of three-quarters of a century of warfare, which had begun in 1689. The first act in the long contest was King William's War, 1689 to 1697. In America, New England was the chief battlefront, and Indians were often goaded into attacking English settlements such as the one at Haverhill. This particular manifestation of French–English rivalry produced no victor or lasting peace settlement.

Similarly, the second and third segments of this murderous rivalry, Queen Anne's War, 1701 to 1714, and King George's War, 1739 to 1748, were inconclusive. Again, some Indian tribes allied themselves with the French in attacking the English colonists. Some of the bloodiest attacks by Indians were on Deerfield, a tiny frontier town in northwest Massachusetts. That rare and scholarly chronicler, George Sheldon, writing his classic two-volume history of Deerfield, in 1896, viewed the colonists with awe and the Indians with sympathy. He included innumerable eyewitness accounts and descriptions handed down through his own family, which—since he had been born in 1818—he heard directly from his grandparents. For example, he wrote of the attack on the home of Benoni Stebbins, a neighbor of his ancestor, John Sheldon:

> It was occupied by Sergt. Stebbins, his wife and five children; David Hoyt, his wife and child; and probably Joseph Catlin with his wife and child. . . . Desperate attempts were now made to set the house on fire, which cost the lives of a Macqua chief and several of his men.

The fury of the assailants increased with their losses but they were forced to leave the field and take shelter in the Sheldon house and the meetinghouse. From these covers they continued to shower their bullets upon the heroic garrison. . . . Sergt. Stebbins was killed. Mrs. Hoyt was wounded, and also a soldier. . . .

In all the wars of New England, there is not a more gallant act recorded than this defense of an unfortified house, by seven men and a few women, for three hours, against, not only the fury and wiles of an unorganized horde of savages but also a large force of French soldiers, under officers of the line trained in the wars of France.

In this same Deerfield massacre of 1704, Sheldon reports the murder of Mary Allen, whose "captors finding her an incumbrance in their hasty retreat, probably knocked her on the head in the woods, where her body became the prey of wild beast, the scalp being retained, to grace their triumphant reception at home."

Other captives—notably children—astounded Sheldon by their refusal to return home even when freed. "A hothouse civilization," must be all that Europeans offered their people, he concluded, adding that the children must have loved nature and the simple life in contrast to the highly touted excellence of Western civilization. He cited as the most conspicuous example of this strong attachment to the Indian way of life the very young daughter of John Williams. Not released with her father who had also been taken prisoner in the early 1700s, she lived with her captors, learned their habits and customs, and eventually married one of them. She steadfastly declined to return home permanently. And in 1740, on a visit to her Deerfield birthplace, she indignantly repulsed the attempts of her friends to redeem her, insisting that she preferred life as an Indian.

When Deerfield was again attacked in 1746, the most vivid and informative eyewitness account was written by Lucy

Terry, a sixteen-year-old slave belonging to Ensign Ebenezer Wells. Succinctly, in twenty-eight homespun lines, America's first Negro poet described the deaths of seven men and one woman:

> *August 'twas the twenty-fifth,*
> *Seventeen hundred forty-six,*
> *The Indians did in ambush lay,*
> *Some very valiant men to slay,*
> *The names of whom I'll not leave out:*
> *Samuel Allen like a hero fout,*
> *And though he was so brave and bold,*
> *His face no more shall be behold.*
>
> *Eleazer Hawks was killed outright*
> *Before he had time to fight,—*
> *Before he did the Indians see,*
> *Was shot and killed immediately.*
>
> *Oliver Amsden he was slain,*
> *Which caused his friends much grief and pain.*
> *Simeon Amsden they found dead*
> *Not many rods distant from his head.*
>
> *Adonijah Gillett, we do hear,*
> *Did lose his life which was so dear.*
> *John Sadler fled across the water,*
> *And thus escaped the dreadful slaughter.*
>
> *Eunice Allen sees the Indians coming,*
> *And hopes to save herself by running;*
> *And had not her petticoat stopped her,*
> *The awful creatures had not cotched her,*
> *Nor tommy hawked her on the head,*
> *And left her on the ground for dead.*

*Young Samuel Allen, Oh, lack-a-day!*
*Was taken and carried to Canada.*

Historian Sheldon calls this poem "Bars Fight" (Bars was the name of an area in the town), "the fullest contemporary account of that bloody tragedy which has been preserved."

Another nineteenth-century historian, William Fowler, told the story of a Mrs. Hendee of Royalton, Vermont, working alone in the field in the years before the Revolution, since her husband was absent on military duty. The Indians attacked her house and carried off her children across the White River. Waxing florid and Victorian, Fowler recounts in his *Woman on the American Frontier,* published in 1878:

> With pallid face, flashing eyes, and lips compressed, maternal love dominating every fear, she strode into the Indian camp, regardless of the tomahawks menacingly flourished round her head, boldly demanded the release of her little ones, and persevered in her alternate upbraidings and supplications, till her request was granted.

However, Fowler continues, rescuing her own children was not enough, so she returned across the deep and wide river to the Indian camp and demanded the release of no less than fifteen captured children of other settlers. Not only did she succeed in her mission, but she so impressed the Indians with her bravery that they offered the services of a strong young Indian to carry her on his back across the river—though the fifteen children were apparently allowed to wade or swim.

All of these Indian–colonist confrontations were total war. Women were involved every bit as much as men, since homes proved no sanctuary in attack. There was, quite simply, no such person as a protected noncombatant.

# · *Part IV* ·

---

# FROM
# BRITISH COLONISTS
# TO
# AMERICAN RESIDENTS

---

Pastel portrait of Thomas Moore as a child, c. 1725, by Henrietta Johnston, America's first woman painter. *Courtesy of the Collection of the Virginia Museum of Fine Arts.*

# CHAPTER NINE

# Business and Professions

Midwifery, imported from Europe and the direct ancestor of modern obstetrics, was a specialty practiced almost exclusively by women. Jane Sharp of England, a skilled midwife for thirty years who published the authoritative handbook *The Compleat Midwife's Companion* in 1671, strongly advised against admitting men to the field since "the art of midwifery chiefly concerns us." And when Captain Francis Raynes of Wells, Maine, in 1675 announced himself as that wonderful anomaly, the male midwife, the town publicly scolded him and fined him fifty shillings "for presuming to act the part of a midwife."

Occupying positions of greatest dignity in the colonial period, midwives raised the status of women in general. In the early years of Massachusetts Bay colony, several Boston women took the bold step of petitioning the court on behalf of midwife Alice Tilly, accused of ministering badly to several women and children. Mary Coggan, Margery Colborne, Anne Cotton, Lydia Oliver, Elinor Shrimpton, and Elizabeth Winthrop asserted that the magistrates and many other men might speak from mere hearsay, but "we and many more of us can speak from experience."

Always on call to give or save life, midwives were also frequently summoned by courts to testify as experts on questions of doubtful pregnancy, or called into court as reliable witnesses on such matters as age, bastardy, or infanticide. In his diary for December 13, 1711, William Byrd of Virginia wrote: "About ten o'clock I went to the capitol where a jury of matrons were impanelled to inquire if Betty Jordan was quick with child, and their verdict was that she was quick."

When science and education found their way into medicine in the mid-eighteenth century[1] and men began taking over the midwife's functions, husbands bitterly resented their fellow males as intruders—despite the fact that these carefully trained *accoucheurs* had higher standards of cleanliness and sanitation, and could use forceps and perform Cesarean operations when necessary. However, before men took over completely, several women entered the record books for living to remarkably old age and assisting at multiple births. Dorchester, Massachusetts, records show that "old widow Wiat" lived to "the great age of ninety-four years," having helped deliver "upwards of one thousand and one hundred children." In Charles Town, South Carolina, Elizabeth Philips brought some three thousand children into the world by the time of her death in 1761 at the age of seventy. Two years later, in the frontier settlement of Marlboro, Vermont, the wife of Thomas Whitmore died at the age of eighty-seven, having officiated at the birth of more than two thousand infants and "never lost a patient," according to Zadock Thompson in his 1853 *History of Vermont*. And in 1771, seventy-six-year-old Catherine Blaikley of Williamsburg, Virginia, died, credited by the *Virginia Gazette* with delivering more than three thousand babies.

The practice of medicine, too, was on a decidedly unprofessional level and largely in the hands of women. In fact, very

---

[1] Dr. William B. Shippen of Philadelphia gave a course for midwives in 1765, open to both sexes. He discussed anatomy, pregnancy, birth labor—both normal and complicated—and diseases affecting women and children.

few men were educated as professional physicians until the late eighteenth century. Every mother knew the uses of herbs and medicinal cures, unhesitatingly taking care of her own family or that of a neighbor whose wife was sick. Of the several women reported to have called themselves physicians and surgeons during the colonial period, a few have risen from anonymity: Anne Mountfort Eliot, mother of six, who served as doctor of Roxbury, Massachusetts, until her death in 1687; Elizabeth King of Southold, Long Island, who undertook the duties of chief physician from 1740 till she died in 1780; and a Mrs. Levingstone mentioned by William Byrd in an account of his 1732 visit to the frontier settlement of Fredericksburg where he was a guest of Colonel Harry Willis:

> Besides Colonel Willis, who is the top man of the place, there are only one merchant, a tailor, a smith, and an ordinary [tavern] keeper . . . though I must not forget Mrs. Levingstone, who acts here in the double capacity of a doctress and a coffee woman.

The near-miraculous cure effected by an anonymous but "notable female doctress" was mentioned in a report by John Clayton, rector of Crofton at Wakefield in Yorkshire, England. Writing to the Royal Society on May 12, 1688, about his voyage to Virginia he noted:

> A gentlewoman that was a notable female doctress told me that a neighbor being bit by a rattlesnake swelled excessively. Some days afterwards she was sent for, who found him swelled beyond what she had thought it had been possible for the skin to contain, and very thirsty. She gave him oriental Bezoar shaved, with a strong Decoction of the aforesaid Dittany, whereby she recovered the person.

In the Maryland archives, historian Julia Cherry Spruill found several references to lawsuits brought by Katherine

Hebden and her husband Thomas to collect payment due for her medical services in the 1640s. At least four times she was successful in suits instituted by her in her own name or by her husband on her behalf. Other lawsuits to force payment for medical services rendered in Maryland in the years 1640 to 1660 were won by Mary Bradnox, Mary Vanderdonck, and the wife of Oliver Spry.

Information on women being paid as nurses is spotty, though Julia Spruill has found a few notations of payment to women for their nursing services, one as early as 1659, when the Maryland provincial court ordered Calvert county to pay Mary Gillford for attending to a sick boy. And in 1685, a Mrs. Robinson received a monthly fee of one hundred pounds of tobacco on orders from the Christ Church Parish in Middlesex county, Virginia, for taking care of an old sick man, Thomas Wilson. Throughout the colonial period, women nursed disabled soldiers, and during the French and Indian War, 1756 to 1763, women nurses even accompanied the armies, also doing their cooking and washing. There were a few cases of nursing services performed by women for private patients in the seventeenth century, and by the eighteenth century women occasionally advertised their nursing abilities. Still, every mother had her own stock of herbs and medicinal cures for her own family, and so the most effective and experienced nurses continued to be the women of each individual household.

Fortunately, the climate of the colonies was much more healthful than that of the Old World and thereby contributed to the relative longevity of the population. Nevertheless, trading centers, such as Boston and New York, constantly suffered from epidemics of smallpox, yellow fever, and dysentery brought in from the West Indies or Europe. To reduce the spread of germs, many towns began passing strict sanitation laws to deal with garbage, butcher shops, and human refuse. But it was a losing battle. People themselves were breeding grounds for disease, since for more than the first 150 years of settlement personal cleanliness was an unknown concept, a luxury for the future. Soap made from animal grease and wood ashes was hard on the skin. Equally difficult, water had to be carried from great distances and so had to be carefully conserved. And most of the population had only one set of clothes, meaning that these could seldom if ever be removed for washing, drying, and ironing.

Meanwhile, the same combination of newness, wilderness, and colonial status that radically changed the routine and business outlook of men in the English colonies made some women achieve or reach for a new degree of financial independence. In New York, for example, the shrewd merchandising of Margaret Philipse, shipowner and international trader, made diarist Jaspar Danckers burst out that she was not only the most stingy and greedy of women but of all traders in general. When he was sent out by Holland in 1679 to survey the New York area to find a place to plant a new colony (this was fifteen years after the conquest of New Netherland by the English, who renamed the area New York), Danckers had sailed on her ship, the *Charles*, on which she owned all the cargo and exercised complete authority over crew and passengers.

She had engaged in the shipping business almost from the date of her arrival in the New World from Holland, sometime during the year 1659. Though married to Peter Rudolphus shortly after landing and, after his death, to Fredrick Philipse, she carried on her business under her maiden name of Hardenbrook—which she would do till her own death in 1690, though perversely history would insist on recording her as Margaret Philipse. From her first husband, a wealthy merchant trader, she had inherited enough money to help expand the business ventures of her second husband, making him one of the colony's richest men. At the same time she herself carried on trade with Holland, exchanging American furs for Dutch merchandise, which she then offered for sale in the colony. Though mother of three sons and a daughter and married for some twenty-eight years to Philipse, she made frequent trips between America and Holland.

Teaching was a profession that attracted many women. Very early in the colonial period, the widow Margery Hoar Flynt of Braintree, Massachusetts, ran a boarding school for girls, emphasizing dancing, needlework, household arts, and music lessons. When she died in March 1687, her tombstone memorialized her as "a gentlewoman of piety, prudence, and peculiarly accomplished for instructing young gentlewomen, many being sent to her from other towns, especially from Boston."

In Boston during the years 1706 to 1776 Robert Francis Seybolt found several women advertising themselves as teachers. In his study *The Private Schools of Colonial Boston,* published in 1935 and based largely on newspaper announcements, he discusses, for example, Mistress Mary Turfrey of Boston's South End. She proposed to board young gentlewomen, adding her desire to discuss terms with any gentleman who desired to put his daughters "under her education" (here the word *education* is close to the Latin *educare* meaning "to rear, to bring up," leading to the conclusion that she was conducting a finishing school). Another woman, Mrs. Collins, in 1736 promised to teach French to "any young ladies or other persons." That same year, Margaret Mackellwen proposed to teach pastry-making, painting on glass, and embroidery. Just six years later in 1742, an obviously indomitable Mrs. Condy opened her school for teaching arts and crafts, promising to supply prospective customers with materials "whether they learn of her or not . . . and cheaper than those which come from London."

Equally at home merchandising or teaching, Elizabeth Murray in 1751 informed one and all that she would board young ladies and teach Dresden, and would also sell all kinds of material, "newest fashion caps," necklaces and earrings, women's shoes, stockings, gloves, thread, needles, and pins. Elizabeth Cain in 1755 combined the ability to clean gloves with running a school "where all sorts of work may be taught," and spinning. "That most ingenious art of painting on gauze and cat-gutt" as well as artificial-flower-making could be learned from Mrs. Elizabeth Courtney in 1767, who added, apparently thinking to supplement her income if the turnout was not large enough: "English feather muffs and tippets to be had cheap and gauze washed, to look as well as new." A sad story appeared in the advertisement of an un-named couple who had been enticed to Boston from Ireland by their relative, who was nowhere to be found. Thus, he would teach the three Rs, Italian bookkeeping, and the classics, while she, a good seamstress who could also read and write, "understands housework extremely well" and "would engage in a good family as house maid or child's maid."

Similar advertising was found in Southern newspapers, be-ginning with the Widow Varnod, who in 1734 announced the establishment of a French school for young females in South Carolina. In Annapolis, Maryland, Mary Ann March and her daughter taught embroidery and sampler work in the early 1750s, and in the same town in 1754, Mary Salisbury pro-posed opening a boarding school for girls who wished to learn French and fancy needlework. Also in Annapolis a Mrs. Polk in 1774 announced the opening of a school to meet mornings between the hours of eight and one. She, too, would teach fancy embroidery and needlework, and for those girls who for whatever reason could not come to her, she offered to meet at their homes at whatever hour they found convenient.

Occasionally, women taught in town-supported schools, but in the lower grades, the only age level for which their own meager education was thought to equip them. For example, the town records of Dedham, Massachusetts, for the eighteen years from 1757 to 1775 list nineteen women teachers.

Never in New England, but further south, including Philadelphia, indentured females were sometimes promoted to the
role of governess. Also, some daughters of wealthy planters
assumed this position.

Just prior to the Revolution, Philip Fithian, tutor at one of
Virginia's grandest plantations, described two young govern-
esses working not too far away. In his journal he praised Miss
Garrot, governess for the daughters of Colonel Tayloe:
"chatty, satirical, neat, civil," with the happy facility of making "many merry remarks at dinner." However, he sneered at
the strange appearance of the other, young Sally Panton from
England, who taught English, French, and writing to Miss
Turburville, a friend of Fithian's tutees. For some reason forever lost except to fiction's imagination, Mistress Panton, with
a comfortable legacy of fifty pounds sterling back in England,
had uprooted herself to settle in Virginia where she was
miserably homesick and discontent.

Whereas back home in Europe, the somewhat rigid social
order placed certain occupations beyond the reach of upper-
class women, the freer and upwardly mobile American society,
especially in the towns, gave women opportunity to enter all
kinds of businesses and occupations without losing social
standing. In addition to working as teachers, nurses, and midwives, women managed shops, crafted articles for sale, and
were also employed as tavern keepers. Spinning, weaving, lace-
making, and samplers brought good profits even in the earliest
years, as did the sale of homemade jelly, bread, cakes, and
gingerbread. If all else failed, women could always—like
Judith Manigault of South Carolina in 1685—take in children
or adults as paying boarders.

Several colonial women deserve inclusion in a special hall
of fame honoring high achievers during the first half of the
eighteenth century. So named should be Hannah Williams,
Sibylla Masters, Sarah Kemble Knight, Henrietta Johnston,
Elizabeth (Eliza) Lucas Pinckney, Jane Colden, and Martha

Logan. One other, the highly successful counterfeiter, Mary Peck Butterworth, can either be omitted—conspicuously by way of disgrace—or can be used to leaven the group as a scapegrace.

Hannah Williams of South Carolina became the New World's first woman scientist a generation after the founding of the Royal Society in England in 1662, when science was in its infancy and concerned mainly with collecting and describing natural phenomena. Along with Paul Dudley and Cotton Mather of Massachusetts, she set about collecting all sorts of specimens. In 1705 she sent to England several kinds of lizards, scorpions, and snakes in a bottle, as well as many insects, birds, pressed leaves, and a wild bees' nest.

In the early 1700s Sibylla Masters matched her Quaker husband's achievements (he had served successively as alderman and mayor of Philadelphia and Provincial Councillor) with her own as mother of four children and creator of two important inventions. She developed a method to pulverize corn into meal by using a process of stamping rather than the customary one of grinding. In 1715 she voyaged to England on her own to obtain a patent. Returning to Philadelphia, she tried selling the cornmeal as a cure for consumption, but sales were disappointing. So she turned her ingenuity to a second invention, a special process for weaving straw, and proceeded to market and advertise hats, bonnets, baskets, chairs, and stools, which were all made by the new method. She may or may not have been the first American woman inventor. But there is no question that she was ingenious in developing her special techniques, patenting her two inventions and marketing the resulting products—and that she thus made a great contribution to the country's industrial and economic progress.

A contemporary, thirty-nine-year-old Sarah Kemble Knight of Boston, set out by herself to supervise distribution of an estate in New York. Either already a widow or about to be bereaved in two years—depending on which historian is read—she left her one and only child, sixteen-year-old Elizabeth, in charge at home.

Over a period of five months, she made the round trip by horse to New York, via Rhode Island, New Haven, and Westchester county—a journey considered extremely hazardous for an experienced, well-armed giant, let alone for an ordinary-sized, unaccompanied amateur traveler. All along the way she kept a journal (her greatest claim to fame), amounting eventually to some ten thousand words, scintillating, humorous, and full of invaluable firsthand observation on the social, economic, and political conditions of the long-settled Northeast.

Sarah Knight's journal gives the reader a strong suspicion that she undertook her journey out of sheer curiosity to see the world beyond Boston, or to prove that a woman had the courage and stamina to hazard a journey completely on her own through woods filled with hostile Indians and wild animals, without maps to chart her way. One time, all alone, not knowing the direction and surrounded by what she called "terrifying darkness," she commented that all this "was enough to startle a more masculine courage."[2]

Apparently, she had to deal with shyster types who tried to distract her by providing all kinds of amusements after she at great risk had finally arrived at her destination. However, she accomplished her mission and returned home on March 3, 1705, happy to find "kind relations and friends flocking in to welcome me and hear the story of my transactions and travails. . . ."

Positively, this could not have been the end of Sarah Knight's career, though the only evidence backing such a presumption is the lofty title forever bestowed on her—"Madam"

[2] Sarah Kemble Knight's many-faceted personality cannot be confined to a single chapter. Her journal will be considered separately in Chapter Eleven, "Arts and Letters."

Sarah Knight. Some have speculated that she acquired it as director of a writing school that included Benjamin Franklin and Samuel Mather, son of Cotton Mather, among its pupils. However, there is no record or trace of her in any Boston classroom, so perhaps the title was self-conferred. On the other hand, records for the time are admittedly scanty, and Hannah Mather Crocker (1752–1829), daughter of Samuel Mather, writing her strongly feminist tract, *Observations on the Real Rights of Women,* in 1818, was the first to mention Sarah Knight in print, calling her "a smart, witty, sensible woman," who in her day had exerted "considerable influence." Further, historical detectives have deduced that Sarah Knight's ability to read and write, as well as the literary references made in her journal, indicate a classical education so rare for a female in her day—her dates are 1666 to 1727—that she undoubtedly would have put it to special use.

Down south, Elizabeth (Eliza) Lucas Pinckney of South Carolina had by the middle of the eighteenth century successfully undertaken the culture of silkworms—and at one time gave the Princess of Wales, mother of King George III, a dress woven from silk grown on her own plantation. In addition, she found a way to raise indigo in the local soil, a crop abandoned seventy years earlier as unsuitable for the area.

Her life was very much affected by—and in turn actually influenced—England's striving for empire. Her father, a lieutenant colonel in the British army, had to leave his two daughters and their ailing mother alone on their newly settled plantation, seventeen miles outside of Charles Town, when conflict erupted between Spain and England in 1739. She described her new responsibilities to a friend: "I have the business of three plantations to transact, which requires much writing and more business and fatigue of other sorts than you can imagine," but, she reasoned, "it was unavoidable as my mama's bad state of health prevents her going through any fatigue."

Still in her teens when she supervised experiments leading to the successful growing of indigo, she helped to make her colony self-sufficient up to the time of the Revolution, when war cut off trade. (After the Revolution, sometime around 1800, cotton replaced indigo as South Carolina's chief crop.) At the same time, by growing indigo in English America, she strengthened England on the world scene, freeing the mother country from the need to import this dye—used in the important cloth industry—from her enemy France. Eliza Lucas's success was superlatively timed, since the spilling over of European wars onto the high seas and into America meant that South Carolina's one staple, rice, could no longer be exported to the continent of Europe, its main market.

To her father, Eliza Lucas wrote in 1744: "We please ourselves with the prospect of exporting in a few years a good quantity of [indigo] from hence, and supplying our Mother Country with a manufacture for which she has so great a demand, and which she is now supplied with from the French colonies and many thousand pounds per annum thereby lost to the nation." She distributed seeds from her early crops to many local planters, so that very shortly the total crop reached first forty thousand pounds for shipment to England, then soon afterward one hundred thousand pounds, at which point Parliament bestowed a special bounty on the colony.

Educated in England, Eliza Lucas could quote Virgil, Plutarch, Shakespeare, and Milton, speak French, and even play an occasional tune on that ostensibly masculine instrument, the flute. She was a whirlwind who rose at five each morning and equated sleep with death: "The longer time we are awake, the longer we live," she concluded at the age of twenty. "Thus then I have the advantage over the sleepers in point of long life." In her spare time she tutored her younger sister Polly, as well as two young Negro girls, whom she hoped would then teach the other young black children. And for her own amusement she sometimes wrote verse. In a 1742 letter she wrote:

> I promised to tell you when the mocking bird began to
> sing. The little warbler has done wonders. The first time
> he opened his soft pipe this spring he inspired me with
> the spirit of rhyming and produced the three following lines
> while I was lacing my stays:

> *Sing on thou charming mimic of the feathered kind,*
> *And let the rational a lesson learn from thee,*
> *To mimic (not defects) but harmony.*

Then mocking herself she added: "If you let any mortal besides yourself see this exquisite piece of poetry, you shall never have a line more than this specimen, and how great will be your loss, you who have seen the above may judge."

Her carefully preserved letter book[3] is a gold mine of information about colonial life, the role of women, and, of course, the many accomplishments of the writer herself. For example, as she succeeded in her plantation enterprises, she developed a strong sense of independence. Thus, when her father wrote to suggest two men as possible husbands, she replied that she liked neither, preferred the single life instead. Referring to the first, she called him "the old gentleman" and told her father politely but firmly "that the riches of Peru and Chile if he had them put together could not purchase a sufficient esteem for him to make him my husband." As for the second prospect, she wrote reprovingly: "You know, Sir, I have so slight a knowledge of him I can form no judgment of him, and a case of such consequences requires the nicest distinction of humors and sentiments." However, by the time she reached

---

[3] Many contemporary businessmen and private correspondents kept a copybook of their letters just as Eliza Lucas Pinckney did. She would have used her letter book for drafting outgoing correspondence, recording memoranda, or copying a completed letter.

the age of twenty-two she changed her mind, and on May 27, 1744, married Colonel Charles Pinckney, twenty-three years her senior, whose wife had died four months earlier.

The birth of her first child, Charles Cotesworth Pinckney (who would eventually represent South Carolina at the Constitutional Convention of 1787), occasioned a letter ordering a newly developed toy from London with which the child could, she concluded, "play himself into learning." And she wrote of her plan to teach her son to read letters by the time he began to speak.

Another letter tells of her study of law, which she hopes "will make me useful to any of our poor neighbors." She writes of drawing up two wills, but tells of how she balked at drawing a marriage settlement for a wealthy widow: "It was out of my depth and I absolutely refused it, so she got an abler hand to do it. Indeed she could afford it. But I could not get off from being one of the trustees to her settlement, and an old gentleman the other."

Eventually, Eliza Pinckney mothered three sons (one of whom died shortly after birth) and one daughter. In the early 1750s the family moved to London, on Colonel Pinckney's insistence that only in the motherland would his young sons obtain the education necessary for their future position as upper-class colonists. To pay expenses he served as commissioner representing South Carolina to the British Board of Trade. However, renewed war with France convinced him to return home with his wife and daughter, though he left his sons behind to finish school.

One month after his arrival in South Carolina, Colonel Pinckney contracted malaria and died three weeks later on July 12, 1758. Henceforth, Eliza Pinckney took complete charge of the plantation, now greatly enlarged by the combination of her own and her late husband's holdings and wealth, and never remarried. When she died of cancer on May 26, 1793, in Philadelphia where she had gone seeking cure by a highly recommended medical specialist, George Washington served as pallbearer at his own request. He had met her two years previously on his tour of the South.

In a related field, Jane Colden was a distinguished mid-eighteenth-century botanist, one of ten children of Cadwalader Colden, lieutenant governor of New York, who had himself been educated at the University of Edinburgh in medicine. He encouraged her to read widely and taught her the recently published Linnaean system, to the point where she joined him in corresponding with the noted Swedish naturalist Karl von Linné (whose name is sometimes Latinized as Linnaeus). Partly because she never learned botanical Latin, she was able to popularize botany by describing plants in English. By 1757 she produced a catalog fully describing more than three hundred local specimens, illustrated with her own sketches of living plants and ink impressions she had taken of leaves. When the young Scottish botanist William Rutherford visited Dr. Colden he was impressed with her accomplishments as a fellow professional—as well as her creativity in the kitchen: "She has discovered a great number of plants never before described, and has given them properties and virtues, many of which are found useful in medicine, and she draws and colors them with great beauty. N. B. She makes the best cheese I ever ate in America."

At the interestingly late age of thirty-five, she married Dr. William Farquhar, March 12, 1759. Unhappily, she died just seven years later in 1766.

A contemporary, Martha Logan of Charles Town, South Carolina, was a dealer in nursery plants, a well-known horticulturist, and author of *The Gardener's Calendar*. Her gardening was both a hobby and a source of income since she sold seeds for vegetables, flowers, and fruit trees, and corresponded extensively with Pennsylvania botanist John Bartram, whom she had met in 1760. Earlier she had managed a boarding school, with a master to teach writing and arithmetic, while she herself took charge of classes in reading, drawing, and needlework. Newspaper advertisements in the local *Gazette* reveal some of her additional activities: selling her own estate as well as other properties, and acting as attorney for her son.

Her life was long, full, and independent. Left fatherless (almost nothing is known about her mother) at the age of thirteen, she married George Logan Jr. the following year. The couple lived on a plantation that Martha had inherited from her father, ten miles from Charles Town. She had eight children in the years between 1720 and 1736. Two of her children died before reaching adulthood. She herself lived on to the age of seventy-five, dying on June 28, 1779.

The colonial period's female scoundrel was Mary Peck Butterworth of Rehoboth, Massachusetts. The summer of 1716, when she was thirty, she organized her relatives into a cottage industry in her own kitchen. Here the handicraft product was counterfeit money made by a unique process. Instead of the conventional but easily detected copper plate, she devised a method of placing cloth containing a perfect facsimile of paper money on exactly sized clean paper. She would then transfer the image by means of a hot iron, and carefully darken the tracing with a pen. Afterward, she presumably destroyed the incriminating muslin by fire. She sold the bogus bills at half their face value, making so much profit that she, her husband, and their five children had moved into a new, larger home by 1722. Betrayal by the wife of one of her cohorts led to her arrest and imprisonment in 1723. However, charges had to be dropped when no actual evidence could be found, and the case became only the word of Mary Butterworth—who vigorously denied everything—against that of her chief accuser. She was released from jail to become an apparently respectable housewife, who in 1725 added twin boys to her family. She lived on quietly, but long, dying in 1775 at the age of eighty-nine.

Nowhere in the colonies was there any onus attached to women who worked for a living either outside the home or in honest, cottage-type industry within the home. And especially among the Puritans, idleness or ignoring one's calling were the real sins, so that women, too, were expected to do whatever needed to be done during the early years of settlement. Later on it was the absolute duty of the married woman to help the family by earning additional money or to contribute skills to the community (especially in the case of wealthy women who needed no extra funds). In addition, work for pay was positively encouraged among single women—those who were unmarried, widowed, or deserted by their husbands.

# CHAPTER TEN

# "Femes Sole"

Everyone exalted marriage for providing stability, security, and children. Even so, unmarried women or widows (traditionally labeled "femes sole," from the old French, meaning "women alone") were still receiving most of the economic, social, and political concessions granted to females before the Revolution.

In all colonies, the single woman's most notable achievement in business outside the home was land management—largely ignored by historians, who emphasized war and politics rather than land and agriculture. In addition to early and conspicuous examples, such as the presumably unmarried Elizabeth Poole of Taunton, Massachusetts, and Margaret and Mary Brent of Maryland, and the widow Lady Deborah Moody of Gravesend, Long Island, many other lesser known women owned land on exactly the same terms as men.

For example, the account of Elizabeth Digges's activities is filled with superlatives. As the widow of Virginia's onetime governor Edward Digges, she was her colony's wealthiest woman planter in the seventeenth century. The 108 slaves she owned were the greatest number held by any one person in Virginia, and her personal property had the highest valuation in York county—1,102 pounds when her estate was inventoried in 1699. Another Southern landowning widow of note was Rebecca Axtell of South Carolina, whose husband had died shortly after their immigration. She organized the plantation well enough to obtain an additional grant of a thousand acres in 1705.

In the eighteenth-century North, Mary Warenbuer Ferree, a widowed French Huguenot, brought her grown children to Pennsylvania after obtaining title from Queen Anne to two thousand acres of land in New Strasburg, Lancaster county, in 1711. In New York, Cornelia de Peyster owned seven lots as well as five houses at her death in 1730. At least one woman, Rebecca Wells of Philadelphia, was a real estate agent who on January 20, 1757, advertised a house for rent and two lots for sale. And Chappaquiddick Island of Martha's Vineyard, Massachusetts, was advertised for sale in 1771 by the uniquely named Marcy Cheese.

Haddonfield, New Jersey, took its name from still another female landed proprietor. Elizabeth Haddon (1680–1762), a Quaker from the age of seventeen, met William Penn while she was still a young girl. Impressed with his description of adventures with Indians in wild Pennsylvania, she persuaded her father to emigrate to the New World and buy a large tract of land in New Jersey. However, at the last minute John Haddon, a wealthy London blacksmith and manufacturer of ship anchors, decided to remain in England. Young Elizabeth decided to go anyway, and departed in 1700 when she was twenty, with a widow chosen to act as her housekeeper and companion.

Her new home was in a part of the forest that had been cleared but was three miles from the nearest house. In 1702, two years after her arrival, she is said to have proposed marriage to preacher John Estaugh, and when he accepted, married him—a union that lasted forty years till his death. Three different times she returned across the Atlantic to visit her aged parents. She survived her husband by twenty years, never remarrying. After her death the monthly meeting of Haddonfield published a testimonial to her:

She was endowed with great natural abilities . . . whereby she became qualified to act in the affairs of the church, and was a serviceable member, having been clerk to the woman's meeting nearly fifty years, greatly to their satisfaction. She was a sincere sympathizer with the afflicted; of a benevolent disposition and in distributing to the poor, was desirous to do it in a way most profitable and durable to them. . . . Though in a state of affluence as to this world's wealth, she was an example of plainness and moderation. Her heart and house were open to her friends, whom to entertain seemed one of her greatest pleasures.

Women property owners were given permission to vote in Massachusetts by the end of the seventeenth century.[1] Under the Provincial Charter granted by King William in 1691, women who held property voted for all elective officers—and this continued up to 1780, the date of adoption of the constitution of Massachusetts, one of the thirteen newly independent states. Women landowners appeared on polling lists in Boston, Cambridge, Scituate, Weston, and Worcester. For example, of 193 names listed as voters for the March 1775 town meeting in Worcester, Massachusetts, three were women: Sarah Chandler, Mary Stearns, and Mary Walker. In addition, names of women turned up on tax rolls and on formal petitions to the colony for permission to build or repair property. They could vote on the use and distribution of common land, improvements for the town, and new roads. In practice, the right to vote depended only on property ownership—and those allowed to hold land included all males and those females who were unmarried or widowed. (Sometime

[1] In the Plymouth colony Governor William Bradford had been forced to lay to rest the rumor that Plymouth had gone so far on the path to democracy as to grant the vote to women and children. On September 8, 1623, he had to write a reassuring letter of denial to the parent company in England.

around the age of twenty-one, a child could inherit property and participate in government on the town level. The status of freeman and the consequent right to participate in the wider colony government were granted sometime between the ages of twenty-five and forty.)

Vermont, settled in 1724 by English who came mainly from Massachusetts and Connecticut, included the names of women property owners on its polling lists, as did Wetherfield and Windsor, Connecticut. However, other colonies were not so liberal. Virginia, South Carolina, Delaware, and Georgia specifically restricted voting to men. And in the remaining seven colonies, the exclusion of women was taken as a matter of course.

Nevertheless, there is at least one example of an eighteenth-century widow who, after standing up successfully for her personal rights, asserted for herself the privilege of involvement in colonial politics. The recently widowed Elizabeth Turgis, before her marriage to Governor Joseph Blake of South Carolina, insisted on two clauses in the prenuptial contract. One would insure financial security for her two daughters. The other would guarantee them an education based on standards she herself would set.

Perhaps the strength acquired in taking that strong stand carried over to her self-inclusion in local politics. After her second husband died in 1700, she wrapped the mantle of wife of the late governor about herself and attempted to exert influence on such weighty matters as taxation and free speech. She wrote a letter to the Lords Proprietor of the colony back in England complaining that the combination of heavy taxes and suppression of the right to protest would soon be "a fatal discouragement of the further and better settlement of this part of your Lordships' province." When Daniel Defoe— famous as author of *Robinson Crusoe,* publicist, and advocate of education for women—quoted her letter in England, her words received wide publicity and serious consideration.

All too abruptly, the story of the activities of Lady Elizabeth Blake ends here. There are no written records of additional stands taken by this woman of strong convictions—though it would be fair to surmise that she went on speaking them. Equally disappointing, Lady Elizabeth effected no immediate changes. Yet her letter, pointing to the need for local political control, becomes one more foundation stone supporting the eventual demand for American independence, a little more than two generations later.

In the neighboring colony of Georgia, Mary Musgrove, through personal intelligence and land ownership, helped to keep the area English rather than Spanish. Mary Musgrove, whose original name was Coosaponakeesa, was the daughter of an English trader and a Creek mother, reputed to be the sister of Old Brim, "Emperor of the Creeks."

After her marriage, she became known to history forevermore as Mary Musgrove (there is no record of her father's name), though she was twice widowed and subsequently married first Jacob Matthews, formerly her indentured servant, then Thomas Bosomworth.

Her ability to speak both English and the Creek language, along with her influence over the Indians and her skill in diplomacy, made her invaluable to Georgia's governor, James Ogelthorpe. He paid her one hundred pounds annually for her aid and advice in treating with the Indians, not only to keep them on friendly terms with the colony, but to watch and report on the movements of the always threatening Spaniards in neighboring Florida.

She owned a great deal of valuable land and commanded the support and services of many Indian traders. As a result, she supplied hungry Georgians with food and provisions, and recruited Indian warriors to serve with Ogelthorpe as he successfully repelled the Spanish in the early 1740s.

Ogelthorpe left the colony in 1743, giving Mary Musgrove a diamond ring from his own finger and two hundred pounds before his departure. Subsequently, she worked to keep the Creeks from allying either with the Spanish or the French against England.

Her fourth husband, Thomas Bosomworth, is blamed for a month-long Creek terrorization of Savannah in the summer of 1749. Considered unscrupulous and uneducated by contemporary observers and later historians, he had a get-rich-quick scheme in the cattle business for which he needed additional lands and great amounts of money. Accordingly, he persuaded his wife to make additional financial and territorial claims for her past services. Since she had amply demonstrated her power over the Creeks, when she and her husband went in person to England in 1754 to press her claims, the government listened, and finally in 1759 granted the Bosomworths St. Catherine's Island and a bounty of 2,100 pounds for past services. The couple built a huge manor house on the island as well as a cattle ranch. But Mary lived only a few years longer, dying sometime around 1763, survived by no children. (Her offspring, all by her first husband, had died at birth or shortly afterward.)

A northern contemporary of Mary Musgrove was Madame Montour, her first name unknown and her dates only surmised as being from 1684 to 1752. She carried herself with dignity, had great force of character, and was thought by contemporaries to be the daughter of a French father and an Indian woman—all of which apparently accounts for the title. Frequently, she acted as interpreter in negotiations between the Iroquois and the colonies of New York and Pennsylvania, and worked diligently to preserve peace despite the attempts of the governor of Canada to enlist her on the side of the French. Of her four children, one, Andrew, settled near the whites in Carlisle, where he had been given a large area of land. During the French and Indian War (1756–1763) he was an English major in command of a large Indian contingent. Honoring both Madame Montour and her son, modern-day Pennsylvania has named a county, a town, and a mountain after them.

As English colonists became American residents, women expanded their activities to include business as well as land-owning. Generally speaking, they were propelled into this new role by the advent of prosperity, stability, and the equal-ing out of the male-female ratio. Elisabeth Anthony Dexter, in her landmark book *Colonial Women of Affairs* (published in 1924 and still unsurpassed for information on colonial women in business), estimated that women accounted for 9½ percent of Boston's merchants by 1773. She based this figure on newspaper ads.

The very first woman shopkeeper had been a Mrs. Goose of Salem, Massachusetts, who sold groceries in 1643. She attracted history's attention in a will noting that one Joanna Cummins owed Mrs. Goose money for having purchased a pound of sugar. A somewhat later Massachusetts shopkeeper was Mrs. Mary Tappan Avery. On April 4, 1690, Judge Samuel Sewall of Boston, who had the remarkable facility of being able to detail every event occurring around him, noted in his diary that her shop had been attached for debt—and presumably closed.

As early as 1692, the Massachusetts General Court had taken note and special care of women in business, writing into law that while every unmarried person should be attached to a family, this requirement should not "hinder any single woman of good repute from the exercise of any lawful trade or employment for a livelihood, whereunto she shall have the allowance and approbation of the selectmen." In other words, Massachusetts was specifically writing into law the traditional though largely unwritten "feme sole" concept that unmarried or widowed women had complete freedom to buy and sell on their own responsibility, to sue and be sued, to act in a legal capacity as administrator or executor of an estate, and to have power of attorney to sign and receive documents. In line with this concept, the widow frequently acted as executor of her husband's estate, or a daughter served in the same capacity. And sometimes a woman with no apparent claim of married or blood relationship was chosen as executor. Women were allowed to will their businesses to their children or to anyone else they chose, and in the same way sometimes themselves inherited a business.

Examples of career women abounded in all colonies—aided and abetted by the dire shortage of labor, which forced the use of every skill regardless of the sex of its possessor, and at equal pay. (England, in contrast, had an oversupply of labor and generally—though there were exceptions—excluded women, whether married, widowed, or spinster, from business or labor, or exploited them with wages a fraction of those paid to men.) Thus, Mary Farmer of Philadelphia, widowed in 1685 shortly after her arrival in America with her husband from County Tipperary, Ireland, took to merchandising limestone completely on her own. For two years, till her own death in 1687, she earned a good living. Admiringly, Dr. Nicholas More, who was the first speaker of the Pennsylvania provincial assembly and later that colony's first chief justice and one of five commissioners appointed by William Penn to govern the area, wrote of her thriving business: "Madame Farmer has found out as good limestone on the Schuylkill as any in the world, and is building with it. She offers to sell 10,000 bushels at six pence the bushel."

A few women pursued highly unusual occupations. Some were barbers, usually substituting for sick, deceased, or temporarily absent husbands or fathers. Then there were morticians, booksellers, owners of ladies' or gentlemen's specialty shops, and those who made household goods for sale from glass, wood, and metal. On King Street, Boston, the widowed Joanna Perry owned and managed a bookstore till her death in 1725. And in New York, an enterprising merchant, Mrs.

Samuel Bourdet, carried a complete line of European finery for the ladies, and, to keep their husbands from being bored while waiting, displayed saws, firearms, and hinges.

Inaugurating colonial forerunners of the dermatologist's office or the beauty salon, many women advertised their skill at curing skin diseases and beautifying the ugly. A Mrs. Edwards founded the New York cosmetics industry in 1736 as she touted her miraculous product in the local newspaper:

> An admirable beautifying wash for hands, face, and neck, it makes the skin soft, smooth, and plump. It likewise takes away redness, freckles, skin-burnings, or pimples, and cures postules, itchings, ring worms . . . and other like deformities of the face and skin (entirely free from any corroding quality) and brings to an exquisite beauty, with lip salve and tooth powder, all sold very cheap.

According to eighteenth-century newspaper ads and announcements, there must have been untold numbers of female dealers in musical instruments, hardware, cutlery, groceries, farm products, wine, alcohol, dry goods, and millinery—and at least one female-owned blacksmith shop. On November 21, 1734, the widow Mankin of Market Street, Philadelphia, inserted the following ad for goods recently received and currently on sale in her drugstore: "Lately arrived, a select parcel from London, consisting chiefly of such things as are principally used in the modern practice of physic, being a great variety of materia medica, both simple and compound. . . ." Also in Philadelphia, just a few years later in 1741 and 1742, there were three newspaper ads for goods sold in bakeries run by women.

One woman is named in a listing of one hundred manufacturers around Boston. She was Mary Jackson, a widow, who advertised in the *Boston Newsletter* for June 21, 1750, that she made and sold—wholesale and retail—such utensils as brass and copper saucepans, baking pans, fish kettles, stew pans, coffee pots, copper drinking pots, and teakettles.

Chair caners included Sarah Goodwin of Boston, who advertised her wares many times in the years between 1745 and 1756, and the widow Gale of Philadelphia who advertised at least once, in the *Pennsylvania Gazette* for December 5, 1754. Also in Philadelphia, Mary Emerson carried on a variety of enterprises—selling new and secondhand furniture, silvering mirrors, and doing carpentry. And many Quaker City widows advertised themselves as continuing the businesses of their late husbands: Margaret Paschal, cutlery; Elizabeth Russell, coach-making; and Sarah Jewell, rope-making. Back in Massachusetts, Mary Salmon of Boston in 1754 made known her intention to proceed with her late husband's business—horseshoeing—and in the *Essex County Gazette* for April 14, 1772, Anna Jones announced that she would henceforth manage her husband's distillery and would provide customers with "the best of spirits."

In her search through Southern newspapers, Julia Spruill found many women who specialized in gourmet foods and condiments. For example, a Mrs. Bell in Charles Town, South Carolina, in the 1730s advertised good anchovies at reasonable rates; Anne Forrester announced her stock of pickled herrings and coffee in the 1760s; and Sarah Saxby offered customers vinegar, ketchup, and mushrooms. In Annapolis, Maryland, in the 1750s, Elizabeth Marriott sold Cheshire cheese and Lisbon lemons.

In the *Maryland Gazette* for May 27, 1746, Catherine Pritchard invited customers to purchase West India rum at her home, while Susannah Gates of Charles Town advertised in the *South Carolina Gazette* for December 19, 1741, her intention to manage the wine and rum shop of her late husband.

Sarah and Lucy Weaver of South Carolina may have inaugurated the practice of using newspaper ads to sell dry goods in 1735. The second such advertiser was Sarah Packe of Williamsburg, Virginia, who in 1737 described her stock of women's accessories as well as hatbands and gloves for men. Over and again, as in the North, announcements appeared that recent widows would carry on the husband's businesses—for instance, Catherine Dalbiac of Virginia, who in the 1740s intended to carry on as a dry goods merchant.

Certainly a varied stock was the one advertised by Anne Waller on March 1, 1749, in the *Virginia Gazette*—dry goods, gold watches, guns, and pistols.

In all colonies, north and south, at a time when the tavern substituted for the modern hotel,[2] widows sometimes preserved their only legacy, the home, by providing meals and overnight accommodations for travelers. In 1714, when the population of Boston was around ten thousand, twelve of the town's thirty-four innkeepers were women, one of the four common victuallers was a woman, and seventeen of forty-one liquor retailers were women. When husbands were still alive, however, they sometimes would not allow wives to run taverns alone, or to house male guests even in a jointly run, husband-wife venture if the husband was temporarily absent on business—and this despite the couple's desperate need for extra revenue.

Southern planters followed the practice of inviting all comers to dine and spend the night, but this by no means replaced the tavern either in towns or in the backwoods where distances between plantations were reckoned in days, some-

---

[2] However, these taverns had distinctively eighteenth-century features. For example, Sarah Knight, who on her round trip from Boston to New York in 1705 frequently picked up postriders along the way to serve as her guide, casually mentions sharing a room at night with one such male. The shortage of space allowed no segregation of sexes.

times weeks. As early as the 1650s, Ann Moore of Northumberland county, Virginia, received a license to operate a tavern where she could sell wine and beer. And eighteenth-century southern newspapers repeatedly carried notices of taverns operated by women.

Several of George Washington's sleeping places were taverns operated by women, a Mrs. Hawkins and a Mrs. Chew in Alexandria, Virginia, and a Mrs. Brough in Hampton. In Annapolis, Maryland, Washington is on record as having paid Anne Howard a shilling and twopence for his stay on October 29, 1774. Frequently, Martha and George Washington stayed with Elizabeth Dawson of Williamsburg, the widow of the former president of the College of William and Mary, who had converted her gracious home into a luxurious tavern.

There were other widows who, out of dire necessity to support their families, entered those most exclusively masculine of all early trades and professions—printing and journalism. In 1695, Dinah Nuthead became the first woman to operate a printing shop in the colonies. Though herself illiterate and unable even to sign her own name, she received permission from the Maryland legislature, after her husband's death, to "print blanks, bills, bonds, writs, warrants of attorney, letters of administration, and other necessary blanks useful for the public offices of this province." The obstacles facing her were mountainous. First of all, the printing was still done on a wooden press similar to the one used by Johann Gutenberg in the fifteenth century. It required the type for each letter and word to be set painstakingly by hand. Thus, she would have had either to set the type herself as well as take care of the business end of the shop (attracting customers and paying bills), or incur the expense of hiring employees. Her second problem was that her husband, who had been public printer of Maryland, left no will, only a printing press and type appraised for the paltry sum of five pounds, plus almost one hundred pounds of outstanding debts. The exact details of how she managed have been lost in history, but somehow with two young children, William and Susannah, to support she eked out a living by supplying printed legal forms until she remarried, about a year later.

In the first half of the eighteenth century, four women entered the fields of printing and journalism, all distinguishing themselves by carrying on successfully the important though difficult and complicated work of their late husbands. Anna Catherine Maul Zenger of New York and Elizabeth Timothy of South Carolina vie for honors as the earliest.

During the nine-month period between November 1734 and August 1735, while her husband was in prison for libeling William Cosby, the governor of New York, thirty-seven-year-old Anna Zenger continued to publish the *New York Weekly Journal,* which Zenger himself edited within the confines of his cell. This required supreme courage on the part of both husband and wife, for the *Journal,* a struggling newspaper, was under attack by the royally instituted government, presumably backed by the power of England. Happily, in the end Zenger was acquitted and resumed all responsibilities for publication until his death eleven years later on July 28, 1746. Then, for the next two and a half years Anna Zenger took over, sometimes supplementing her income by selling various goods she had received as payment in kind for services —such as the time she advertised "very good canary wine." By early 1749, her son John Jr., now fully trained, assumed control of the *Journal* and she turned to managing a book shop. Both Zengers, husband and wife, had arrived in New York around 1710, at about the age of thirteen, with their parents who had been forced to flee from the Palatinate to the Netherlands to England to America—a memory that might well have colored their determination to stand up for freedom of the press.

Elizabeth Timothy is thought to have been a Huguenot refugee from Holland, where she received an education that

Anna Zenger consulting with her imprisoned husband. *Courtesy of the National Park Service, U.S. Department of the Interior.*

included training in accounting. Her birthday, maiden name, and date of marriage are uncertain, though she is known to have arrived in Philadelphia in September 1731 from Rotterdam, along with her husband Lewis and their four children. Two years later the family moved to Charles Town, South Carolina, where Lewis Timothy (sometimes spelled Louis

Timothee) took over publication of the one-year-old *South Carolina Gazette,* a weekly he ran in partnership with Benjamin Franklin.

When Lewis Timothy died in December 1738, his widow took over publication of the *Gazette,* South Carolina's first permanent newspaper, which rapidly became an indispensable link in communication with the other colonies and the world beyond. A near-contemporary newspaper publisher, Isaiah Thomas of Boston (1749–1831), wrote in his 1810 *History of Printing in America* that regularly for ten years, 1738 to 1748, Elizabeth Timothy published the *Gazette* every Monday and Thursday (semiweekly, in contrast to her husband's weekly publication). And Benjamin Franklin praised her in his autobiography, remarking that she was a better accountant than her late husband. In fact, she organized the business so well that she was able to support her family and eventually buy out Benjamin Franklin's interest in the business. By 1748, she gave the management of the *Gazette* and the printing business to her eldest son, Peter, occupying herself instead with the running of a book and stationery store. A wealth of wordly goods at her death in 1757 indicated great financial success. In her will she disposed of three houses, a large land area, and eight slaves.

Cornelia Smith, a native of New York City who married Andrew Bradford of Philadelphia in 1740, took over the publication of her husband's newspaper, the *American Weekly Mercury,* just one week after his death in 1742. Though she had inherited wealth from her father as well as from her husband and had no money worries, she managed the late Andrew Bradford's printing press and real estate holdings, and supervised his share of the Durham Iron Works. The printing shop, in common with others in colonial America, also sold clothing, medicine, commercial stationery, and a number of books imported from England. In addition, she did bookbinding, sold "good English glue" wholesale and retail, and made lampblack on the premsies for sale. Her will, made shortly before her death in August 1755, reveals her ownership of a great deal of property in New York, Philadelphia, and Germantown, Pennsylvania, some inherited from her husband or relatives, some purchased in her own name during the thirteen years since her husband's death. With no surviving children, she bequeathed this property to five nieces and nephews, and freed her two black slaves.

Ann Smith Franklin is thought to have been the first New England woman printer and the second anywhere in North America (after Dinah Nuthead in 1695). At the age of twenty-seven, in 1723, she married James Franklin, the brother of Benjamin Franklin and publisher of the *New England Courant,* a Boston newspaper. Early in 1727, because of various difficulties, the family, which by that time included one son, James Jr., and two daughters, Elizabeth and Mary, moved to Newport, Rhode Island, and set up that colony's first printing press. When her husband died shortly after their twelfth wedding anniversary, Anna Franklin took over the running of the press, becoming in 1744 the first woman in America to have her imprint on the title page of a book (*The Charter Granted by His Majesty King Charles II to . . . Rhode Island and Providence Plantations . . .*). She continued her management till 1748 when her son, apprenticed to his Uncle Benjamin in Philadelphia, had learned enough to assume responsibility. However, Ann Smith Franklin continued to take an active part in the business until 1757, when she tried retiring. The early death of her son in 1762, shortly after he had founded the *Newport Mercury,* forced her return to full-time work. In addition to resuming her duties as newspaper publisher, she took on work as official colony printer, producing folios of legislative acts and laws, and also printed various religious monographs and her own almanacs (under her husband's pen name of "Poor Robin"). She died on April 19, 1763, eulogized in a long editorial printed in her newspaper, which afterward came under the direction of a business partner, Samuel Hall.

In addition to moneymaking pursuits such as land management, business, printing, and newspaper publishing, the field of religion also beckoned to women during the generation before the Revolution. In South Carolina, the spirit of Anne Hutchinson was revived in Sophia Hume. She was a granddaughter of Mary Fisher, who had been whipped and then deported from Boston in 1656, along with Anne Austin, as the first Quakers to arrive in the colonies. Brought up in a prosperous home, Sophia Wigington was at first more interested in art, music, books, and elaborate clothes than in following the Quakerism of her grandmother, or of her mother Susannah Bayley, who had converted from Anglicanism when the girl was seventeen.

Her own serious illnesses and the death of her husband Robert Hume in 1737, when she was thirty-five, convinced her that she must abandon frivolity for simplicity, and convert from Anglicanism to Quakerism. In 1747 she published a sermon, *Exhortation to the Inhabitants of the Province of South Carolina,* and thereafter devoted herself to Quakerism, a sect in which women as well as men were "acknowledged," not appointed, as ministers without salary. Her sermon was reprinted five times, and she traveled widely, north to Philadelphia and many times across the ocean to London, preaching her message denouncing love of luxury and exhorting a return to religious strength. She preached actively until sometime in 1768 when she retired. She died six years later in 1774 at the age of seventy-two, one of the best-known women preachers of her day.

During this same period another religious woman, Mrs. Barbara Ruckle Heck (in this case her husband was still living), together with her cousin Philip Embury and a British army officer, Captain Thomas Webb, founded the Methodist church in America. Sometimes called "mother of American

Methodism," she had arrived in America from County Limerick, Ireland, where her German parents had fled in 1709 in the course of Queen Anne's War. Like many, the Ruckle family abandoned their German Protestantism but found Anglicanism difficult to accept. In the 1740s, along with two other families, the Hecks and the Emburys, they were inspired by the sermons of John Wesley, founder of Methodism.

At the age of twenty-six, in 1760, Barbara Ruckle married Paul Heck and migrated from Ireland to New York City with her new husband, her cousin Philip Embury and his wife, and other friends. At her urging, the Hecks, the Emburys, and the Webbs, sometime in 1766, organized a Methodist society like the one they had known in Ireland. Though Barbara Ruckle herself never preached, she organized the first Methodist meetings in this country and assumed responsibility for erecting the first Methodist church here. In the early days of Methodism in the British Isles, John Wesley had encouraged women preachers, but as the movement grew and male preachers became available, females were no longer asked to mount the pulpit.

At least once, the self-confidence women attained from their success in the outer world burst into print. Following an organizational meeting, a group of widows wrote a letter to John Peter Zenger who, perhaps influenced by his independent wife, duly printed their plea and plaint in the *New Work Weekly Journal* for January 21, 1733:

> We are the housekeepers, pay our taxes, carry on trade, and most of us are she merchants, and as we in some measure contribute to the support of government, we ought to be entitled to some of the sweets of it. But we find ourselves entirely neglected, while the husbands that live in our neighborhood are daily invited to dine at court. We have the vanity to think we can be full as entertaining, and make as brave a defense in case of an invasion and perhaps not turn tail as soon as some of them. . . .

A similar demand for equality with men was versified and printed in the *Virginia Gazette* for October 22, 1736, under the title "The Lady's Complaint":

> *Equal laws let custom find*
> *And neither sex oppress.*
> *More freedom grant to womankind*
> *Or give to mankind less.*

Unhappily, there is no record that either the letter or the verse brought any immediate results. However, over and again women—particularly widows—proved that they could transform a going business into a growing business. This, of course, raises the question of why, if they could do this in the second place, after inheriting an enterprise from their husbands, they could not also do so in the first place, completely on their own, making something where once was absolutely nothing.

# *Arts and Letters*

When Anne Bradstreet received recognition as the New World's first woman writer in the 1650s, she had only the nine female muses of the ancient Greeks for company.[1] But in the 1700s, artistically talented women appeared on the scene in increasing numbers. Remarkable since America was busy scoring its greatest success in the pragmatic art of colonization, and creativity was viewed as a luxury for long-established cultures only.

Often talked about but never seen is the collection, *Songs for the Nursery or Mother Goose's Melodies for Children,* supposed to have been printed in Boston in 1719. Mother

[1] A generation later and almost a continent away, there was another New World woman poet, a young Spanish nun, Sor Juana Ines de la Cruz of Mexico. She was born in 1651, the year after Anne Bradstreet's poems were published under the title *The Tenth Muse Lately Sprung up in America.* . . . Either there was some communication allowing contemporaries to know of the two women, or it was pure coincidence, but, like Anne Bradstreet, Sor Juana was also known as "The Tenth Muse." She died at age forty-three in 1695, the author of what many critics now consider the greatest poetry written in Spanish America. For further information about Sor Juana, see Irene Nicholson, *A Guide to Mexican Poetry,* Judith Thurman, *I Became Alone,* and Benjamin Keen, editor, *Readings in Latin American Civilization.*

Goose's works have been proclaimed early American originals, but have also been claimed as traditional tales handed down from ancient England, Italy, Scandinavia, and Spain. In fact, the French in 1650 included this line in a volume of rhymes: *"Comme un conte de la Mère Oye"* ("like a Mother Goose story"). In any case, Boston today reveres the remains of Mother Goose, appropriately memorialized with a gravestone in the venerable Old Granary Burying Ground. A Mary Goose was nominated for this honor and the stone marked with her name, plus the information that she was married to Isaac Goose and died at the age of forty-two on October 9, 1690. Other sources have found other names: Elizabeth Foster or Elizabeth Foster Vergoose or Vertigoose or Goose. And she has been given another set of dates, 1665 to 1757, which means that she would have lived much longer into the eighteenth century and died at the very old age of ninety-two, instead of forty-two.

But all researchers agree at least that the singer of the nursery rhymes was indeed a woman, and that she was a mother and grandmother—and mother-in-law of Boston printer Thomas Fleet, who is said to have published the 1719 book.

Maybe a neighbor of Mother Goose, and certainly deserving equal renown, was the redoubtable Sarah Kemble Knight, who by herself in 1704–1705 made a five-month round trip between Boston and New York on business. Throughout, she kept a journal, full of invaluable commentary and observations on food, clothing, customs, houses, and local government—interspersed with spontaneous rhymes and humor that promote her writing to literature.

For example, one time she described an uncomfortably long ride of what her guide called twenty-two miles, but which she insisted had to be at least thirty, with no place to feed the horses and no rest stops for travelers. When she complained bitterly, a local guide offered encouragement, saying that Mr. Devill a few miles further on offered good accommodations:

> But I questioned whether we ought to go to the devil to be helped out of affliction. However, like the rest of deluded souls that post to the infernal den, we made all possible speed to this devil's habitation, where alighting, in full assurance of good accommodation, we were going in. But meeting his two daughters, as I supposed twins, they so nearly resembled each other, both in features and habit, and looked as old as the devil himself, and quite as ugly, we desired entertainment, but could hardly get a word out of them, till with our importunity, telling them our necessity, etc., they called the old sophister, who was as sparing of his words as his daughters had been, and no, or none, was the replies he made to our demands. He differed only in this from the old fellow in the other country: he let us depart. However, I thought it proper to warn poor travelers to endeavour to avoid falling into circumstances like ours, which at our next stage I sat down and did as followeth:

> *May all that dread the cruel fiend of night*
> *Keep on, and not at this curs't mansion light.*
> *'Tis hell, 'tis hell! and devils here do dwell:*
> *Here dwells the devil—surely this's hell.*
> *Nothing but wants: a drop to cool your tongue*
> *Can't be procured these cruel fiends among.*
> *Plenty of horrid grins and looks severe,*
> *Hunger and thirst, but pity's banished here—*
> *The right hand keep, if hell on earth you fear!*

Wherever she went, Sarah Knight wrote down as much as she could observe of local geography, politics, and people. About Indians, she alerted future anthropologists to their having many wives, and to the ease of divorce among them, initiated by either male or female just by "saying *stand away*."

(Italics hers.) She then makes a comment about marital practice in her own society: "And indeed these uncomely *stand aways* are too much in vogue among the English in this indulgent colony as their records plentifully prove, and that on very trivial matters, of which some have been told me, but are not proper to be related by a female pen, though some of that foolish sex have had too large a share in the story." (Eighteenth-century newspapers reveal a constant stream of colonial men and women running away and abandoning their marriage partners and children.)

She demonstrates a profound political awareness, an understanding of the rules by which people live together in society. Commenting on unspecified crimes committed by the Indians, she shows that the English continually punished Indians for misdeeds perpetrated on what the colonists now considered their own land, though they ignored the same activities carried out by Indians on Indian property.

Nothing escaped her attention. Though female and therefore a member of what she herself had labeled "that foolish sex," she knew enough about the political system in Massachusetts to be able to draw a comparison with that of Connecticut, which she found very similar, though she disapproved of the neighbor colony's rigid punishments for minor offenses. Thus, she emerges as a political and economic feminist, whose demonstrated independence and writing form a strong bridge from Puritanism to later Revolutionary-inspired agitation for equal rights and status.

Down south, Henrietta Johnston of Charles Town, South Carolina, was active for about twenty years as America's first pastelist and perhaps the New World's first woman artist. Beginning around 1708, she helped her financially hard-pressed husband, the Reverend Gideon Johnston, by earning money for creating more than forty portraits in dry colored chalk of local officials and the well-to-do citizenry.

She is known to have been born and married in Dublin, Ireland, and both she and her husband—a Trinity College graduate—were highly literate. Apparently, after her husband drowned in Charles Town harbor in 1716, she supported herself, three sons, and two daughters by painting, continuing to work until her own death in March 1729. Except for these facts, the rest of her life remains a mystery, including the extent of her artistic training and the source of her knowledge about the brand new pastel technique, first practiced by the Italian painter Rosalba Carriera (1675–1757).

Interestingly, other known women artists were also all from South Carolina. Historian Julia Cherry Spruill found widow Mary Roberts advertising "face painting," or portraits, in the *South Carolina Gazette* for February 9, 1734. On December 31, 1772, a Miss Reid announced her intention in the same newspaper to paint "portraits in crayones." And in 1773 Laetitia Sage Bambridge, formerly of Philadelphia, where she had studied with Charles Peale, advertised herself as a painter of portraits and miniatures.

However, most artistically inclined females, North and South, confined themselves anonymously to needlecraft, wall and furniture decoration, painting on gowns, hangings, and glassware. In addition, they worked on embroidery and the so-called Liberty Quilts.

In Pennsylvania, Quaker frontierswoman Susanna Wright wrote poetry. At the same time, she cultivated her own silkworms and ran her widowed father's sizable household; she herself never married. Also, she acted as unpaid attorney for many of her neighbors, drawing up indentures, deeds, and wills, and arbitrating disputes about land and cattle. Born in England, where her father had been educated as a doctor and where she herself attended schools until her late teens, she served as community physician in Lancaster. Possessor of one of Pennsylvania's most extensive libraries, she knew French,

Latin, and Italian, and a great deal of natural philosophy. Unfortunately, her poetry, known to be pleasantly simple and rhythmic, has all but disappeared.

Another Pennsylvanian, twenty-year-old Elizabeth Graeme, turned to writing to console herself after the breaking off of her engagement to Benjamin Franklin's son William in 1757. (Holding opposite political views, both fathers had worked hard to prevent the match.) Her poetic translation from the French of François Fénelon's 1699 masterpiece *Télémaque*, as well as circulation of her private journal and letters, gave her immediate acceptance into Philadelphia's intellectual circle. Well educated by her parents, widely read, and supremely intelligent, she began giving Saturday evening parties—during the 1760s when she was still less than thirty—which were the equivalent of continental literary salons. Sadly, her unhappy marriage to a younger Scotsman, Henry Hugh Ferguson, on April 21, 1772, and the unproved charge that she was involved in near-treasonous activity during the war made her later years painful and unproductive of further writing. Her husband returned to England without her after the war, and she died childless at the age of sixty on February 23, 1801.

A near contemporary, Charlotte Ramsay Lennox (1720–1804), was the first American-born woman to write a play—*The Sister,* in 1769. However, this country's claim to her talents is based only on her birth and adolescence here. In 1735, at the age of fifteen, she moved to London where her work was later produced with an epilogue written by Oliver Goldsmith, famous dramatist, novelist, and poet. English biographer James Boswell mentions her with praise seven different times in his *Life of Johnson.*

Similarly, Anne Grant, author of *Memoirs of an American Lady,* spent only her young years in America. But in this case the New World may have a better claim. Her book includes pointed descriptions and comments on Indians and colonial society as well as her youthful recollections of Madame

Margarita Schuyler, who married her cousin. Born 1755 in Scotland, the daughter of Duncan MacVicar, officer in a Highland regiment, Anne sailed with her mother for New York, where her father was stationed with the Highlanders in 1757 when she was about two. By the age of six, she had learned the Old Testament thoroughly and was familiarizing herself with Milton's *Paradise Lost* and beginning to write poetry. At thirteen she returned to Scotland, and at twenty-four married Reverend James Grant, military chaplain and scholar. Apparently, she used conversations with Madame Schuyler (who like herself was a Tory) to supplement her own personal recollections before finally having her book published in 1808. For example, disputing those who called Indians savages, she wrote:

> On the Mohawk River, about forty miles from Albany
> . . . were the once renowned Five Nations, whom anyone
> who remembers them while they were a people, will hesitate
> to call savages. Were they savages who had fixed habita-
> tion; who cultivated rich fields; who built castles (for so
> they called their not incommodious wooden houses, sur-
> rounded with palisadoes); who planted maize and beans, and
> showed considerable ingenuity in constructing and adorning
> their canoes, arms, and clothing? They who had wise though
> unwritten laws, and conducted their wars, treaties, and
> alliances with deep and sound policy . . . whose language
> was sonorous, musical, and expressive, who possessed gener-
> ous and elevated sentiments, heroic fortitude, and unstained
> probity. . . .

At an earlier date, Jane Colman Turell (1708–1735), daughter of a strict Boston minister, wrote poetry in her teens, married her father's protégé, Ebeneezer Turell, at the age of eighteen, had four children—three of whom died at birth— and herself died at the early age of twenty-seven. Shortly after her death, her husband wrote the *Memoirs of the Life and*

*Death of the Pious and Ingenious Mrs. Jane Turell,* promoting her to recognition by posterity as he commented in part:

> Before she had seen eighteen, she had read and (in some measure) digested all the English poetry and polite pieces in prose, printed and manuscripts, in her father's well furnished library, and much she borrowed of her friends and acquaintances. She had such a thirst after knowledge that the leisure of the day did not suffice, but she spent whole nights in reading.

Then he added words enshrining her as an early feminist:

> I find she was sometimes fired with a laudable ambition of raising the honor of her sex, who are therefore under obligations to her; and all will be ready to own she had a fine genious, and is to be placed among those who have excelled.

Her best-known poem is the one she wrote at the age of sixteen, "To her honored father, on his being chosen President of Harvard College," beginning with these lines:

> *Sir,*
> *An infant muse begs leave beneath your feet,*
> *To lay the first essays of her poetic wit:*
> *That under your protection she may raise*
> *Her song to some exalted pitch of praise.*

The poetry of Phillis Wheatley, 1753–1784, caused a sensation during her own lifetime and had a renascence both in the years preceding the Civil War and again in the twentieth century. A Boston slave, she was shipped from Africa in 1761 when she was about seven and purchased by a well-to-do tailor, John Wheatley, to serve his wife, Susannah. Mary Wheatley, their daughter, took the frail youngster under her

Phillis Wheatley, from an engraving for her book of poetry, published 1773. *Courtesy of the Brown University Library.*

own wing, providing education in disciplines taught to few white children of either sex: grammar, geography both ancient and modern, astronomy, history, and enough Latin to read the ancient Roman poet, Horace, with ease.

Phillis Wheatley was given instructions to ignore her light housekeeping tasks should she feel poetically inspired, was treated as a member of the family, allowed to use local libraries, and invited to join in conversations with the city's most respected citizens. In the early 1770s, apparently as a result of the marriage of Mary Wheatley and Reverend John Lathrop, the Old South Meeting House, making a rare exception, allowed Phillis Wheatley to become a baptized communicant, though a slave. But her health took a turn for the worse in 1773, and in response to the family physician's recommendation for sea air, Phillis joined Mary's twin brother Nathaniel in a long-planned voyage to England.

In England her literary talent and wide reading, as well as her exotic beauty, made her the darling of the aristocracy. She stayed at the home of the Countess of Huntingdon, who had already had one of her poems printed, and who is thought to have made arrangements for the publication of her only book of poetry. Brook Watson, the Lord Mayor of London, gave her Milton's *Paradise Lost* in folio edition, and Lord Dartmouth, newly appointed Secretary for North America, to whom she had dedicated a poem, praised her publicly.

In the Dartmouth poem she hailed his appointment, optimistically predicting more friendship for the American colonies than his predecessors had shown, and inserted some of her own feelings as a slave (roman hers):

> *No more,* America, *in mournful strain*
> *Of wrongs, and grievance unredress'd complain,*
> *No longer shalt thou dread the iron chain,*
> *Which wanton* Tyranny *with lawless hand*
> *Had made, and with it meant t' enslave the land.*

*Should you, my lord, while you peruse my song,*
*Wonder from whence my love of* Freedom *sprung,*
*Whence flow these wishes for the common good,*
*By feeling, fears alone best understood,*
*I, young in life, by seeming cruel fate*
*Was snatched from* Africa's *fancy'd happy seat:*
*What pangs excruciating must molest,*
*What sorrows labour in my parent's breast?*
*Steel'd was that soul and by no misery mov'd*
*That from a father seiz'd his babe belov'd:*
*Such, such my case. And can I but pray*
*Others may never feel tyrannic sway.*

When her mistress back in Boston became seriously ill, Phillis Wheatley felt it her duty to return home after spending some five weeks in London (where, before her sudden departure, plans were under way to present her at court). Mrs. Wheatley died in 1774 and her husband soon afterward. Mary had her own life and family responsibilities, Nathaniel remained in England, and Phillis, left all alone, married a ne'er-do-well, free Negro, John Peters, in April 1778. In the end he deserted her and their one living child—two others had already died—and she had to support herself and the child by working in a cheap boarding house. She and her baby died in Boston on December 5, 1784. A few days later the *Independent Chronicle* ran her obituary:

Last Lord's Day died Mrs. Phillis Peters (formerly Phillis Wheatley), aged 31, known to the world by her celebrated miscellaneous poems. Her funeral is to be this afternoon, at four o'clock, from the house lately improved by Mrs. Todd, nearly opposite Dr. Bulfinch's at West Boston, where her friends and acquaintances are desired to attend.

During her lifetime Phillis Wheatley had received written praise from Thomas Paine, George Washington (to whom she had dedicated a poem and who responded gratefully), and John Hancock. In Philadelphia, Benjamin Rush, doctor, statesman, and sometime ally of women demanding better education, wrote:

> There is now in the town of Boston a free Negro girl, about eighteen years of age, who has been but nine years in the country, whose singular genius and accomplishments are such as not only do honor to her sex, but to human nature.

In 1833 Lydia Maria Child, Massachusetts author, abolitionist, and reformer, mentioned Phillis Wheatley favorably in her book, *An Appeal in Favor of That Class of Americans called Africans,* one of the first antislavery tracts. And Caroline May in her 1848 study, *The American Female Poets,* included a couplet written by Phillis Wheatley:

> *Remember, Christians, Negroes black as Cain,*
> *May be refined, and join the angelic train.*

Then, in this book published thirteen years before the Civil War, Caroline May took subtle notice of the strong case Phillis Wheatley's life and poetic achievements made against human enslavement:

> She made so great a sensation in her time that we must not omit a notice of her in our history of American female poetry, although the specimens we give of her talents may not be considered so wonderful as the sensation they caused. . . . Peace be to her memory.

Happily, in the twentieth century there have been several publications of the complete poems of Phillis Wheatley, and she is invariably included in the history of the United States at the time of the Revolution.

Another American woman, Patience Lovell Wright, also

attracted the attention of England's high and mighty. Left as a widow with three of her five children still alive, this forty-seven-year-old New Jersey Quaker decided to pursue her moderately successful career in wax sculpture across the sea in London. Introduced to English society by Benjamin Franklin soon after her arrival in 1772, she rapidly became an idol of the English aristocracy—and maybe a spy for the colonial rebels. Now considered America's first professional sculptor, her most famous work, a life-size image of Prime Minister William Pitt, Earl of Chatham, who opposed the king's colonial policies, is presently on display in Westminster Abbey, in a room devoted to wax effigies celebrating England's heroic past.

The unsubstantiated but heavily rumored story about her espionage activities contends that she became privy to all sorts of secret information as she chatted with her famous subjects in the course of modeling their faces and figures. At first she is supposed to have passed on this information to Pitt, whom she greatly admired and trusted as a true friend of America. And later she presumably made reports to Benjamin Franklin and wrote letters full of planned enemy moves to the Continental Congress. If the story has any basis in fact, then the legend may well be true that she sent her notes to America concealed in the wax effigies of such prominent personages as Lord North, sculpted for the wax museum operated in Philadelphia by her sister Rachel Wells. The best evidence to support these activities is an anonymous letter, written in 1785 and included in the Franklin papers, quoting John Hancock as praising her efforts on behalf of the American cause.

Actually, her well-known eccentricity may have allowed her to get away with such activities, even though she was an outspoken opponent of Britain's war against America. For example, when the king and queen came to visit her studio to watch her at work she would often forget herself and address them as George and Charlotte. She had no inhibitions about

Wax effigy of Prime Minister William Penn, by
Patience Lovell Wright. *Courtesy of the Dean
and Chapter of Westminster.*

swearing or using coarse language in public, and her style of dress varied from outlandish to slovenly.

Though she lacked formal education, she could converse easily with the intellectuals in England, such as historian Catherine Macaulay or the three expatriate American painters, John Singleton Copley, Gilbert Stuart, and Benjamin West. Whether or not she was an American spy, she definitely opened her London home to American prisoners-of-war during the Revolution. She always made plain her intention to return to America, vowing that she would never let her bones rest in England; but in 1786 at the age of sixty-one, she died suddenly after a fall and was buried in London.

Back in America, women shared equal recognition with men on the stage in the eighteenth century. Mrs. Hallam was leading lady and wife of the manager of Lewis Hallam's American Company, the chief theatrical group in colonial America. They presented Shakespeare's *Merchant of Venice* at Williamsburg, Virginia, on September 5, 1752, and subsequently played before various audiences throughout Virginia. They then toured New York, Philadelphia, Charles Town, and Jamaica, where Lewis Hallam died. In 1758 his widow married the new manager of the company, David Douglass. Recognized as America's most talented stage performer in the years 1752 to 1766, Mrs. Douglass played a long series of Shakespearean female leads: Gertrude in *Hamlet,* Lady Macbeth in *Macbeth,* Portia in *The Merchant of Venice,* Lady Anne in *Richard III,* and Juliet in *Romeo and Juliet.*

Almost nothing is known of Mrs. Douglass's early life; not even her first name is known. And for her late life, historians differ as to whether to call her Mrs. Hallam or Mrs. Douglass. She had two daughters: Helen, who went on stage in America; and Isabella, who remained in England, where she performed as comedian and singer. Her son Lewis Hallam Jr. became the company's leading man. Mrs. Hallam-Douglass died sometime in the spring or summer of 1774 and was probably buried in Philadelphia—in a cemetery long since destroyed.

Her successor as America's greatest leading lady was Margaret Cheer, who during the mid-1760s often replaced Mrs. Hallam-Douglass when she was indisposed. However, Margaret Cheer's stage career was very short. She retired about a year after her marriage in 1768 to a Scottish nobleman.

Mrs. Hallam-Douglass's niece, Sarah Hallam, joined the company sometime in 1765 and later took over as leading lady, until 1774 when the Continental Congress voted to discontinue theatrical productions as overly distracting and expensive in the troublous times of the Revolution. She played such roles as Juliet, Polly in John Gay's *Beggar's Opera,* and Imogen in William Congreve's *Love for Love.* With the demise of the theater, she ran a fashionable boarding school for girls in Williamsburg after 1774.

Two more women who belong to any discussion of colonial arts and letters are Mercy Warren (1728–1814) and Abigail Adams (1744–1818). Mrs. Warren wrote a three-volume eyewitness history of the American Revolution, including incisive character sketches of leaders on both sides as well as her own moving and intelligent reactions to the Declaration of Independence, Indian policy, and the gore of war. She also wrote poetry and masterful plays demolishing the British by satire. Her good friend, Abigail Adams, sixteen years younger, wrote two volumes of delightfully literate letters—some critics include her letters with the best literature ever produced in the West—discussing everything from wartime inflation to woman's place in society.

Both women lived long, productive lives—Abigail Adams to age seventy-four and Mercy Warren to eighty-six—taking leading roles in literature, politics, and society, and thus cannot be easily categorized or confined to a single chapter. Instead, they will appear many times and at the greater length their many accomplishments demand in the pages ahead.

## · Part V ·

---

# REVOLUTION

---

"A Society of Patriotic Ladies at Edenton, N.C.," 1775. *Courtesy of the Collection of the Library of Congress.*

# CHAPTER TWELVE

# Hostility to England

Female hostility to England accompanied or maybe even preceded male hostility. Long before men adapted the Dutch aphorism, "Taxation without representation is tyranny," to the colonial–British relationship, women were forming clubs, organizing boycotts, refusing to drink tea or to wear clothes imported from the mother country. Their passive resistance increased in effectiveness to the point where an observant British officer remarked to the British commanding general, Lord Charles Cornwallis at Charles Town, South Carolina: "We may destroy all the men in America and we shall still have all we can do to defeat the women."

Elizabeth Ellet, who in 1846 collected all the reminiscences she could find about the role of women during the Revolution—interviewing survivors, reading diaries and letters, conversing at length with daughters and sons, nieces and nephews, cousins and friends—came to enthusiastic conclusions about the contribution of women in arousing revolutionary fervor. Proceeding from the premise that women discussed politics with their husbands, all visitors to their homes, and other women, and so were well informed, she conjectured that "patriotic mothers nursed the infancy of freedom." She contended that they talked of little else than the wrongs and the tyranny visited on the colonists by England, with the result that sons grew up determined to improve society, to win back their "invaded rights" and then defend them to the utmost.

While this kind of domestic inspiration may well have occurred, it was by its very nature unrecorded and so must remain mere conjecture. Other female actions, however, were carefully noted at the time. For example, as early as 1749, three hundred "young female spinsters" set up their spinning wheels right in the middle of Boston Common. For a whole day they sat turning out flax, demonstrating how colonial industry could be promoted—and in the process catching the attention of all Atlantic coast newspapers as well as of Parliament. Somewhere, someone must have been struck with the thought that economic self-sufficiency would bring greater concessions and respect from the mother country. In fact, an anonymous New Jersey newspaper writer in 1758 encouraged women to spin and weave for the economic independence of the colony, assuring them as an added attraction that they were bound to snare good husbands as a result of their demonstrated competence in spinning. Historian Kathleen Bruce in 1929 inferred that the Non-Importation Agreement signed in 1769 was the result of abundant manufacture of cloth by women, meaning that there was no longer a dire need for imports.

In the 1760s, five Salem women traders banded together to oppose stamp taxes (though two other female merchants joined two businessmen in continuing to import British goods, much to the annoyance of an advertiser in the local Essex County *Gazette* for November 13, 1770, who castigated all four publicly for having broken the boycott agreement and "thus taken an ungenerous advantage of their fellow traders"). In Philadelphia, 1765, and Providence, Rhode Island, 1766, newspapers mention women joining in the boycotts of British goods.

But to keep women from looking lopsidedly patriotic compared to the men—at a time when one-third of the population were patriots; one-fifth to one-third, loyalists; and the rest apathetic—there is the case of Anne Matthews of Virginia. She signed the Agreement but was caught selling imported goods anyway. With her son as partner, she had been operating a successful shop, inherited from her late husband, for eleven years, from 1755 to 1766. The authorities ignored Benjamin Matthews's disclaimer that he had had nothing to do with the violation, that his mother must have sold the goods while he was out of town. Both mother and son were publicized as "Violators of the Resolutions" and the public told to stay away from them.

More reassuring to patriotic hearts were the 426 women of Boston—300 as mistresses of families and 126 unclassified females—who signed an agreement on January 31, 1770, not to serve or drink any tea until repeal of the hated tea tax. This was 46½ months, or almost four years, before the Boston Tea Party of December 16, 1773. Also, there was Bostonian Sarah Bradlee Fulton who earned the sobriquet "Mother of the Boston Tea Party" (again without further information, leaving details to be filled in by lively use of the imagination). And three scholarly and enthusiastic historians, Alice Morse Earle and Alice Brown in the 1890s and Kathleen Bruce in 1929, concluded that America changed from a tea-drinking to a coffee-drinking nation because women of the Revolutionary era refused to serve tea to their families or friends, invariably substituting coffee, imported with no assistance—or tax—from England. Alice Brown used a letter written by John Adams to his wife Abigail to support her contention. In 1774 he reported:

> When I first came to this house it was late in the afternoon, and I had ridden thirty-five miles at least. "Madam" said I to Mrs. Huston, "is it lawful for a weary traveler to refresh himself with a dish of tea, provided it has been honestly smuggled, or paid no duties?" "No sir," said she, "we

have renounced all tea in this place, but I'll make you coffee." Accordingly I have drunk coffee every afternoon since and have borne it very well. Tea must be universally renounced, and I must be weaned, and the sooner the better.

His wife Abigail had already denounced and renounced tea— quite on her own—as the "weed of slavery."

With great ingenuity, if questionable flavor, women were making "Liberty Tea" from currant, raspberry, sage, and strawberry leaves. Tea-drinking, after all, was such an ingrained habit that every lady invited for an afternoon visit carried along her own teacup, saucer, and spoon.

At least one foreigner observer added further evidence supporting the historians' contention. She was Baroness Frederika von Riedesel, who accompanied her husband, the Hessian mercenary commander, on a six-year tour of duty for the British. In her journal she wrote that when she made tea for her family as they stopped to rest in a Virginia tavern, she noted that the woman of the house "watched us greedily, for the Americans loved tea very much, but had decided not to drink any more, because the tea tax was the cause of the war."

With more patriotism than poetry, someone billing herself as "a young woman of Virginia, 1774" wrote seven verses titled "Virginia Banishing Tea":

> *Begone, pernicious baneful tea,*
> *With all Pandora's ills possessed.*
> *Hyson,[1] no more beguiled by thee*
> *My noble sons shall be oppressed.*
>
> *To Britain fly, where gold enslaves,*
> *And venal men their birth-right sell;*

[1] A kind of green tea from China.

*Tell North and his bribed clan of knaves,*
*Their bloody acts were made in hell.*

In the wake of the Stamp Act furor, many groups called "Daughters of Liberty" formed, some having as many as sixty to seventy members. Seventeen young women met to organize their activities, spinning yarn and weaving cloth, at the home of Dean Ephraim Bowen in Providence, 1766, and by their second meeting they had to move to the courthouse for more room. Writing in her diary, twelve-year-old Anna Winslow of Boston got swept up on the opposite side to her father, who eventually joined the Tories and went into permanent exile. She declared, "As I am (as we say) a daughter of liberty, I choose to wear as much of our manufactory as possible."

The name Daughters of Liberty almost became generic, meaning females taking any kind of stand against the mother country. Groups of women regularly held spinning and weaving bees to replace British cloth with homespun. The idea caught on, and even the prestigious sons of Harvard (where until just prior to the Revolution students were graduated in order of social rank instead of alphabetically) began to take their degrees wearing homespun, as did the president of Brown and its first graduating class in 1769. When the Sons of Liberty were holding meetings every day and every evening, young girls issued a proud declaration: "We, the daughters of those Patriots who have appeared for the public interest, do now with pleasure engage with them in denying ourselves the drinking of foreign tea."

In the Massachusetts *Gazette* for November 9, 1767, there appeared a poem carrying the theme further but throwing the burden on men by renouncing marriage to any man who did not similarly boycott British manufactures:

*What if homespun they say is not quite as gay*
*As brocades, yet be not in a passion,*

*For when once it is known this is much wore in town,*
*One and all will cry out "'Tis the fashion."*
*And as one and all agree that you'll not married be*
*To such as will wear London factory,*
*But at first sight refuse, till e'en such you do choose*
*As encourage our own manufactory.*

Perhaps the most famous boycott of British goods was undertaken by Penelope Barker, leader of a group of fifty-one Edenton, North Carolina, women. On October 25, 1774, the female Edentonians proclaimed:

As we cannot be indifferent on any occasion that appears to affect the peace and happiness of our country, and as it has been thought necessary for the public good to enter into several particular resolves, by meeting of members of deputies from the whole province, it is a duty that we owe not only to our near and dear relations and connections, but to ourselves who are essentially interested in their welfare, to do everything as far as lies in our power to testify our sincere adherence to the same, and we do therefore accordingly subscribe this paper as a witness of our fixed intentions and solemn determination to do so.

The many spirited reactions in England to the Edenton women indicated their effectiveness. A London newspaper published a highly unflattering caricature, captioned simply— as though these women needed no further identification— "The Ladies of Edenton, North Carolina."

And from London, Arthur Iredell sent a strongly mocking letter to his brother James in North Carolina:

Is there a female Congress at Edenton too? I hope not, for we Englishmen are afraid of the male Congress, but if the ladies who have ever, since the Amazonian era, been esteemed the most formidable enemies, if they, I say, should attack us the most fatal consequence is to be dreaded. So dextrous in the handling of a dart, each wound they give is mortal; whilst we, so unhappily formed by Nature, the more we strive to conquer them the more are conquered! The Edenton ladies, conscious I suppose of this superiority on their side, by former experience, are willing, I imagine, to crush us to atoms by their omnipotency; the only security on our side to prevent the impending ruin that I can perceive is the probability that there are few places in America which possess so much female artillery as in Edenton.

Quilting bees, which had started as an afternoon's diversion for idle ladies, very often became forums for exchanging gossip, plotting politics, and planning boycotts. However, newspapers were a more direct means of spreading propaganda.[2] "In establishing American independence the pen and the press had a merit equal to that of the sword," according to David Ramsay, author of *The History of the American Revolution,* published in 1789. And there were at least six newspapers owned by women in the Revolutionary period (out of some forty published in the colonies), five supporting the colonies and one the British.

One owner was Sarah Updike Goddard, descended on both sides from early colonial settlers, her paternal grandfather having left Germany for Long Island during the course of the Thirty Years War, in 1635, and her maternal ancestors having settled in early Rhode Island. Her education had included the usual 3 Rs, plus tutoring in French and Latin. At around the age of thirty-five she married a New London, Connecticut, doctor and had four children, of whom a daughter Mary Katherine and a son William survived to adulthood. Her son

[2] Typically, newspapers at this time consisted of one large sheet of paper folded in the middle to make four pages, and included "letters to the printer," editorials, foreign and domestic news, official notices and advertisements (these latter two to make ends meet).

founded the first printing press in Providence and the first newspaper there, the *Providence Gazette,* in June 1762 with a 300-pound loan from his mother, a widow since 1757, when her husband died leaving her a goodly estate of 780 pounds.

Discouraged at the lack of subscribers and harassed by the Stamp Tax, William abandoned the *Gazette* in 1765 and moved to New York. Mrs. Goddard took over control of the printing office, and on August 9, 1766—five months after repeal of the Stamp Act—resumed publication of the Providence *Gazette,* thus becoming the city's second printer and newspaper publisher. She continued successfully until November 1768, when she sold out to one of her son's friends, John Carter. She also gave up her successful bookstore and bookbindery, where she had distinguished herself by publishing in 1766 the first colonial edition of the *Letters of Lady Mary Wortley Montague,* the work of the English feminist, poet, and medical pioneer who had introduced smallpox vaccination into Britain in 1718. (Lady Mary had died in 1762). In 1768 Mrs. Goddard moved to Philadelphia, where she again gave her son financial support, this time helping him to publish the Pennsylvania *Chronicle.* Occasionally, during her son's absence on business, she would take over supervision of the shop, right up to her death at about age seventy on January 5, 1770.

Her daughter Mary Katherine, who had frequently worked in the printing shop, took over publication of the Baltimore, Maryland, *Journal* in February 1774. It had been under the supervision of her restlessly active brother William, strongly involved in anti-British activities since the imposition of the Stamp Tax of 1765. He had founded the Baltimore newspaper shortly before deciding to abandon the *Chronicle* in Philadelphia. Mary Katherine was well trained to take over in Baltimore, since she had had early supervision by her mother and later received further experience by managing her

Mary Katherine Goddard. *Courtesy of the New York Public Library.*

brother's Philadelphia newspaper at a time when he had owned one of the largest print shops in the colonies.

William abandoned the Baltimore *Journal* because he was called to Annapolis to set up a colonial post office in opposition to the British postal system. Mary Katherine assumed full responsibility for the newspaper during the difficult years of the Revolutionary War. Sometimes she had to reduce the size of the paper, but she generally got it out on time. In her spare hours she did job printing, ran a bookstore, and took over the duties of postmistress at Baltimore (presumably the first colonial postmistress and definitely the first female to serve in such a post after the Declaration of Independence).

She served as Annapolis postmistress (it was quite common for a newspaper publisher to run the post office, too) until 1789, when she was forced out after fourteen years. Grounds for her dismissal were that the job was too difficult for a woman. Too much travel involved, they said, since someone—a male—was needed to supervise the southern postal system.

Mary Katherine Goddard's newspaper had one of the largest circulations of any on the continent, and she continued to publish until 1784, when in the course of a bitter, though unexplained, quarrel with her brother she turned the paper back to him. During her years as publisher, Congress authorized her to print official copies of the Declaration of Independence, the first to include the names of the signers, for distribution to state legislatures, January 18, 1777. She lived on to the age of seventy-eight, apparently unmarried and childless.

Another newspaperwoman was Anna Catherine Hoof Green. A Dutch woman, she married Jonas Green of the pioneer Green printing family from Boston in 1738 and had six sons and eight daughters, though only six of the children—three sons and three daughters—reached maturity. While her husband fought the Stamp Tax, Anna Catherine earned extra money selling coffee and chocolate at their home in the local post office. As her children matured, she began working in the print shop where her husband published the Annapolis *Gazette,* which he had founded, and where he also did all the official government printing for Maryland. When he died in 1767, she carried on, though for more than a year she received none of the official allowance granted her husband as public printer. However, in 1768 the legislature voted to appoint her to her late husband's position at the same rate of pay, "nine hundred and forty-eight dollars and one-half dollar" and after that 48,000 pounds of tobacco per annum for years when the Assembly was in session, and 36,109 pounds for other years. Experts agree that her printing work was some of the best done in the colonies. For eight years she printed public notices, almanacs, political pamphlets, satirical pieces, and, of course, the *Gazette.* The *Gazette* was the only Maryland newspaper until the inauguration of William Goddard's Maryland *Journal* on August 20, 1773, so that for six years Anna Catherine Green was responsible for maintaining communication between Maryland and the northern colonies, where the vehement protests against England were occurring along with organization of boycotts. She also reported local events and agitation. Her political role preparing the colony for Revolution was crucial, especially since she opened her columns to all sides of any issue, educating her readers through frank and open discussion, assiduously avoiding libelous attacks on individuals. At her death on March 23, 1775, at around the age of fifty-five, her more radically minded son Frederick succeeded her in the business, though he continued to respect her rules for publication.

Still further south, Clementina Rind became editor of the Virginia *Gazette* on the death of her husband William in August 1773. An apprentice and later partner of Jonas Green in publishing the Maryland *Gazette,* William Rind had founded his own newspaper on May 16, 1766, at the urging of several Virginia liberals. Like the Greens he encouraged all points of view and used the motto: "Open to all parties, but influenced by none." Despite high costs and shortages of supplies, his paper prospered and won great respect in the colony.

When Clementina Rind took over publication, she announced her action as being in the interests of supporting her four sons and one daughter. She carefully printed all news of foreign and domestic events, developments in the field of science, essays, poetry—and her own opinions. One time she unhesitatingly branded "with infamy" Parliament's "despotic proceedings." The House of Burgesses made Mrs. Rind her husband's successor as official printer for an annual stipend of 450 pounds, despite the strong claims for the position made by rival publishers. Shortly after having set an important precedent in refusing to publish an anonymous attack against highly placed individuals—unless the author allowed his name to be signed to the article—she died. She lived for only thirty-four years, served as newspaper publisher and official Virginia printer for only one year, but made enough of an impression to be eulogized at her death on September 25, 1774, as a woman who combined writing ability with personal courage, diverse interests, and careful critical judgment.

Back north in Boston, the hotbed of the Revolution, Margaret Draper published the pro-British *Massachusetts Gazette and Boston News Letter*. She had inherited the paper from her Tory husband, Richard Draper, who died on June 5, 1774. Whereas his obituary characterized him as having "equanimity of temper," a rival newspaper accused her of "palpable falsehoods" and "a malignant heart" toward her country. She published a pro-British series of arguments by Daniel Leonard, solicitor general to the customs board, under the pseudonym "Massachusettsensis." John Adams answered him as "Novanglus" in the columns of another newspaper, the Boston *Gazette*. The British evacuation of Boston on March 17, 1776, put an end to Margaret Draper's publications. Her paper was the oldest in America and the last to be pro-Tory.

"Massachusettsensis" appeared in one of the three satirical plays written in the years 1772 to 1775 by Mercy Warren, Massachusetts historian, poet, intellectual, and sister of James Otis who proposed the Stamp Act Congress. Twice, royal governor Thomas Hutchinson was her special target, first in *The Adulateur*, dealing with the Boston Massacre of 1770, and again in *The Defeat. The Group*, published April 18, 1775, the day before the battle of Lexington and Concord and, with special permission, performed on stage in 1775 (the others were printed to be read not acted), pilloried prominent Tories. Mrs. Warren bestowed on her high-and-mighty antagonists such names as Judge Meagre, Brigadier Hum Humbug, Sir Sparrow Spendall, Hector Mushroom, Beau Trumps, Simple

Sapling, and Crusty Crowbar. Dupe was Secretary of State, and Collateralis, a new-made Judge.

She described this "group" as "attended by a swarm of court sycophants, hungry harpies, and unprincipled danglers, collected from the neighbouring villages, hovering over the stage in the shape of locusts led by Massachusettsensis in the form of a basilisk [a legendary dragon who breathes death]. . . . The whole supported by a mighty army and navy, from Blunderland, for the laudable purpose of enslaving its best friends."

Montrose J. Moses, editor of *Representative Plays by American Dramatists, Volume I, 1765–1819,* selected *The Group* for inclusion "as being an excellent example of the partisan writing done at the time of our American Revolution. . . ." Mercy Warren's good friend John Adams had written to her husband in 1773 that her pen had "no equal that I know of in this country."

At one point, Mercy Warren turned to satiric verse to chasten women who failed to grasp the significance of the struggle between America and England:

> *The state may totter on proud ruin's brink,*
> *The sword be brandished or the bark may sink;*
> *Yet shall Clarissa check her wanton pride,*
> *And lay her female ornaments aside?*
> *If 't would save the nation from the curse*
> *Of standing troops, or name a plague still worse,*
> *Few can this choice delicious draught give up*
> *Though all Medea's poisons fill the cup.*

As propagandist and staunch patriot, Mercy Warren was definitely among the one-third of the American population who supported the colonies against England. Thus, her poignant description of the doubts and fears as well as the hopes attendant on proclaiming the Declaration of Independence is all the more remarkable. In her eyewitness three-volume *History of the Rise, Progress, and Termination of the American Revolution,* she gives posterity an insight into the contemporary emotions underlying the challenge of an infant nation to a worldwide empire:

> The allegiance of thirteen states at once withdrawn by a solemn declaration, from a government towards which they had looked with the highest veneration; whose authority they had acknowledged, whose laws they had obeyed, whose protection they had claimed for more than a century and a half —was a consideration of solemnity, a bold resolution, an experiment of hazard: especially when the infancy of the colonies as a nation, without wealth, resources, or allies, was contrasted with the strength, riches and power of Great Britain. The timid trembled at the idea of final separation; the disciples of passive obedience were shocked by a reflection of a breach of faith to their ancient sovereign; and the enemies to the general freedom of mankind were incensed to madness or involved in despair. But these classes bore a small proportion to those who resented the rejection of their petitions, and coolly surveyed the impending dangers, that threatened themselves and their children, which rendered it clear to their apprehension that this step was necessary to their political salvation. They considered themselves no longer bound by any moral tie, to render fealty to a sovereign thus disposed to encroach on their civil freedom, which they could now secure only by a social compact among themselves, and which they determined to maintain, or perish in the attempt.

Judged by her writings, Mercy Warren thought of herself not as a feminist but as the possessor of masculine intelligence within a female body. More than likely her repeated use of the word "they" referred to men only. But women were involved in every step, battle, and aspect of the war that followed the Declaration of Independence on July 4, 1776.

# CHAPTER THIRTEEN

# Heroics and Patriotism

Betsy Ross attracts such blinding limelight that most other Revolutionary heroines remain obscured. Unfortunately, though she was a very real person and actually lived during the time of the Revolution, she turns out to be nothing more than a legend perpetrated by her grandson William J. Canby, ballyhooed in time for the national centennial a century ago.

In an address to the Pennsylvania Historic Society, William Canby revealed that when he was eleven years old his grandmother on her deathbed had told him the story of her making the first American flag. He presented no documentation other than sworn affidavits from her daughter, granddaughter, and niece, claiming that they had heard the same story from her lips but not testifying that they had actually seen her make the flag.

At the time, there was strong opposition to the mythologizing of Betsy Ross. Opponents pointed out that though George Washington was supposed to have asked her to make the first flag, he was not in Philadelphia at the time of the allegedly authorized visit to her upholstery shop by a secret committee of the Continental Congress. Nor are there any existing records showing payment to Mrs. Ross for making such a flag, though it is quite possible that later on, after the first flag was designed and produced, she too joined the many local seam-stresses who made Stars and Stripes.[1]

However, collectors of social history can be grateful that Betsy Ross's life has been thoroughly researched, even if for a specious reason. According to actual records she was born Elizabeth Griscom on January 1, 1752, eighth of the seventeen children of Samuel and Rebecca James Griscom. A fourth-generation American, she was a Quaker, who, like other female children in her parents' sect, probably attended the Friends' School on South Fourth Street. Her marriage to an Anglican upholsterer, John Ross, caused her to be read out of Quaker meeting in 1774. Together with her husband, she set up an upholstery shop in Philadelphia.

But she was ill-starred in marriage. Her first husband was killed in an explosion while serving with the state militia in 1776. She returned to the Quaker fold as a member of a fringe group, the Society of Free Quakers, known as "The Fighting Quakers," since they rejected total pacifism. Seventeen months after being widowed, she married Joseph Ashburn, a sailor who was soon afterward captured in war at sea and imprisoned in England where he died in 1782. She had two children by him: Zillah, who died young, and Eliza, born in 1781. Consoled by John Claypoole, a family friend, after the death of her second husband, she married him in 1783 and had five daughters, of whom four survived. Her third husband, a sometime employee at the United States Customs House, suffered from paralysis after the turn of the nineteenth century and died in August 1817. Betsy Ross Ashburn Claypoole lived on until January 30, 1836, supporting herself as

---

[1] William Henry Egle, writing his *Pennsylvania Women in the American Revolution* in 1898, and seemingly including every single wife and mother about whom he could find even minuscle information, made no mention of Betsy Ross Ashburn Claypoole.

an able seamstress, a skill she had apparently learned in her youth from her mother.

Betsy Ross thus demonstrates the prevalency of frequent remarriage and large numbers of children, and the need for women to support themselves financially by learning a skill. But beyond this she will probably remain forever in history textbooks as a Revolutionary heroine, if only because of the convenient availability of Charles H. Weisberger's painting of the 1890s, *Birth of Our Nation's Flag,* which pictures her showing her creation to the congressional committee.

However, more concrete evidence backs the claims of heroism for other legendary females of the Revolutionary era. Elizabeth Ellet, who compiled the first list of heroines and spies in 1848, found 160 women who qualified. Most conspicuous in this category was nineteen-year-old Deborah Sampson, who disguised herself as a boy "Timothy Thayer" and joined the Continental Army. At a time when many young, still beardless males were being recruited, she had no trouble entering the ranks in clothing borrowed from one Samuel Leonard. She was tall—five feet eight inches—and bound her breasts to flatten her chest. However, somehow she was recognized and forced to return to civilian life.

Again, in 1782, she succeeded in enlisting and joined the Fourth Massachusetts Regiment as infantry Private Robert Shurtleff. She was shipped out to West Point where she served for eighteen months, participated in several battles, and was wounded in Tarrytown, New York. Later, suffering from yellow fever and hospitalized, she was discovered to be a female by Dr. Barnabas Binney and dismissed from service.

She married farmer Benjamin Gannet of Sharon, Massachusetts, in 1784, and bore three children. But she showed little taste for settling down permanently. A combination of a relatively good education (she had attended Middleborough Public School part time in her youth and had also been privately tutored), adventurous ancestry (her mother was descended from Governor William Bradford of Plymouth colony and her father from Miles Standish), and discontent with her early lot in life (because of a disastrous turn in family finances her mother had had to bind her out as an indentured servant from ten to eighteen), plus a six-month stint as teacher in her old school, made her supremely daring.

Besides, her unusual wartime career got special recognition in the 1790s. On January 20, 1792, the Massachusetts General Court voted to pay her 34 pounds for past services in the United States army where she "did actually perform the duty of a soldier." The all-male legislature added approvingly:

> The said Deborah exhibited an extraordinary instance of female heroism, by discharging the duties of a faithful, gallant soldier, and at the same time preserving the virtue and chastity of her sex unsuspected and unblemished, and was discharged from the service with a fair and honorable character. . . .

Soon afterward, publicized and praised lavishly in a thinly disguised fictional biography *The Female Review,* written by Herman Mann in 1797, she went on to become perhaps the first woman lecturer in the United States. She addressed sizable audiences in Massachusetts, Rhode Island, and New York, each time bringing the session to an end by dressing as a soldier and performing a military drill on stage.

Paul Revere, calling her "a woman of handsome talents, good morals, a dutiful wife, and an affectionate parent," helped her to obtain an army pension in 1804. After her death on April 29, 1827, at the age of sixty-seven, her husband petitioned Congress for an increased pension, on the grounds that he had burdensome medical bills as a result of her service-connected sickness. A year after his death, Congress on July 7, 1838, responded with an "Act for the relief of the heirs of Deborah Gannett, a soldier of the Revolution," paying a total sum of $466.66 to her three children.

Another woman renowned for military bravado is, of course, the somewhat legendary Molly Pitcher. Like many other women at the time, twenty-four-year-old Mary Ludwig Hays followed her husband of nine years to his military camp in New Jersey. Typically, she made army life more amenable for the soldiers by helping with the cooking, laundry, and nursing. She earned her nickname Molly Pitcher at the battle of Monmouth, on June 28, 1778, when she used a pitcher or pail to carry water from a local spring to the thirsty and exhausted soldiers. When her husband fell in battle, either wounded or prostrate from the extreme heat, she was said to have loaded his cannon, missing not a single round, and helping win the American victory. Pennsylvania historian William Henry Egle wrote in 1898 that George Washington personally thanked her for her actions.

Long after the Revolution, on February 21, 1822, the Pennsylvania legislature granted her a pension: forty dollars paid immediately and an annuity of forty dollars. At the time the legislature acted, she had been widowed and remarried to another war veteran, John McCauley, who had also died, forcing her to earn a living as a charwoman. Significantly, despite having been married to two Revolutionary soldiers, she was given the pension for her own "services during the Revolutionary war," not for being the widow of two army men. Like Betsy Ross, her legendary fame—based incidentally on much firmer support than that of Betsy Ross—took flight at the time of the centennial in 1876. And at the beginning of the twentieth century, in 1916, New Jersey included Molly Pitcher on the battle monument at Monmouth, showing her barefoot, tending the cannon, with a pitcher at her side.

Another "Captain Molly" was Margaret Corbin (1751–1800), who similarly followed her husband to camp, helped make the soldiers more comfortable, and took over his battle post. During the September 1776 battle of Harlem Heights, New York, her husband was wounded fatally by the Hessians, and she herself was felled by three shots, which left her permanently disabled, unable to use one arm. She, too, received a military pension from Congress, the first woman in the United States to be awarded such a grant. In July 1779, Congress unanimously resolved:

> That Margaret Corbin, who was wounded and utterly disabled at Fort Washington while she heroically filled the post of her husband, who was killed by her side serving a piece of artillery, do receive during her natural life, or continuance of said disability, one-half the monthly pay drawn by a soldier in the service of these states; and that she now receive out of public stores, one suit of clothes or value thereof in money.

Also rumored to have helped the Army was Lydia Darragh, who supposedly overheard British plans and reported the details to the Americans. Historians suspect the authenticity of the legend because there is no contemporary reference to it, nor was it mentioned in her newspaper obituary. However, it makes as good historical fiction as George Washington and the cherry tree. According to the story, several British soldiers on the night of December 2, 1777, requisitioned the Darragh home in Philadelphia for a secret meeting—probably because William and Lydia Darragh as Quakers were considered pacifists and neutrals. One officer strongly suggested, perhaps commanded, that Lydia should make sure that all members of her family go to bed early, close the doors to their rooms, and emerge only in the morning. She did as told, but, suspicious and alarmed over the extensive precautions, stole out of her own room to listen at the keyhole, where she overheard marching orders and plans for a British attack against Washington, who was camped at Whitemarsh, near Chestnut Hill, Pennsylvania. Returning to bed she pretended to sleep, slyly delaying an answer until after several knocks, when the commanding officer came to her door to inform her of the men's departure.

Without a word to anyone about her nighttime adventure, she left the house the next morning on the pretext—according to one version of her story—of going to the local mill for flour, or—according to another version—of visiting her younger children, who were staying outside the city for safety. Since the British were quite used to her comings and goings, for either of these two reasons, she easily obtained a pass through their lines. Fearful for the safety of her eldest son, a soldier serving under Washington, she was determined to warn the Patriots of the impending attacks and so began walking the thirteen-mile road to their encampment. Along the way, she met Colonel Thomas Craig, a friend, gave him the details, and allowed him to accompany her to a nearby house for safety. The result of her successful mission was that the American soldiers were prepared for the attack and so held the British to an inconclusive standstill.

The legend of Lydia Darragh, like that of Betsy Ross, is gossamer thin, but similarly makes a contribution to the social history of her time. Born in Ireland, where she married clergyman William Darragh, she migrated with him to Philadelphia, where they both joined the Society of Friends. They had nine children, of whom five reached adulthood. She worked as a midwife and nurse, and at one time during 1766 advertised her intention to open a funeral home. Her business acumen was strong enough to enable her to leave an estate of more than 1,600 pounds when she died in 1789 at around the age of sixty, some six years after the death of her husband.

Back north in Connecticut, twenty-two-year-old Deborah Champion was a female version of Paul Revere. With her trusted servant Aristarchus, she rode for two days from her home in Connecticut to George Washington in Boston with urgent dispatches. She insured a definite place in history for herself by writing an account of her mission. At one point she commented: "We met few people on the road, almost all men being with the army and only the very old men and the women at work in the villages and farms. Dear heart, but war is a cruel thing!"

After resting at her uncle's home along the way, where she also secured fresh horses, she and Aristarchus continued northward:

> I heard that it would be almost impossible to avoid the British unless by going so far out of the way that too much time would be lost, so I plucked up what courage I could and secreting my papers in a small pocket in the saddle-bags, under all the eatables mother had filled them with, I rode on, determined to ride all night. It was late at night, or rather very early in the morning, that I heard the call of the sentry and knew that now, if at all, the danger point was reached, but pulling my calash still farther over my face, I went on with what boldness I could muster. Suddenly I was ordered to halt; as I couldn't help myself, I did so. I could almost hear Aristarchus's teeth rattle in his mouth, but I knew he would obey my instructions and if I was detained would try to find the way alone. A soldier in a red coat proceeded to take me to headquarters, but I told him it was too early to wake the captain, and to please to let me pass for I had been sent in urgent haste to see a friend in need, which was true if ambiguous. To my joy, he let me go, saying: "Well, you are only an old woman anyway," evidently as glad to get rid of me as I of him.

She reached General Washington and gave him the papers.

Another female rider in the night was sixteen-year-old Sybil Ludington of Fredericksburg, New York. For forty miles, on April 26, 1777, she rode her horse, Star, stick in hand to prod

him, to knock at each militiaman's door along the route.
Thanks to her nighttime alarm, a large number of men gathered at the home of her father, Colonel Ludington, and
marched out to help force some newly arrived British troops
back to their ships.

One of the best female spy adventure stories concerns
young Emily Geiger of South Carolina. She had offered to
deliver a message from General Nathaniel Greene, who was
under siege by the British, to General Thomas Sumter, from
whom Greene wanted immediate help and reinforcements.
Intercepted on her way from Greene's army by British Lord
Rawdon's scouts, she was put under guard because of the
direction she was following from Greene's headquarters and
because she could not seem to lie without blushing. But before
an old town woman could arrive to search her (it was considered more proper for the matron to search the girl than for
a male soldier to do so), Emily ate the piece of paper containing the message. After the search revealed nothing, she was set
free, followed a roundabout route to General Sumter—in
order to put off possible detection—and delivered the message
orally.

Other women made similarly important contributions to
the war effort, though until recently their contributions were
ignored or minimized, probably because during Victorian
days women were thought incapable of enduring suffering or
displaying courage. For example, there was Rebecca Motte of
South Carolina, who encouraged American soldiers to burn
her house, which the British were using as their headquarters.

And in neighboring Georgia there was cross-eyed, forty-
plus-year-old "Aunt Nancy" Hart, six feet tall and illiterate.
She fed four, five, or six attacking British soldiers who invaded
her home and commanded a meal—the number of intruders
depending on the account of her legendary exploit. While she
was feeding her unwelcome dinner guests and plying them
with liquor, she confiscated their rifles and sent her young

daughter (one of her eight children) off on an errand, supposedly to fetch water but actually to bring back some Patriot troops. When the soliders at last caught on to her ruse, she threw two rifles out the window and used another to hold the soldiers at bay until her daughter finally returned with military reinforcements.

Nancy Hart had a reputation for aiming a rifle as well as any sharpshooter in the frontier area of Georgia, where the fighting between the British and the Patriots was so severe that it was dubbed "The War of Extermination." She lived till 1830, when she was around ninety. Twenty-three years later, in 1853, Georgia named a county for her.

In the North, at Menotomy (present-day Arlington, Massachusetts), an old woman known only as Mother Batherick interrupted her dandelion picking to take six British soldiers prisoner on their way from Boston to Lexington and Concord. As she handed them over to Captain Ephraim Frost, she remarked: "If you ever live to get back, you tell King George that an old women took six of his grenadiers prisoners."

William C. Nell in 1855, possibly the first black historian of the Revolution, in his carefully researched study, *The Colored Patriots of the American Revolution,* told the sad story of a young Virginia slave girl who "was employed in running bullets for the Americans. Her patriotism was but miserably rewarded, for she was held as a slave till she was about eighty years of age, when she fled to Canada for freedom, where, under monarchical institutions and laws, she is protected in her old age. No one can reasonably rebuke her for the utterance of an earnest 'God Save the Queen.'" (Such a story must have added power to abolitionist propaganda in those years just before the Civil War of 1861.)

In neighboring North Carolina, white women, daughters of the state's most respected families, pledged to refuse any suitors who had not answered the nation's call to military service. They may or may not have been following advice published sporadically throughout the colonies by men who sometimes used female pseudonyms. For example, the *Pennsylvania Evening Post* for May 8, 1778, carried an article signed "Belinda" but actually written by Governor William Livingston of neighboring New Jersey:

> I do not remember whether your gazette has hitherto given us the production of any woman correspondent. Indeed nothing but the most pressing call of my country could have induced me to appear in print. But rather than suffer your sex to be caught by the bait of that archfoe to American liberty, Lord North, I think ours ought, to a woman, to draw their pens, and to enter our solemn protest against it. Nay the fair ones in our neighborhood have already entered into a resolve for every mother to disown her son, and refuse the caresses of her husband, and for every maiden to reject the addresses of her gallant, where such husband, son, or gallant, shows the least symptoms of being imposed upon by this flimsy subterfuge, which I call the dying speech, and last refuge of Great Britain, pronounced and grunted out by her great oracle, and little politician, who now appears ready to hang himself, for having brought the nation to the brink of that ruin from which he cannot deliver her. You will be kind enough to correct my spelling, a part of my education in which I have been much neglected. I am your sincere friend. BELINDA.

The most effective propaganda, however, rose out of the martyrdom of Jane McCrea, which helped turn the tide of war to the American favor. At the battle of Saratoga in 1777, her brutal death at the hands of British General John Burgoyne's Indian allies whipped Americans into a frenzy, and across the sea made Edmund Burke take to the floor of Parliament to denounce the policy of using Indians to slaughter Americans.

At around the age of twenty-four, Jane McCrea was tall, slim, and beautiful, with long silken hair. The daughter of

Scotch-Irish Presbyterian minister James McCrea and his wife, Mary Graham McCrea, she belonged to her father's first brood of seven, and had five half brothers and half sisters by his second marriage after the death of her own mother. This large family of twelve living children, with half the males on the Patriot side and half supporting the British, strongly indicates the civil war aspect of the Revolution. Jane herself was to be married to a Tory officer, David Jones.

Mercy Warren, contemporary historian of the Revolution, tells the story "of the barbarous murder of a Miss McCrea" as she heard it:

> This beautiful young lady, dressed in her bridal habiliments, in order to be married the same evening to an officer of character in Burgoyne's own regiment, while her heart glowed in expectation of a speedy union with the beloved object of her affections, was induced to leave a house near Fort Edward, with the idea of being escorted to the present residence of her intended husband, and was massacred on the way, in all the cold-blooded ferocity of savage manners. Her father had uniformly been a zealous loyalist, but it was not always in the power of the most humane of the British officers to protect the innocent from the barbarity of their savage friends.
>
> General Burgoyne was shocked by the tragic circumstances that attended the fate of this lovely, unfortunate girl; but he attempted to palliate the crime, though he did not neglect an endeavor to inflict due punishment on the perpetrators. Yet such was the temper of his Indian adherents that instead of inflicting death he was obliged to pardon the guilty chiefs, notwithstanding the cry of justice, and the grief and resentment of her lover. The best coloring that could be given the affecting tale was that two of the principal warriors, under a pretense of guarding her person had, in a mad quarrel between themselves, which was best entitled to the prize or to the honor of the escort, made the blooming beauty,

shivering in the distress of innocence, youth, and despair, the victim of their fury. The helpless maid was butchered and scalped, and her bleeding corpse left in the woods to excite the tear of every beholder.

The immediate effect of finding the mutilated corpse of Jane McCrea was to turn many from being undecided neutrals to becoming strong supporters of the American cause. And this in an area known to supply as many soldiers to the British army as all other colonies combined. Subsequently, Jane McCrea became the folk heroine of legend and ballad (an 1893 publication *Ballads and Poems Relating to the Burgoyne Campaign,* William L. Stone, editor, devotes 80 pages to "Ballads on the Death of Jane McCrea," in a book of 274 pages).

Her first appearance as a legend came the very next year after her death, in 1778, in "America Independent" by Philip Freneau, who has been called the poet of the Revolution:

> *Full many a corpse lies mouldering on the plain*
> *That ne'er shall see its little brood again:*
> *See, yonder lies, all breathless, cold, and pale,*
> *Drench'd in her gore, Lavinia[2] of the vale;*

---

[2] Lavinia is an allusion to Jane McCrea. In Roman mythology, Lavinia was the daughter of Latinus, ruler of Latium at the mouth of the Tiber. When the Trojan leader Aeneas arrived on the scene, Latinus felt certain that he should marry Lavinia and the couple would then produce the race that would rule the world. However, the goddess Juno intervened, persuading a former suitor Turnus, ruler of a neighboring kingdom, to make war on his rival. But Turnus was defeated by Aeneas in a series of bloody battles even though he had at his disposal all the forces of his own kingdom and those of the Latins. Aeneas and Lavinia then married and together founded the Roman race.

*The cruel Indian seiz'd life away,*
*As the next morn began her bridal day!*
*This deed alone our just revenge would claim,*
*Did not ten thousand more your sons defame.*

The fate of Jane McCrea inflamed poets long after her murder. In 1787 Yale graduate Joel Barlow published his epic poem "The Vision of Columbus," which includes in the sixth book the story of Jane McCrea. A later admirer, Lura Boies (1835–1859) of Saratoga county, New York, is described as a precocious intellectual who devoted her few leisure hours to writing verse, which included her 3,600-word rhymed eulogy "Jane McCrea." More famous was Sarah Josepha Hale (1788–1879), nineteenth-century poet who created "Mary's Little Lamb" and served as editor of *Godey's Lady's Book.* The opening of her sixteen-line poem "Lines on Jane McCrea" gives a good indication of the tone:

*Oh! very beautiful was she,*
*A loveliness most rare to see.*

In retrospect, the death of Jane McCrea has been given large amounts of credit for the decisive victory by the Americans at Saratoga, which impelled the French to enter on their side and finally assured American victory and independence. Some have said that her martyrdom did for the Middle States what Lexington and Concord had done for New England in arousing anti-British fervor.

Another woman, Mary Brant, was involved in the war effort on the other side. She in fact helped to keep the Indians on the side of the British during the Revolution. An exception to the general rule that Indians would not leave their tribes to live with Europeans, she was the daughter of a Mohawk sachem and became the common-law wife of Sir William

Johnson. He was one of colonial America's wealthiest and most influential leaders, and Superintendent for Indian Affairs of the Northern Colonies. After the death of Sir William's first wife in 1759, Mary had nine children by him, all of whom he acknowledged as his "natural" children. She contributed to the success of his negotiations with the Indians by her ability to keep them pacified.

For fifteen years she lived in luxury, presiding as mistress of Sir William's large estate, Johnson Hall. After his death in 1774, however, his eldest son by his first marriage took over, dispossessing his stepmother. She went to live elsewhere, on land bequeathed her by Sir William.

During the war, Mary Brant gave the British information on American troop movements and provided food and ammunition. Forced by the Americans to abandon her land, she went further west, where she used her influence to keep the Cayugas and Senecas as British allies; her power to do so is a good example of the dominant role of women among the Iroquois tribes.

After the Peace of Paris in 1783, she went to live in Ontario, where several of her daughters married Canadian officers. For her services during the war the Loyalist Claims Commission in London compensated her for the loss of her New York lands, and the British government granted her an annual pension of one hundred pounds. She died on April 16, 1796, at the age of sixty.

Meanwhile, back at war, even weddings served as opportunities for propaganda. For example, not a word is wasted in this description of Jenny Roan's marriage to William Clingan Jr., as reported in the *Pennsylvania Packet* for June 11, 1778:

> Was married, last Thursday, Mr. William Clingan, Jr., of Donegal, to Miss Jenny Roan, of Londonderry, both of the county of Lancaster—a sober sensible agreeable young

couple and very sincere Whigs. This marriage promises as much happiness as the state of things in our sinful world will admit.

. . . After the marriage [ceremony] was ended, a motion was made, and heartily agreed to by all present, that the young unmarried ladies should form themselves into an association by the name of the "Whig Association of the Unmarried Ladies of America," in which they should pledge their honor that they would never give their hand in marriage to any gentleman until he had first proved himself a patriot, in readily turning out when called to defend his country from slavery, by a spirited and brave conduct, as they would not wish to be the mothers of a race of slaves and cowards.

# CHAPTER FOURTEEN

# War and Women

While many women served on the battlefield—on both sides—during the war, others served with equal distinction at home. All through the Revolution, women left a record of their heroism and fears, hopes and feelings. Their own writings, together with reports and reminiscences by others, give a whole new dimension to the period, helping us feel as it must have felt to be living at that time.

For example, William Fowler, in his 1878 account of *Woman on the American Frontier,* quoted the story of a mother's heroism he had heard from an old man who had long since passed the age of eighty:

My father was in the army during the whole eight years of the Revolutionary War,[1] at first as a common soldier, afterwards as an officer. My mother had the sole charge of us four little ones. Our house was a poor one, and far from neighbors. I have a keen remembrance of the terrible cold of some of those winters. The snow lay so deep and long, that it was difficult to cut or draw fuel from the woods,

---

[1] The war began with the battle of Lexington and Concord on April 19, 1775, and ended with the British surrender at Yorktown, Virginia, on October 19, 1781. After almost two years of negotiations, the peace treaty was signed at Paris on September 3, 1783.

or to get our corn to the mill, when we had any. My mother
was the possessor of a coffee-mill. In that she ground wheat,
and made coarse bread, which we ate, and were thankful. It
was not always we could be allowed as much, even of this, as
our keen appetites craved. Many is the time that we have
gone to bed, with only a drink of water for our supper, in
which a little molasses had been mingled. We patiently received it, for we knew our mother did as well for us as she
could; and we hoped to have something better in the morning. . . .

When my father was permitted to come home, his stay
was short, and he had not much to leave us, for the pay of

British cartoon on poverty in the colonies during the Revolution. *Courtesy of the Collection of the Library of Congress.*

those who achieved our liberties was slight, and irregularly given. Yet when he went, my mother ever bade him farewell with a cheerful face, and told him not to be anxious about his children, for she would watch over them night and day. . . . Sometimes we wondered that she did not mention the cold weather, or our short meals, or her hard work, that we little ones might be clothed, and fed, and taught. But she would not weaken his hands, or sadden his heart, for she said a soldier's life was harder than all. . . .

As a result of the absence of the husband-provider, many women made and sold homespun products, and built up businesses making linsey-woolseys, blue-and-white blankets, and linen sheets. One Mrs. Smith, sister of Silas Deane (who as diplomatic agent in France obtained commercial and military aid for the Americans), needed money for food for her six small children in the absence of her husband, army Captain Ebenezer Smith. She sewed and sold clothes to her neighbors in a tiny Berkshire Hills village in Massachusetts, for her farm soil was too sterile to produce edible crops. And though lacework seems hardly to fit into the picture of a population poorly fed, clothed, and housed because of war, Hannah Adams—later to win a reputation as America's first woman to write for a living—earned money during the years from 1776 to 1783 by making and selling this delicate material. (In fact, she earned more money this way than she would later from her excellent histories.)

Other female handiwork was more practical. Women produced food by doing heavy farm labor, manufactured bullets from their pewter ware when there was a shortage of lead, and spun, wove, and made military supplies for hospitals. In South Carolina—according to Tory Louisa Susannah Wells, who returned to England in 1778 and the following year wrote an account of her discomfort in America—women used thorns of native bushes for the pins they could no longer obtain. And with British manufactures totally boycotted, she had to work hard to keep her clothes in one piece: "I used to darn my stockings with the ravellings of another, and we flossed out our old silk gowns to spin together with cotton to knit our gloves."

In Philadelphia, Esther DeBerdt Reed and Sarah Franklin Bache organized women to help supply destitute soldiers with clothing. Their efforts at raising money through various charitable enterprises resulted in a profit of 7,500 dollars in coined money (i.e., not hopelessly inflated paper money), which they then used to purchase materials. In addition, they convinced more than sixteen hundred donors to contribute over 300,000 dollars, which they used to buy material from which, at the suggestion of George Washington, they themselves made shirts for soldiers. By December 26, 1780, they had given the army 2,005 shirts by Sarah's own count.

Sarah Bache was the youngest of the three children of Benjamin Franklin and Deborah Read. In 1767, at the age of twenty-four, she had married Philadelphia merchant Richard Bache, and in the years from 1769 to 1788 she had eight children, of whom four boys and three girls survived infancy. By her own account she had to flee the approaching British army in September 1777, just four days after giving birth to a second daughter. Whereas the official entertaining she did for her father (her mother died in 1774) was a cooperative contribution, her organizing efforts on behalf of the army were her own achievement. She took the job over when the founder, Esther Reed, died in 1780. Sarah herself lived on to 1808.

Esther DeBerdt Reed had arrived in Philadelphia from her native London in 1770 with her new husband and her mother. While giving birth to a total of six children—five of whom survived—she organized the fund-raising drive for the Continental Army and attempted through letters to rouse enthusiasm for similar efforts in other Pennsylvania communities and in Trenton, New Jersey. But without her on-the-spot direction, other towns only halfheartedly followed suit. In 1780 she fell seriously ill, first with smallpox and then with dysentery, which killed her in September 1780 when she was thirty-three. (Along with war injuries, these two diseases wreaked havoc and death in all the colonies.)

The patriotic efforts of Sarah Bache and Esther Reed help allay some nasty aspersions cast on Philadelphia women. In 1898, for instance, Pennsylvania historian William Henry Egle wrote:

> While the dames of the Quaker City were lavishing their smiles upon the officers of the British army, . . . backwoods women were spinning the flax they had raised to make the material to clothe their fathers and brothers, husbands and sons, wintering at Valley Forge.

A contemporary diary written by Philadelphia Quaker Elizabeth Drinker goes far to explain the behavior of many Philadelphia women. The adherence of the sizable Quaker community to nonviolence and their refusal to take an oath of allegiance made them appear to support the Tories. Thus, Elizabeth's husband Henry was locked up by the Americans and then banished from the city in September 1777. Six months later, on March 31, 1778, four women, including Elizabeth Drinker, were delegated to ask Congress for return of their Quaker husbands. They set off on April 5, 1778, met and dined with General George Washington on April 6. He gave them a pass through the lines, saying he could do no more. However, on April 27 the husbands were freed to return home, never having learned what the charges against them were. Still, the experience did not change Elizabeth Drinker's thinking. On May 18, 1778, she wrote of the land being "so greatly desolated and death and sore destruction have overtaken and now impend over so many."

Another letter written by a woman reveals that Massachusetts, so-called hotbed of the Revolution, had its share of

British sympathizers. Hannah Quincy of Braintree, just outside Boston, felt compelled to write an impassioned letter on May 11, 1775, to her brother Samuel, about to abandon his wife, family, and homeland to live in England:

> . . . Let reason take the helm. Disregard all greatness but greatness of the soul. Then the little trappings that royalty can confer will lose their lustre, that false lustre, which, I fear, inclines you to the prerogative side. Spare me, and do not call what I have written impertinent, but ascribe it to the anxiety of a sister, really distressed for thee. I behold you leaving your country, "a land flowing with milk and honey," and in which, as yet, iniquity of all kinds is punished . . . for a country where evil works are committed with impunity. Can you expect there to work uprightly? Can you take fire into your bosom and not be burned?

Except for this letter and a diary note written by John Adams, Hannah Quincy has inexplicably disappeared from history's view. Meeting Hannah long before he had met his future wife Abigail Smith, John wrote admiringly that she "makes observations on actions, characters and events in Homer, Milton, Pope's poems and plays, romances, etc., that she reads and asks questions about them in company . . . , questions that prove a thinking mind."

Abigail Smith married John Adams on October 25, 1764, when she was one month short of being twenty and he was twenty-nine. A decade later, her husband's years-long absences commenced, first to the Continental Congress in Philadelphia and subsequently as a diplomat in Europe. These absences produced volumes of some of the most gracefully literate and informative letters ever to have been written—and though Abigail Adams as a member of the upper middle class may or may not have been typical, much of her comment has a ring of universal experience. She covered every relevant subject: the scarcity of food, clothing, and medicine; profiteering; the political theory and morality supporting independence; warfare; and the effect of rampant inflation both on the individual family and on the government in its attempts to raise an army and to buy ammunition.

She wrote of the battle of Bunker Hill, June 17, 1775, making a comment with which historians now universally agree: "The day—perhaps the decisive day—is come, on which the fate of America depends." Though the Americans won no victory, they held off the British, causing them twice the casualties suffered by the Patriots. Equally or more important, the standoff filled the Americans with confidence that they could ultimately best the British.[2]

In that same letter, penned the day after Bunker Hill, she wrote:

> How many have fallen, we know not. The constant roar of the canon is so distressing that we cannot eat, drink, or sleep. May we be supported and sustained in the dreadful conflict.

A week later, still frightened but turning a beautiful phrase, she asked:

> Does every member feel for us? Can they realize what we suffer? And can they believe, with what patience and fortitude we endure the conflict? Nor do we even tremble at the frowns of power.

Along with war, Boston in 1775 was afflicted with a severe epidemic. Mourning and grieving, Abigail wrote to her husband on October 1, 1775, about the death of her mother:

[2] A few representative quotes follow, a mere smattering but full of the flavor of Abigail Adams's writing. Only the complete, unexcerpted volumes of her letters can do her justice (see bibliography) —or alternatively, the current publication of the *Adams Family Correspondence,* edited by L. H. Butterfield.

Have pity upon me. Have pity upon me, O thou my beloved, for the hand of God presseth me sore. . . . How can I tell you (O my bursting heart!) that my dear mother has left me?—this day, about five o' clock. . . .

After sustaining sixteen days' severe conflict, nature fainted and she fell asleep. Blessed spirit! where art thou? At times, I am almost ready to faint under the severe and heavy stroke, separated from thee, who used to be a comforter to me in affliction. . . .

'Tis a dreadful time with the whole province. Sickness and death are in almost every family. I have no more shockand terrible idea of any distemper, except the plague, than this.

Her grandson, Charles Adams, who annotated and published her letters in 1848, observed that the sickness referred to was dysentery, which had first attacked the British soldiers in their cramped Boston quarters and then spread to the inhabitants in and around the capital. Abigail Adams and her children were ill but recovered. Her mother, her husband's brother, and a domestic servant all died from the disease.

Abigail wrote of being lonely and doing her husband's chores as well as her own, on April 11, 1776:

I find it necessary to be the directress of our husbandry. I hope in time to have the reputation of being as good a farmeress as my partner has of being a good statesman. . . .

Teasingly, her husband responded that neighbors might find his affairs in better order during his absence. And, in fact, grandson Charles Adams, in his introductory memoir to her letters, credits Abigail with saving John from the bankruptcy that befell so many of his political peers.

Asking the questions that needed to be asked—and answered—by those preparing to write and promulgate the Declaration of Independence, she had displayed a keen understanding of politics on November 27, 1775:

> If we separate from Britain, what code of laws will be
> established? How shall we be governed so as to retain our
> liberties? Can any government be free which is not ad-
> ministered by general stated laws? Who will give them force
> and energy? . . .
>
> When I consider these things, and the prejudices of people
> in favor of ancient customs and regulations, I feel anxious
> for the fate of our monarchy or democracy, or whatever is to
> take place. I soon get lost in a labyrinth of perplexities; but,
> whatever occurs, may justice and righteousness be the
> stability of our times, and order rise out of confusion.

Sounding for all the world like a Victorian husband talking
to his little woman, she concludes before going on to family
chitchat: "I believe I have tired you with politics; as to news
we have not any at all."

Two months before the Declaration of Independence, on
May 7, 1776, she veers from politics in general to specific
recommendations:

> I cannot say that I think you are very generous to the
> ladies; for whilst you are proclaiming peace and goodwill to
> men, emancipating all nations, you insist upon retaining an
> absolute power over wives. But you must remember that
> arbitrary power is like most other things which are very
> hard, very liable to be broken; and notwithstanding all your
> wise laws and maxims, we have it in our power not only to
> free ourselves, but to subdue our masters, and without vio-
> lence throw both your natural and legal authority at our feet.

By July 31, 1777, profiteering on coffee and sugar turned
women into a raging mob. Abigail described their attack on a
local merchant:

You must know that there is a great scarcity of sugar and coffee, articles which the female part of the state is very loath to give up, especially whilst they consider the scarcity occasioned by the merchants having secreted a large quantity. There had been much rout and noise in the town for several weeks. Some stores had been opened by a number of people, and the coffee and sugar carried into the market and dealt out by pounds. It was rumored that an eminent, wealthy, stingy merchant (who is a bachelor) had a hogshead of coffee in his store, which he refused to sell to the committee under six shillings per pound. A number of females, some say a hundred, some say more, assembled with a cart and trucks, marched down to the warehouse, and demanded the keys, which he refused to deliver. Upon which, one of them, seized him by his neck and tossed him into the cart. Upon his finding no quarter, he delivered the keys, when they tipped up the cart and discharged him; then opened the warehouse, hoisted out the coffee themselves, put it into the truck, and drove off. . . . A large concourse of men stood amazed, silent spectators of the whole transaction.

Once again reporting the course of rampant inflation, she wrote on October 15, 1780:

You tell me to send you prices current. . . . Beef, eight dollars per pound; mutton, nine; lamb, six, seven, and eight. Butter twelve dollars per pound; cheese, ten. Sheep's wool, thirty dollars per pound, flax twenty. . . . Money scarce, *enormous* taxes.

Some of the same complaints made by Abigail Adams appeared in verse form by "Anonymous Molly Gutridge":

> *For salt is all the farmer's cry.*
> *If we've no salt we sure must die.*
> *We cannot get bread nor yet meat.*

*We see the world is nought but cheat.*

. . . . . . . . . . .

*These times will learn us to be wise.*
*We now do eat what we despis'd.*
*I now have something more to say.*
*We must go up and down the Bay.*
*To get a fish a-days to fry,*
*We can't get fat were we to die.*

Another kind of verse came from the sorrow-worn pen of Anne Eliza Bleecker (1752–1783), whose life in New York was stalked by war, first the French and Indian War from 1756 to 1763, and then the Revolution. Seventeen when she married John J. Bleecker of New Rochelle in 1769, she moved with him to Tomhanick, an isolated little village eighteen miles from Albany. When the British army led by General Burgoyne approached in 1777, her husband left for Albany to make arrangements to move his wife and two young daughters—four-year-old Margaretta and an infant, Abella, there out of the path of the invaders. In his absence, Anne Bleecker heard rumors that the British were no more than two miles away, and so fled the town, hoping to reach Albany and safety. She carried her baby and held her four-year-old by the hand; the three were accompanied by a maid. After a frightening walk through the wilderness and an overnight rest in a garret, she met her husband coming to fetch her, and went with him to Albany. Her baby died a few days later, engendering her poignant poetic lament, "Written on the Retreat from Burgoyne":

*Was it for this, with thee, a pleasing load,*
*I sadly wandered through the hostile wood—*
*When I thought Fortune's spite could do no more,*
*To see thee perish on a foreign shore?*

*Oh my loved babe! my treasures left behind,*
*Ne'er sunk a cloud of grief upon my mind;*
*Rich in my children, on my arms I bore*
*My living treasures from the scalper's power:*
*When I sat down to rest, beneath some shade,*
*On the soft grass how innocent she played,*
*While her sweet sister from the fragrant wild*
*Collects the flowers to please my precious child,*
*Unconscious of her danger, laughing roves,*
*Nor dreads the painted savage in the groves!*
*Soon as the spires of Albany appeared,*
*With fallacies my rising grief I cheered:*
*"Resigned I bear," said I, "Heaven's just reproof,*
*Content to dwell beneath a stranger's roof—*
*Content my babes should eat dependent bread,*
*Or by the labor of my hands be fed.*
*What though my houses, lands, and goods, are gone,*
*My babes remain—these I can call my own!—*
*But soon my beloved Abella hung her head—*
*From her soft cheek the bright carnation fled;*
*Her smooth transparent skin too plainly showed*
*How fierce through every vein the fever glowed.*
*In bitter anguish o'er her limbs I hung,*
*I wept and sighed, but sorrow chained my tongue;*
*At length her languid eyes closed from the day,*
*The idol of my soul was torn away;*
*Her spirit fled and left me ghastly clay!*
*Then—then my soul rejected all relief,*
*Comfort I wished not, for I loved my grief.*
*Nor shall the mollifying hand of Time*
*Which wipes off common sorrows, cancel mine.*

War brought her further anxieties in the summer of 1781. Her husband, serving in the Patriot militia, was captured by the British and taken toward the Canadian border and imprisonment, only to be rescued unexpectedly at the last moment. Not long afterward, she suffered a kind of nervous breakdown, which she described as making her physically weak and mentally depressed. She never completely recovered and died two years later at the age of thirty-one.

Also in New York, Grace Barclay, surrounded by Tories, used letters to sort out her own largely antiwar sentiments. Thus, in September of 1776, writing from British-occupied Long Island to her husband, an American officer in battle, she pondered the effects of brother fighting brother:

> We love this our native land, the native country of my mother, of both your parents. Her cause seems to us a righteous one. She is overtaxed, oppressed, insulted; my father feels this; he is indignant at it; yet . . . he *hates* the sin, while he *loves* the sinner. They seem (the English) the foes of our own household to him; brother lifting up sword against brother, in unnatural warfare, which he prays may speedily come to an end.

By December, 1776, she revealed even more intense hatred for warfare:

> Oh, dear husband, war is a weariness! Its effects sicken the soul. Every hour some fresh account of murder, robbery, wounding, destroying, depredating! When will this unnatural warfare be at an end?

Later that same month, she wrote to her husband acknowledging that as a woman she perhaps viewed war differently, but no less patriotically. She insisted:

> My womanish fears, as you name them, get the better of me. The disparity between the contending parties is so immense. . . .
> What is this struggle of the Colonies? Is it a war of

aggression, of cupidity, or conquest, of fierce passion, for tyranny and despotic sway? No—it is the noble endeavor, the strong purpose, founded in inalienable right, to throw off a galling yoke unjustly and perseveringly imposed. It is the cry of humanity against oppression, usurped power, insolence and rapacity. Will it prevail or will it be smothered? Will those evils, from which our fathers fled to this new-found country, like hydra-headed monsters raise here their heads, nor be smitten?

Her January 1778 reaction on hearing of the alliance with France is distinctly from a woman's point of view:

> Just received the joyful news of the Treaty of Alliance with France. My heart beats tremulously with hope and expectation, and yet I scarcely know what to hope for. Can I, a woman, wife, and mother, delight in warfare or desire the destruction of the children of a common origin? No! May God of his merciful goodness grant a speedy termination of the war! This be my prevailing, my fervent prayer.

Putting first things first, she wrote in October 1780: "There is a rumor of a great battle fought at the South and the Continentals victorious. I cannot vouch for the truth of it. My first thought and prayer is my husband's safety; the next for our country."

Unlike Grace Barclay, many women refused to stay at home while their husbands fought. They accompanied them to the battlefield—even those who were pregnant or had to drag children along. As a matter of fact, they showed up in such great numbers that George Washington on August 4, 1777, felt forced to issue a directive limiting camp followers:

> In the present marching state of the army, every incumbrance proves greatly prejudicial to the service: the

multitude of women in particular, especially those who are pregnant, or have children, are a clog upon every movement. The Commander-in-Chief therefore earnestly recommends it to the officers commanding brigades and corps, to use every reasonable method in their power to get rid of all such as are not absolutely necessary; and the admission or continuance of any, who shall, or may have come to the Army since its arrival in Pennsylvania, is positively forbidden, to which point the officers will give particular attention.

And yet Washington himself had sent for his wife Martha at the very outset of hostilities. In November 1775, shortly after taking command of the Continental Army at Cambridge, he requested that she spend the winter with him at headquarters. Washington had weighed the personal dangers to his wife against the morale-building effect of her eventual arrival —which would demonstrate to the troops and to the enemy that he intended to dig in and not be forced to yield ground. Apparently he decided that Martha's arrival was bound to set a good example for other women by showing her strong Patriot allegiance.

Massachusetts was only the first in a series of campsites to which Martha Washington followed her husband. Even at death-stalked Valley Forge she stayed the winter, occupying herself along with other camp women by sewing or knitting clothes for the soldiers, or visiting the wounded, and occasionally acting as the general's secretary in transmitting official orders or letters.

In her three-volume history of the Revolution, Mercy Warren described officers' sending for their wives at Valley Forge:

> The commander in chief, and several of the principal officers of the American army, in defiance of danger, either to themselves or to such tender connections, sent for their ladies from the different states to which they belonged, to

pass the remainder of the winter, and by their presence to enliven the gloomy appearance of a hutted village in the woods, inhabited only by a hungry and half-naked soldier.

In a rare instance of allowing compassion to intrude on strict narration, she added in a footnote: "Nothing but the inexperience of the American ladies, and their confidence in the judgment of their husbands, could justify this hazard to their person, and to their feelings of delicacy."

Possibly twenty thousand women followed their husbands and lovers into battle camps, an exhausting and dangerous experience. Such a number meant that one out of every ten soldiers was accompanied by a woman. Only generals' wives could expect special treatment. A Martha Washington or Baroness Frederika von Riedesel, wife of the mercenary Hessian commander, were carried everywhere by carriage and could count on sleeping in local manor houses.

In contrast, most women tramped on foot, carrying heavy iron pots, children, and clothing, and slept in the fields alongside their men or in hastily erected barracks. When battle erupted, they scrambled to safety, though some remained to supply water or nursing care, and to hunt for food for their men as well as for themselves. Callously, when peace and quiet returned to the field, they would go around searching dead bodies for articles useful for the living. When their own man was killed, they would frequently change allegiance on the spot, attaching themselves to a new companion, the cost and danger of returning home being insurmountable difficulties.

In a march at Brandywine, Pennsylvania, women revolted at Washington's attempt to hide them or at least to lose them in the rear with the baggage train—this to improve the morale of the local citizenry by displaying Continental soldiers as being as well disciplined as the troops of British General Howe.

A local observer described the results:

> They were spirited off into the quaint, dirty little alley-
> ways and side streets. But they hated it. The army had barely
> passed through the main thoroughfares before these camp
> followers poured after their soldiers again, their hair flying,
> their brows beady with the heat, their belongings slung over
> one shoulder, chattering and yelling in sluttish shrills as
> they went, and spitting in the gutters.

Even so, at the beginning of the war there were fewer
American than British camp followers. Continental soldiers
tended to fight near their homes, and when their area was
finally cleared of the enemy, would leave the service. The
British soldier, in contrast, had enlisted for a long term and
was fighting an ocean away from his family. Temporary
liaisons were more tempting to him. It was only as the war
dragged on that more colonial women, especially those who
were financially hard pressed, began showing up at American
campsites.

At least one general's wife, Baroness Frederika von Riedesel,
wrote journals and letters covering her years (1776 to 1782)
on the battle campaign trail with her husband, the Prussian
who led his troops against the Americans alongside General
Burgoyne. Somewhat perversely, or perhaps simply without
any understanding, she found very pleasant the weeks following the Battle of Bennington, where the Vermont militia had
routed a Hessian force, killing or capturing every one of its
eight hundred men. She wrote contentedly:

> We were very happy during these three weeks! The
> country there was lovely, and we were in the midst of the
> camps of the English and the German [Hessian] troops.
> The place where we lived was called the Red House. I had
> only one room for my husband, myself, and my children,
> in which all of us slept, and a tiny study. My maids slept in

a sort of hall. When the weather was good we had our meals out under the trees, otherwise we had them in the barn, laying boards across barrels for tables. It was here that I ate bear meat for the first time, and it tasted very good to me. Sometimes we had nothing at all; but in spite of everything, I was very happy and satisfied, for I was with my children and was beloved by all about me.

Accompanying her husband to Boston in the fall of 1777, she found the city attractive but its citizens enthusiastically patriotic and its women especially horrid, "casting ugly looks at me, and some of them even spitting when I passed by them." On the other hand, she saw for herself the sorrows of a family with divided loyalties, a Tory brother ready to gun down his Patriot brothers. "With such people we were obliged to live or to see nobody at all," she observed. "I naturally preferred the latter choice."

Interestingly, in 1780 she gave birth to a fourth daughter whom she called America, explaining that if it had been a son the name would have been Americus.

Another aspect of the war comes to light in a letter written to Mercy Warren by Hannah Winthrop, whose husband was professor of science and mathematics at Harvard. She described the flight from Cambridge after the battle of Lexington and Concord on April 19, 1775, asserting that never "will old Time erase the horrors of that midnight":

We were roused from the benign slumbers of the season by beat of drum and ringing of bell with the dire alarm that a thousand of the troops of George the Third were gone forth to murder the peaceful inhabitants of the surrounding villages. A few hours with the dawning day convinced us the bloody purpose was executing; the platoon firing assuring us the rising sun must witness the bloody carnage. Not knowing what the event would be at Cambridge at the return of these bloody ruffians, and seeing another brigade dispatched to the assistance of the former, looking with the ferocity of barbarians, it seemed necessary to retire to some place of safety till the calamity was passed. . . .

After dinner we set out, not knowing whither we went. We were directed to a place called Fresh Pond, about a mile from the town; but what a distressed house did we find there, filled with women whose husbands were gone forth to meet the assailants; seventy or eighty of these, with numbers of infant children, crying and agonizing for the fate of their husbands! In addition to this scene of distress, we were for some time in sight of the battle, the glistening instruments of death proclaiming by an incessant fire that much blood must be shed, that many widowed and orphaned ones be left as monuments of that persecuting barbarity of British tyranny. Another uncomfortable night we passed, some nodding in their chairs, others resting their weary limbs on the floor. The welcome harbingers of day give notice of its dawning light, but bring us news that it is useless to return to Cambridge, as the enemy were advancing up the river and firing on the town. To stay in this place was impracticable.

They decided to flee to Andover, about twenty miles to the north:

We began our pilgrimage alternately walking and riding, the roads filled with frightened women and children, some in carts with their tattered furniture, others on foot fleeing into the woods. But what added greatly to the horror of the scene was our passing through the bloody field at Menotomy [Arlington], which was strewed with the mangled bodies. We met one affectionate father with a cart, looking for his murdered son, and picking up his neighbors who had fallen in battle, in order for their burial.

She concludes that in Andover she feels completely cut off

from society, but that when she thinks of her friends who are still living in Boston she is ashamed of complaining.

Referring to the other side in the war, Mrs. Winthrop's friend Mercy Warren interrupted her three-volume narrative of the Revolution to tell the story of Lady Ackland, wife of Major Ackland, a British officer with General Burgoyne. Two different times Lady Ackland risked her own life to nurse her wounded husband, remaining by his side "to the last moment of his life." Mercy Warren obtained the details of Lady Ackland's story from a narrative passed on by General Burgoyne, whom she quotes as having observed:

> After so long an exposure and agitation of the spirits, exhausted not only for want of rest, but absolutely for want of food, drenched in rain for twelve hours together, that a woman should be capable of delivering herself to the enemy, probably in the night, and uncertain what hands she should fall into, appeared an effort above human nature. . . .

Finally, Mary Quigley Brady represents another—too often unmentioned—aspect of the Revolution. Her family in Pennsylvania was attacked by Indians who, as they had repeatedly done in the past, allied themselves with anyone fighting the settlers on their lands. In this case, they joined forces with the British against the colonists. This reminiscence is based on a memoir written by her son, General Hugh Brady:

> On the 11th of April [1779], not far from his residence, Captain Brady was assassinated by a concealed body of Indians—and thus perished one of the most gallant warriors of the Revolutionary era. . . . This was a terrible blow to his heroic little wife, who was already bowed down with grief on account of the melancholy death at the hands of the Indians of her son James, near Sunbury, the 13th of August, 1778. . . . Hurriedly collecting her children to-

gether, Mrs. Brady fled to the residence of her father in the Cumberland Valley. Here she tarried until October following, when she returned to the Buffalo Valley, upon a tract of land her husband had located. It is stated that when she started homeward Mrs. Brady performed the wonderful feat of carrying her youngest child before her on horseback and leading a cow all the way from Shippensburg. The animal was a gift from a brother. The journey was long, the roads bad, the times perilous, but her energy and perseverance surmounted all, and she and her cow and children arrived in safety.

It should be noted that Mrs. Brady had thirteen children and named her only daughter, who was born August 9, 1778, Liberty, in honor of the Declaration of Independence.

In short, the total warfare of the American Revolution engulfed and battered women left alone to guard home and family as men went off to serve. Sometimes women were in the path of attacks by British and Americans—simultaneously. Starvation, epidemic, and poverty (with the breadwinning husband off to military service) was exacerbated by fear of death on the battlefield for husband and sons, or at home for younger children and the wife herself—to say nothing of galloping inflation, which put purchase of food and clothing beyond her reach.

# CHAPTER FIFTEEN

# Mercy Warren, Patriot, versus Ann Hulton, Loyalist

Two women living in Massachusetts as the Revolution festered and finally burst forth wrote eyewitness accounts of the events that occurred during the years 1767 to 1775—but they started at completely opposite points on the political spectrum.

Mercy Warren, the staunch Patriot whom some have credited with helping to organize the vital Committees of Correspondence (which brought some measure of unity of purpose and action to the colonies), wrote satirical drama and poetry before the outbreak of hostilities in 1775–1776. And at the start of the war she began writing her monumental three-volume history of the Revolution, finally published in 1805. Much of the material from chapter two of her first volume covers the same events as reported by ardent Loyalist Ann Hulton in her personal correspondence.

Ann Hulton had left England to accompany her brother Henry to Massachusetts, where he was commissioner of customs at Boston in 1767 to 1776. She wrote her letters to a Mrs. Adam Lightbody, wife of a Liverpool merchant. Her

Mercy Warren, painted by John Singleton Copley. *Courtesy of the Museum of Fine Arts, Boston, Bequest of Winslow Warren.*

observations on contemporary political events reflect her own strongly Tory point of view, as well as opinions of local British officials with whom she came into contact. She had decided to go to America with all goodwill and high expectations of finding a much better life for herelf there in "Presbyterian" Boston where she would "not be exposed to such a corruption of manners, as in London. . . ." From her own words emerges a portrait of a remarkably intelligent and self-confident woman:

> I shall let the commissioners know that his sister if she goes does not intend to set up for a fine lady, but for something more uncommon, a merchant—a character, however, in which she thinks she can act with greater propriety and advantage, as well as satisfaction to herself. Some useful employment as traffic [commerce] or cultivating a small plantation in the country will be most agreeable to my genius and inclination and best for health. Whatever scheme I pursue I shall submit to his judgment and direction, and shall beware of any partnership, have seen enough of that.

Placing side by side the comments made on identical subjects by these two women produces history crackling with human fears and feelings. Thus, just six days after Ann Hulton arrived in Boston, on June 30, 1768, she was obliged to flee the Sons of Liberty attacking her temporary hostess, a Mrs. Burch:

> We soon found that the mobs here are very different from those in old England where a few lights put into the windows will pacify, or the interposition of a magistrate restrain them, but here . . . no person daring or willing to suppress their outrages, or to punish the most notorious offenders for any crimes whatever, these Sons of Violence after attacking houses, breaking windows, beating, stoning and bruising several gentlemen belonging to the customs,

the collector mortally, and burning his boat, they consulted what was to be done next, and it was agreed to retire for the night, all was ended with a speech from one of the leaders, concluding thus, "We will defend our liberties and property, by the strength of our arm and the help of our God, to your tents O Israel." This is a specimen of the Sons of Liberty, of whom you no doubt have heard, and will hear more.

She explained to her friend in the same letter that the commissioners and their families—about "fifty refugees"—took off that very evening with the protection of several gunboats for safety at Castle William.

Mercy Warren, writing of the same event, agreed that "after this fracas the customs-house officers repaired immediately to Castle William, as did the board of commissioners." She, too, referred to "the inconsiderate rabble," describing the violence in much the same way, though without mentioning any death resulting from beating. But then she objected strongly:

This trivial disturbance was exaggerated until it wore the complexion of a riot of the first magnitude. By the insinuations of the party, and their malignant conduct, it was not strange that in England it was considered as a London mob collected in the streets of Boston with some formidable desperado at their head.

Looking back at the repeal of the Stamp Act in 1766, the two women saw different causes and consequences for this action. Blaming American supporters in Parliament for bringing on the "crisis sooner than expected" and looking on Boston as a kind of ringleader, which the other colonies were only waiting to follow, Ann Hulton fumed:

The poison of disaffection has been infused and spread by inflammatory writers. . . . Lord Camden and Lord Chatham's speeches on the repeal of the Stamp Act, have opened to them a new view of their privileges, and I dare say they are enrolled in their records, as sacred as their charters. . . . The authority and power of the British Parliament to tax them is openly denied. To this purpose the Assembly here sent a petition to his majesty. . . .

On the contrary, Mercy Warren saw the Repeal as part hope and part delusion:

In order to quiet the public mind, the execution of the Stamp Act was pronounced inexpedient by a majority of the House of Commons, and a bill passed for its repeal, on March the 18th, 1766. But a clause was inserted therein, holding up a parliamentary right to make laws binding on the colonies in all cases whatsoever. . . .

A short lived joy was diffused throughout America, even by this delusive appearance of lenity; the people of every description manifested the strongest desire that harmony might be re-established between Great Britain and the colonies. . . . Yet amidst the demonstrations of this lively gratitude, there were some who had sagacity enough to see that the British ministry was not so much instigated by principles of equity, as impelled by necessity. These deemed any relaxation in Parliament an act of justice, rather than favor, and felt more resentment for the manner, than obligation for the design of this partial repeal; their opinion was fully justified by the subsequent conduct of administration.

Fleeing to an island residence outside Boston harbor in order to escape the menacing mob, Ann Hulton viewed the opposition as misinformed massacrers:

The credulity of the common people here is imposed on by a number of lies raised to irritate and inflame them. They believe that the commissioners have an unlimited power given to tax even their lands, and that it is in order to raise a revenue for supporting a number of bishops that are coming over, etc. . . . Every officer of the Crown that does his duty is become obnoxious, and they must either fly or be sacrificed. The attacks are always in the dark, several hundred against one man. . . . As to my brother and Mr. Burch . . . they are prohibited setting foot on shore again at their peril, and in case one of them does, the sexton of each church has orders to give notice by tolling a bell, when all the bells are to ring as for fire to alarm the inhabitants and raise the mob to tear them to pieces. They likewise threaten to drive us hence saying this castle belongs to the province, and not to the King. . . . Should they make this desperate attempt, they might massacre us, but their escape would be impossible. . . .

Mercy Warren's attitude was quite different, but, of course, she was not personally threatened at the time. She lived about forty miles outside Boston, in Plymouth, where nevertheless she heard all the latest news at her home, a meeting place for anti-British leaders such as John and Sam Adams and her brother James Otis. About British tyranny and taxation in general, and arbitrary officials and the threepence-per-pound levy on tea in particular, she exploded:

This inconsiderable duty on teas finally became an object of high importance and altercation; it was not the sum, but the principle that was contested; it manifestly appeared that this was only a financial expedient to raise a revenue from the colonies by imperceptible taxes. The defenders of the privileges and the freedom of the colonies denied all parliamentary right to tax them in any way whatever. They asserted that if the collection of this duty was permitted, it would establish a precedent, and strengthen the claim Parliament had assumed to tax them at pleasure. . . .

In consequence of the new system, a board of customs was instituted and commissioners appointed to sit in Boston to collect the duties; which were, besides other purposes, to supply a fund for the payment of the large salaries annexed to their office. A civil list was soon after established, and the governors of Massachusetts, judges of the superior court, and such other officers as had heretofore depended on the free grants of the representative body, were to be paid out of the revenue chest.

Thus rendered wholly independent of the general assembly, there was no check left on the wanton exercise of power in the crown officers, however disposed they might be to abuse their trust. . . . By a warrant of a writ of assistance from the governor or lieutenant governor, any officer of the revenue was authorized to enter the dwelling of the most respectable inhabitant on the smallest suspicion of a concealment of contraband goods, and to insult, search, or seize, with impunity.

Not quite a year after the arrival of the Hultons, Henry Hulton as a British customs collector was obliged to entertain royal Governor Francis Bernard for tea on July 12, 1768. The only comment Ann Hulton made either about the governor or the conversation was that "His excellency says two more such years as the past and the British Empire is at an end."

Mercy Warren, on the other hand, expressed open contempt for the governor, using the biting language for which she was known in her satirical dramas:

He was a man of little genius, but some learning. He was by education strongly impressed with high ideas of canon and feudal law, and fond of a system of government that had been long obsolete in England, and had never had an existence in America. His disposition was choleric and sanguine, obstinate and designing, yet too open and frank to disguise his intrigues, and too precipitant to bring them to maturity. A revision of colony charters, a resumption of former privileges, and an American revenue were the constant topics of his letters to administration. To prove the necessity of these measures, the most trivial disturbance was magnified to a riot; and to give a pretext to these wicked insinuations it was thought by many that tumults were frequently excited by the indiscretion or malignancy of his own partisans.

Both women were fairly well agreed in their attitude on what history now calls the "Boston Massacre" (following the lead of Paul Revere who gave that title to his engraving of the event). To Ann Hulton, the riot that resulted in the killing of five men was "the rage of a frantic mob," while Mercy Warren saw it as "sudden ferment."

Ann Hulton wrote with a kind of grudging condescension:

> We never thought ourselves more safe from the Sons of Violence than at present. Yet our security and the continuance of it, under a kind of Providence, depends on circumstances, chiefly the authority and support of government. From thence the impartial trial and honorable acquittal of Captain Preston and the soldiers has the most happy effect. It has exposed the conduct of the faction and opened the eyes of the people in general, convinced them that they have been deceived by false opinions, and false representations of facts.

And Mercy Warren expressed pride for Boston's insistence on the rule of law:

> Every method that prudence could dictate was used by a number of influential gentlemen to cool the sudden ferment, to prevent the populace from attempting immediate vengeance, and to prevail on the multitude to retire quietly to their own houses, and wait the decisions of law and equity. They effected their humane purposes; the people dispersed; and Captain Preston and his party were taken into custody of the civil magistrate. A judicial inquiry was afterwards made into their conduct; and so far from being actuated by any partial or undue bias, some of the first counsellors

of law engaged in their defense; and after a fair and legal trial they were acquitted of premeditated murder, by a jury of the county of Suffolk.

On the subject of royal Governor Thomas Hutchinson, lineal descendant of Anne Hutchinson and scholarly historian of Massachusetts Bay, the two women reveal diametrically opposed views. Ann Hulton, who had observed him as acting governor during the Boston Massacre of March 5, 1770, and as full governor in the years 1771 to 1774, which included the Boston Tea Party of December 16, 1773, was full of sympathy and distress at his treatment by his fellow colonists in Massachusetts. Discussing the Tea Party she wrote: "One would have thought . . . that all the malice that earth and hell could raise were pointed against the Governor." .

Mercy Warren for her part made Thomas Hutchinson the focus of another of her trenchant pen portraits—in line with the subtitle of her book which reads: *Interspersed with Biographical, Political and Moral Observations.* (In the course of her history, not a single leader on either side, from battle commanders George Washington and John Burgoyne to statesman-politicians John Adams and Lord Frederick North, escaped her candid, no-holds-barred appraisal.) "Few ages have produced a more fit instrument for the purposes of a corrupt court" than Governor Hutchinson, she insisted:

He was dark, intriguing, insinuating, haughty and ambitious, while the extreme of avarice marked each feature of his character. His abilities were little elevated above the line of mediocrity; yet by dint of industry, exact temperance, and indefatigable labor, he became master of the accomplishments necessary to acquire popular fame. . . .

Raised and distinguished by every honor the people could bestow, he supported for several years the reputation of integrity, . . . and by the appearance of a tenacious regard to the religious institutions of his country, he courted the public eclat with the most profound dissimulation while he engaged the affections of the lower classes by an amiable civility and condescension, without departing from a certain gravity of deportment mistaken by the vulgar for sanctity.

The Boston Tea Party Ann Hulton saw from her position at the center of the action at the customs house. Disgusted, infuriated, and scared, she emphasized the indignities and injuries directed toward petty officials and faceless little people in the aftermath:

> The commissioners of the customs and tea consignees were obliged to seek refuge at the Castle. . . . After destruction of the tea, my brother returned home and the other commissioners left the castle. . . . The tea consignees remain still at the castle. Six weeks since the tea was destroyed, and there is no prospect of their ever returning and residing in Boston with safety. This place, and all the towns about entered into a written agreement not to afford them any shelter or protection, so that they are not only banished from their families and home, but their retreat is cut off, and their interest greatly injured by ruining their trade.
>
> . . . But the most shocking cruelty was exercised a few nights ago upon a poor old man a tidesman, one Malcolm, he is reckoned crazy. A quarrel was picked with him, he was afterward taken, and tarred and feathered. . . . He was stripped stark naked, one of the severest cold nights this winter, his body covered all over with tar, then with feathers, his arm dislocated in tearing off his clothes. He was dragged in a cart with thousands attending, some beating him with clubs and knocking him out of the cart, then in again. They gave him several severe whippings, at different parts of the town. This spectacle of horror and sportive cruelty was exhibited for about five hours. . . . They demanded of him to curse his masters, the King,

Governor, etc., which they could not make him do, but he still cried, "Curse all traitors."

. . . These few instances amongst many serve to show the abject state of government and barbarism of the times. There's no magistrate that dare or will act to suppress the outrages. No person is secure. There are many objects pointed at, at this time, and when once marked out for vengeance, their ruin is certain.

In contrast, Mercy Warren saw the Tea Party not as anarchy but as self-preservation:

A great number of persons, clad like the aborigines of the wilderness, with tomahawks in their hands, and clubs on their shoulders, without the least molestation marched through the streets with silent solemnity, and amidst innumerable spectators, proceeded to the wharves, boarded the ships, demanded the keys, and with much deliberation knocked open the chests, and emptied several thousand weight of the finest teas into the ocean. No opposition was made, though surrounded by the king's ships; all was silence and dismay.

This done, the procession returned through the town in the same order and solemnity as observed in the outset of their attempt. No other order took place, and it was observed, the stillest night ensued that Boston had enjoyed for many months. This unexpected event struck the ministerial party with rage and astonishment; while, as it seemed to be an attack upon private property, many who wished well to the public cause could not fully approve of the measure. Yet perhaps the laws of self-preservation might justify the deed, as the exigencies of the times required extraordinary exertions, and every other method had been tried in vain to avoid this disagreeable alternative. Besides it was alleged, and doubtless it was true, the people were ready to make ample compensation for all damages sustained, whenever the unconstitutional duty should be taken off, and other grievances radically redressed. But there appeared little prospect that any conciliatory advances would soon be made. The officers of government discovered themselves more vindictive than ever: animosities daily increased, and the spirits of the people were irritated to a degree of alienation, even from their tenderest connections, when they happened to differ in political opinion.

The battle of Lexington and Concord on April 19, 1775, turned each woman from eyewitness observer to aggrieved partisan. They both agreed on the British march to Concord, twenty miles from Boston, where ammunition was being stored. From this point, in retelling the story each woman colored her tale with firsthand anger. Perhaps Ann Hulton with her description of "minute companies" and the signal of light shown from one of the steeples in Boston was studied by the poet Longfellow before he wrote his nineteenth-century "Midnight Ride of Paul Revere." In any case, making no attempt to hide her feelings of rage mixed with contempt she reported:

The alarm spread through the country, so that before daybreak the people in general were in arms and on their march to Concord. About daybreak a number of the people appeared before the troops near Lexington. They were called to disperse, when they fired on the troops and ran off, upon which the light infantry pursued them and brought down about fifteen of them. The troops went on to Concord and executed the business they were sent on, and on their return found two or three of their people lying in the agonies of death, scalped and their noses and ears cut off and eyes bored out—which exasperated the soldiers exceedingly—a prodigious number of people now occupying the hills, woods, and stone walls along the road. The light troops drove some parties from the hills, but all the road being enclosed with stone walls served as a cover to the rebels, from whence they fired on the troops still running off whenever they had fired, but still supplied by fresh numbers who came from many parts of the country. In this manner were the troops harassed in their return for seven or eight miles. They were almost exhausted and had expended near the whole of their ammunition when to their great joy they were relieved by a brigade of troops. . . . The troops now combated with fresh ardor and marched in their return with undaunted countenances, receiving sheets of fire all the way from many miles, yet having no visible enemy to combat . . . , *for they never would face them in an open field, but always skulked and fired from behind walls and trees, and out of windows of houses.* [Italicized to emphasize strong partisan flavor.] But this cost them dear for the soldiers entered those dwellings, and put all the men to death. . . . Several officers are wounded and about 100 soldiers. The killed amount to near 50. As to the enemy we can have no exact amount but it is said there was about ten times the number of them engaged, and that near 1000 of them have fallen.

The troops returned to Charlestown about sunset after having some of them marched near 50 miles, and being engaged from daybreak in action, without respite, or refreshment, and about ten in the evening they were brought back to Boston. . . .

Mercy Warren described contemporary astonishment at the attack on "the defenseless peasants of Lexington" . . . "a small village nine miles beyond Cambridge." She continued:

But it being reduced to a certainty that a number of persons had, the evening before, in the environs of Cambridge, been insulted, abused, and stripped by officers in British uniform, and that a considerable armament might be immediately expected in the vicinity, Captain Parker, who commanded a company of militia, ordered them to appear at beat of drum on the parade at Lexington, on the nineteenth. They accordingly obeyed, and were embodied before sunrise.

[British] Colonel Smith who commanded about 800 men came suddenly upon them within a few minutes after, and accosting them in language very unbecoming an officer of his rank, he ordered them to lay down their arms and disperse immediately. He illiberally branded them with the epithets of *rebel* and *traitor;* and before the little party had time, either to resist or to obey, he with wanton precipitations, ordered his troops to fire. Eight men were killed on the spot; and without any concern for his rashness, or little molestation from the inhabitants, Smith proceeded on his rout.

. . . The adjacent villages collected, and prepared to cut off their retreat [from Concord]; but a dispatch had been sent by Col. Smith to inform General Gage that the country was arming and his troops in danger. A battalion under the command of Lord Percy was sent to succour him, and arrived in time to save Smith's corps. . . . Lord Percy came up with the routed corps near the fields of Menotomy [modern-day Arlington]; where barbarities were committed by the king's army, which might have been expected only from a tribe of savages. They entered, rifled, plundered, and burnt several houses; *and in some instances, the aged and infirm fell under the sword of the ruffian; women, with their new-born infants, were obliged to fly naked, to escape the fury of the flames in which their houses were enwrapped.* [Again, italics added.]

The footsteps of the most remorseless nations have seldom been marked with more rancorous and ferocious rage, than may be traced in the transactions of this day; a day never to be forgotten by America.

. . . Notwithstanding their superiority in every respect, several regiments of the best troops in the royal army were seen, to the surprise and joy of every lover of his country, flying before the raw, inexperienced peasantry, who had run hastily together in defense of their lives and liberties . . . .

Unfortunately, Ann Hulton and Mercy Warren never met one another, or read each other's writings. So well informed on both the obvious and the fine points of politics, they might have had some of the Western world's great dialogues on such intricate subjects as manipulating taxation in order to support the motherland's industry, justification for paying official British salaries directly without authorization by the local legislature—or an alternative to war, for which they shared an intense dislike.

In any case, Ann Hulton returned home to England not long after the battle of Lexington and Concord. There she commented on her newfound appreciation of her native country, and in the process painted a bleak picture of Revolutionary Boston:

> It still appears a wonder to me that I am here in my native country, escaped from the dangers and free from dreadful alarms. That I can go to bed without apprehensions of cannonadings, by which I used to be roused, and rise up without anxious thoughts, for supplies and safety by day, and walk out and see plentiful markets and easy countenances, instead of deserted streets, empty marketplaces, or to meet discontented looks and anxious distress.
> . . . Thanks to a kind providence that it was temporary, that the scene is changed both with myself and my friends, for whose safety I have felt more than when I was amidst the alarms and horrors of war.

Mercy Warren remained in Massachusetts, no longer a theater of active warfare after the British evacuation of Dorchester Heights on March 17, 1776. She busied herself with rearing five sons, writing her history, and constantly speaking out. An informed if informal political watchdog, she commented at length on such diverse subjects as maltreatment of the Indian natives and the French Revolution that erupted in 1789.

# · *Part VI* ·

---

## "ALL MEN
## ARE
## CREATED EQUAL"

---

Abigail Smith Adams by C. Schessele. *Courtesy of the Collection of the Library of Congress.*

# CHAPTER SIXTEEN

# *Ladies and Feminists*

The ringing rhetoric of independence spawned feminism—the call for legal, political, and social equality between the sexes.[1] But at the same time prosperity promoted the ideal of the lady, that indolent, ornamental creature whose sole function in life was to display her husband's financial success to the world. Her only place was in the home, her own or someone else's, where she might be seen in all her overdressed, bejeweled splendor.

The ladies and the feminists together (radically opposed images even today) represented no more than five to ten percent of the population. They require special consideration, however, since they wielded great influence, all out of proportion to their small numbers, before the Revolution and after. The so-called lady was the social idol, which every woman in the highly mobile, emerging American society was encouraged to imitate. And as for the feminists, through their writings,

---

[1] Although the word "feminist" was first used only in 1895, the appeal for equality which it defined was as old as man. And in 1776, at the time of the Declaration of Independence that word "man" itself was defined by the Oxford Dictionary as a member of the human race, a human being irrespective of age or sex. Thus British philosopher-historian David Hume could write in 1776: "all men, both male and female."

outspoken pronouncements, and accomplishments, they provided leadership for all women who might wish to follow.

Since the lady rapidly became the nemesis of the feminists, attention should be given to where she came from and how she lived, functioned, and appeared.

To begin, Mercy Warren's complaint about the disappearance of American idealism in post-Revolutionary prosperity probably goes a long way to explain the emergence of the symbol of the lady for earlier periods, as well as for the time of which she writes:

> A sudden accumulation of property by privateering, by speculation, by accident, or fraud, placed many in the lap of affluence, who were without principle, education, or family. These, from a thoughtless ignorance, and the novelty of splendor to which they had been total strangers, suddenly plunged into every kind of dissipation, and grafted the extravagancies of foreigners onto their own passion for squandering what by them had been so easily acquired.
>
> Thus avarice without frugality and profusion without taste were indulged, and soon banished the simplicity and elegance that had formerly reigned: instead of which there was spread in America among the rising generation, a thirst for the accumulation of wealth, unknown to their ancestors. A class who had not had the advantages of the best education, and who had paid little attention to the principles of the Revolution, took the lead in manners. . . .

Typically, the newly emerged lady was ensconced in a completely different setting from the earliest colonial women. Back then, even a magistrate's family huddled together in a cramped dwelling. But by the late eighteenth century, Nomini Hall was a good example of how the top echelon of Virginia lived. Philip Fithian, employed at the estate as tutor for the two sons, nephew, and five daughters of Councillor and Mrs. Robert Carter, included in his *Journal and Letters,* 1767–

*1774* a detailed description of the plantation. In the center stood the brick mansion, seventy-six feet long by forty-four feet wide, two stories high. At an equal distance from each of the four corners of the mansion—which thus became the focal point of a square—stood the coach house, stable, washhouse, and five-room school house, occupied by the two sons, the nephew, and their tutor. Nearby was a row of smaller buildings, containing the bakery, dairy, kitchen, and storehouse. And not mentioned by Fithian, who found further details tedious, were the slave quarters.

The main house was left as a kind of work-free pleasure dome where Mrs. Carter presided, smothered in wealth and swarmed over by slaves. The first floor of the mansion consisted of a ballroom, thirty feet long, and two dining rooms, one for adults and one for all the children. Upstairs were four bedrooms, one set aside for the parents, two always on reserve for guests, and the other for all five daughters to share.[2]

Other plantations, such as Westover, home of the Byrds in Virginia, were even more magnificent and larger. In the towns, Richmond or Charles Town for instance, individual family land area was smaller, but there were Georgian mansions of brick, as well as commodious rambling wooden houses. Both types shared with the plantations a tendency to have a series of outhouses, for kitchen tasks, and slave quarters, and within the main house the same richly paneled walls and grand stairways.

In 1781, a French visitor to America, Abbé Robin, remarked on the contrast between luxury in Annapolis and the meagerness of life in Connecticut:

[2] In all homes, rich and poor, north and south, people slept two or three to a bed, with several beds in each room. Even in wealthy homes where lavish furnishings and *objets d'art* were regularly imported from England, privacy was all but ignored, both for family and for guests.

As we advance towards the South, we observe a sensible difference in the manners and customs of the people. We no longer find, as in Connecticut, houses situated along the road at small distances, just large enough to contain a single family, and the household furniture nothing more than is barely necessary; here are spacious habitations, consisting of different buildings, at some distance from each other, surrounded with plantations that extend beyond the reach of the eye. . . . Their furniture here is constructed out of the most costly kinds of wood, and that most valuable marble, enriched by the elegant devices of the artist's hand.

Generally speaking, the abbé was correct, but in the North he must have seen only the inland farming communities, which were poor, in decided contrast to coastal towns. Farm dwellings consisted of two rooms, housing two families, whereas in Boston, for example, though lot areas were as small, the families of wealthy merchants lived in large homes. Furnishings would be luxurious and include ornate wallpaper, rugs for the floors, chairs, four-poster beds, and draperies.

Definitely, the wealthy southern planter lived more luxuriously than anyone else in the colonies. But somehow the abbé missed seeing that the South, too, had its share of poverty—a fact that made the planter's prosperity stand out even more strikingly. Especially on the constantly expanding frontier, families lived as the first European arrivals in the New World had lived (though with the advantages of having learned from older settlements the lessons necessary for survival and of having available from the established communities certain creature comforts). In this connection, wealthy Colonel William Byrd, surveying the boundary line between Virginia and North Carolina in 1728, had to travel to the backcountry where, he reported, he stayed overnight in a one-room dwelling with a family of nine "who all pigged lovingly together."

This same Colonel Byrd is an excellent source for supporting the generalization that the ladies who lived in mansions

"Tight Lacing, or Fashion before Ease," c. 1777. *Courtesy of Colonial Williamsburg.*

had no worthwhile occupation and so made clothes their main preoccupation. He rose regularly sometime between 5:00 and 7:00 A.M. and observed one day: "Our ladies were not dressed till one o'clock." Another time, when he was up and about by 6:00 A.M., he wrote in his diary that he and his friend the Reverend Dunn "played at billiards and then we read some news while the ladies spent three hours in dressing, according to custom."

Historian Julia Spruill finds the wardrobe of Anne Le Brasseur, widow of a wealthy Charles Town merchant and planter, representative of southern ladies of the aristocracy prior to the Revolution. For ordinary wear she had calico, muslin, and linen, and for special occasions such gowns as one of grosgrain trimmed with gold lace, a white Persian quilted petticoat, brocade shoes with gold laces, and the fanciest of headdresses with ruffles and fringes. Her jewelry included pearls, diamonds, and a gold watch.

England not only set the fashion but sent the clothes worn by these fashionable women (except during the era of the Revolution). And if their outer garments made housework or gardening impractical, their undergarments made these tasks impossible. Tutor Philip Fithian at Nomini Hall reported with astonishment: "Today I saw a phenomenon, Mrs. Carter without stays." Then he went on to explain the apparent reason: a pain in her breasts.

Pointing up the richness of clothes worn by the lady is the contrasting dress of southern lower-class women. Usually former indentured servants, they would start off their years of freedom with a petticoat, a cap and gown of the coarsest and plainest material, and homemade shoes—and sometimes an apron and stockings.

Northern upper-class ladies dressed less lavishly than their southern counterparts, but still far more ornately than the first settlers. In Massachusetts their dress, plain and simple at home, would burst into gay color and ornate material for festive occasions. Quite usual were gowns of velvet, satin, lace, or brocade damask, and on the head a small lace cap. Unlike the Puritans who refused to wear any kind of jewelry, these eighteenth-century New Englanders might very well display their pearls.

Ladies also spent an inordinate amount of time on their hair, having their maids or professional hairdressers make their locks curly, frizzy, or inches high above the scalp. Ointments, curl papers, hot irons, rolls and false hair made of cow tails or horsehair were used, as well as nimble fingers. Nor were gray hairs left untouched. Anna Green Winslow, young Boston diarist, described a fashionable coiffeur, identified only as "D," at work on the head of a local lady:

> How long she was under his operations I know not. I saw him twist and tug and pick and cut off whole locks of gray hair at a slice, (the lady telling him he would have no hair to dress next time,) for the space of an hour and a half. When I left them, he seemed not to be near done.

And Abbé Robin reported that Annapolis ladies considered a French hairdresser a man of great importance. In fact, one local *grande dame* hired her own coiffeur for a thousand crowns a year salary.

So much for how the lady lived and looked. Now to investigate how the law wrote her into American lore.

The Blackstone Code of 1765–1769, which was innocuously presented as a mere codification of already existing law, in fact set women of America back to days of antiquity. "By marriage, the husband and wife are one person in law," Sir William Blackstone expounded. "That is, the very being or legal existence of the woman is suspended during the marriage, or at least is incorporated and consolidated." In other words, man and wife were one person under the law, speaking with one voice, that of the husband.

Actually, the concept dated from time immemorial. However, during the early days of colonization, when women were indispensable for providing and preserving life amid death, no one paid much attention. Instead, when the male-female ratio favored women and when female services were vital to success and stability, men positively catered to their wives, giving them concessions unheard of in the Old World at that time.

But by the late eighteenth century, the thirteen well-established colonies showed intent to treat women no more favorably than had any other society in history, having achieved permanence, prosperity, and a surplus of women.[3] Henceforth, Americans would incorporate into their own legal system the concept of the oneness of husband and wife. This theory went back to English common law in the immediate past, to medieval feudalism further back, and finally to the Old and New Testaments.

Thus, Genesis (2:24):

> Therefore shall a man leave his father and his mother, and shall cleave unto his wife: and they shall be one flesh.

And Jesus speaks in the Gospel according to St. Mark (10:6-8):

> But from the beginning of the creation God made them male and female. For this cause shall a man leave his father and mother, and cleave to his wife. And they twain shall be one flesh: so then they are no more twain, but one flesh.

[3] The first United States census of 1790 showed a surplus of women to men in New England, which had probably existed since the mid-eighteenth century. Furthermore, as whites drove Indians further west and settled inland, more men than women left the settled coastal areas.

The Middle Ages then translated these biblical words on the unity of flesh of husband and wife into the feudal doctrine of coverture or "feme covert," whereby a married woman is legally under the cover, protection, or authority of her husband. In a word, she had no rights, property, or ability to act on her own, and was for all practical purposes legally (as opposed to actually) dead. The concept was incorporated into English common law (law handed down from generation to generation by custom, usage, and court precedent) and finally codified into written law a decade before the American Revolution. The Blackstone code became the law of the land in England and in the American colonies as well.

Around the 1760s there developed a positive mania for writing custom into law, codifying unwritten—and hence flexible—tradition into hard-and-fast rules and laws. And men were in charge of the codification, their position strengthened by the increasing shortage of males and the growth of science and technology along with prosperity.

As a result, the American woman could no longer—as had female colonists in seventeenth-century New England at least—transfer her own real property, sue or be sued in her own name, or give evidence against her husband. She could not even be accused of a crime if she had committed same in the presence of her husband. Instead, the husband would be held responsible as having commanded her to commit the action.

Woman's place was to be in the home only (except during the years of the Revolutionary War, which changed the situation, but only temporarily). No longer could she conduct business in the community, an activity in which she had experienced success prior to the 1760s. When and if attention was paid to educating her, the sole reason was to make her a more interesting conversationalist for her husband and his friends, a much-sought-after guest at business and social gatherings, and a superior hostess in her own home. As for her children, they were no longer her special responsibility. Instead, the father had absolute control over them, the mother deserving only reverence and respect.

Adding to the long-range woe of women was a totally un-planned sequel to all this. Early colonial court records and legislative documents were unavailable in the nineteenth cen-tury, so suffragists assumed that the Blackstone Code had merely written already existing practice into the law of the land. Thus, they were completely unaware of the many con-cessions taken for granted by colonial women, rights and privileges for which nineteenth-century women agitated and which twentieth-century women have still not fully recovered. It was only in 1930 that the pioneer work of a distinguished male scholar, Professor Richard Morris of Columbia, gave feminists a firm base in history. In his book *Studies in the History of American Law,* he devoted seventy-four pages to Chapter III, "Women's Rights in Early American Law."

However, in the late eighteenth century there were still more steps backward for women. At the same time that sci-ence and technology were radically changing every aspect of life, new inventions were bringing about an industrial revolu-tion. For the woman this meant she could no longer add to the family income by working at home in cottage industry, which had often given her vocational training and experience in business. Instead, she had to leave the familiar hearth for the impersonal factory, sometimes at a very early age. In the fac-tory she had little control over her time or her efforts.

As medicine progressed from primitive to scientific, the maternal contributions so necessary to healing were over-looked as men convinced themselves that they alone had the mental capacity to absorb and put to use complex new theories and knowledge. Professions were licensed, specific training was emphasized, and women were barred from the higher education required, on grounds of inferior intelligence and supposed delicacy. By 1820, a Boston doctor put into writing what many had been saying and thinking for more than half a century. He explained the need to replace midwives with well-trained men:

> It is obvious that we cannot instruct women as we do men in the science of medicine; we cannot carry them into the dissecting room and the hospital; . . . and I venture to say that a female could scarce pass through the course of education requisite to prepare her as she ought to be prepared, for the practice of midwivery, without destroying those moral qualities of character which are essential to the office.

Meanwhile, ladies who could read had long had access to a runaway best seller explaining why they should be happy though subordinate, and what to do in every situation, including marriage to an idiot: "First give him the orders you afterwards receive from him." The book was *The Lady's New Year's Gift: or Advice to a Daughter,* written by George Savile, first marquis of Halifax, for his daughter Elizabeth. Between 1688 and 1765 there were fifteen editions in England, and the book was extremely popular in all colonies.

Expanding his advice on handling a husband, Lord Halifax warned his daughter not to let others take charge of her mate. Make sure, he counseled, "if when your husband shall resolve to be an ass . . . he may be *your* ass."

The underlying theme of his book was the difference between the sexes—expressed with sentiments not unknown in the twentieth century:

> You must first lay it down for a foundation in general that there is inequality in the sexes, and that for the better economy of the world, the men who were to be the law givers had the larger share of reason bestowed upon them; by which means your sex is the better prepared for the compliance that is necessary for the better performance of those duties which seem to be most properly assigned to

it. . . . We are made of differing tempers, that our defects may the better be mutually supplied: Your sex wanteth our reason for your conduct and our strength for your protection; ours wanteth your gentleness to soften and to entertain us.

A few sentences later he assured Elizabeth, then twelve years old: "You have more strength in your looks than we have in our laws, and more power by your tears than we have by our arguments."

Other ladies' books and marriage treatises emphasized the wife's duties, seldom mentioned the husband's obligations. Frequently, the writer insisted that the wife existed only for her husband, to give him agreeable and obedient companionship, to mother his children tenderly, and to act as a gracious and attractive hostess to his guests.

"Remember the ladies," Abigail Adams gently warned her husband John, away in Philadelphia helping to declare that "all men are created equal." Probably with the newly promulgated Blackstone Code in mind, she advised him on March 31, 1776:

Do not put such unlimited power into the hands of the husbands. Remember, all men would be tyrants if they could. If particular care and attention is not paid to the ladies, we are determined to foment a rebellion, and will not hold ourselves bound by any laws in which we have no voice or representation.

That your sex are naturally tyrannical is a truth so thoroughly established as to admit of no dispute. . . . Men of sense in all ages abhor those customs which treat us as the vassals of your sex.

Two weeks later on April 14, 1776, John responded with annoying amusement:

As to your extraordinary code of laws, I cannot but laugh. We have been told that our struggle has loosened the bonds of government everywhere; that children and apprentices were disobedient; that schools and colleges were grown turbulent; that Indians slighted their guardians and Negroes grew insolent to their masters. But your letter was the first intimation that another tribe, more numerous and powerful than all the rest, were grown discontented.

But Abigail did not give up easily; she sent an even stronger reiteration on May 7. And this time she seemed to shake John's ancient beliefs, because on May 26, 1776, he wrote a highly significant letter to a James Sullivan:

Whence arises the right of the men to govern the women, without their consent? Why exclude women?

You will say, because their delicacy renders them unfit for practice and experience in the great businesses of life, and the hardy enterprises of war, as well as the arduous cares of state. Besides, their attention is so much engaged with the necessary nurture of their children, that nature has made them fittest for domestic cares. . . .

Your idea that those laws which affect the lives and personal liberty of all, or which inflict corporal punishment, affect those who are not qualified to vote, as well as those who are is just. But so they do women, as well as men; children, as well as adults. . . .

Generally speaking, women and children have as good judgments and as independent minds, as those men who are wholly destitute of property; these last being to all intents and purposes as much dependent upon others, who will please to feed, clothe and employ them, as women are upon their husbands, or children on their parents. . . .

John Adams was certainly far from proclaiming the absolute equality of women with men at this point. But Abigail, too, had some early doubts as to whether women could or should achieve for themselves alone. A letter on education for women, written in July 1776, reflects the idea that women should be educated for the sakes of their husbands and children: "If we mean to have heroes, statesmen, and philosophers, we should have learned women."

However, by the end of June 1778, she had come to the conclusion that education was the greatest single barrier against true equality for women:

> I can hear of the brilliant accomplishments of my sex with pleasure, and rejoice in that liberality of sentiment which acknowledges them. At the same time, I regret the trifling, narrow, constricted education of the females of my own country. . . . In this country, you need not be told how much female education is neglected, nor how fashionable it has been to ridicule female learning. . . .

She then quotes with enthusiastic approval an anonymous, though male, writer who said of women:

> Their senses are generally as quick as ours; their reason as nervous, their judgment as mature and solid. To these natural perfections add but the advantage of acquired learning, what polite and charming creatures would they prove. . . . Nor need we fear to lose our empire over them by thus improving their native abilities; since where there is most learning, sense, and knowledge, there is always observed to be the most modesty and rectitude of manners. . . .

Abigail Adams herself was proof of the connection between erudition and achievement—although other factors have to be noted in her case, such as her strong Puritan heritage, and the need for managing family finances and raising four children during her statesman-diplomat husband's ten years of almost continual absence. The only woman ever to have been the wife of one President ( John Adams, President from 1797 to

1801) and mother of another (John Quincy Adams, President from 1825 to 1829), she had early embraced the liberal Puritanism of the Congregational church of her father, the Reverend William Smith. Sickly as a child, she had had no formal schooling, but benefited from living in a parsonage filled with books and lively conversation. Also, she often visited her maternal grandmother Quincy, whom she credited with filling her full of love of learning.

In her letters, Abigail Adams showed wide reading of history as she referred to the Spartans, Cicero, Nero, Caesar Borgia, and Charles XII of Sweden among others. She quoted from at least three plays by Shakespeare; seventeenth-century poet and dramatist John Dryden; her contemporary Oliver Goldsmith, famous for his novel *The Vicar of Wakefield;* literary critic and poet Alexander Pope; and French dramatist Jean Baptiste Molière, whom she did not particularly enjoy, despite his public acclaim. As for Abigail's political influence over her husband, there is a remark by Albert Gallatin, who would later serve as Secretary of the Treasury under John's arch rival and successor, President Thomas Jefferson: "Mrs. President not of the United States but of a faction," Gallatin called her, looking to insult both Adamses.

Abigail Adams shared her strong interest in politics and a love of history and literature with her good friend, Mercy Otis Warren, who similarly lacked formal education. In Mercy's case, learning came from sitting in on tutorial sessions for her brothers, reading books in the library of her uncle (local minister who acted as tutor for the young Otises), and from her brother James, who often reviewed his lectures at Harvard and his reading assignments with Mercy. Beyond this, it is fun, even if unprovable, to speculate that Mercy Warren's feminist leanings were a throwback to her maternal ancestor, Faith Dotey, famous for preserving her property through the antenuptial agreement she signed in 1667 before remarriage.

In any case, Mercy, like Abigail Adams, chafed at the inferior education available to women:

> I believe it will be found that the deficiency lies not so much in the inferior contexture of female intellect as in the different education bestowed on the sexes, for when the cultivation of the mind is neglected in either, we see ignorance, stupidity, and ferocity of manners equally conspicuous in both. . . . When these temporary distinctions subside we may be equally qualified to taste the full draughts of knowledge and happiness prepared for the upright of every nation and sex.

And to a young friend who had indicated a desire to follow her footsteps and become a historian, Mercy wrote caustically:

> If you have a taste for the study of history let me urge you not to indulge it, lest the picture of human nature in all ages of the world should give your features too serious a cast or by becoming acquainted with the rude state of nature in the earlier ages—the origin of society, the foundations of government, and the rise and fall of empires—you should inadvertently glide into that unpardonable absurdity and sometimes venture to speak when politics happen to be the subject. In short, science of any kind beyond the toilet, the tea, or the card table, is as unnecessary to a lady's figuring in the drawing room as virtue unsully'd by caprice is to the character of the finished gentleman. . . .

Fortunately, Mercy Warren did not follow her own bitter advice; instead, she wrote one of the first three histories of the American Revolution. As a matter of fact, she is the kind of historian who, if given greater exposure, could by herself make history every student's favorite subject. She had no illusions about the past, and no hero was sacrosanct. Thus, George

Washington was a "gentleman . . . of a polite, but not a learned education." John Hancock, who had signed the Declaration of Independence in letters large enough for the king to read without his glasses, was "a gentleman of fortune, of more external accomplishments than real abilities." And her good friend John Adams, when ambassador to England following the Revolution, developed "a partiality for monarchy."

Not surprisingly, Adams refused to have anything to do with her for seven years after this judgment appeared with the publication of her three volumes in 1805, although earlier he had written: "I hope you will continue [our country's history], for there are few persons possessed of more facts or who can record them in a more agreeable manner." Later he complained bitterly to Massachusetts Governor Elbridge Gerry, who eventually effected a reconciliation between John and Mercy: "History is not the province of the ladies."

Mercy Warren was a Jeffersonian, a political position that probably helped cause the breach with John Adams, a strong Federalist. Beginning with the ratification controversy over the Constitution in 1787, they were on opposite sides politically. John favored immediate adoption, but Mercy circularized the unsigned brochure she had written criticizing the document. The President, she objected way back then, had royal powers —the identical criticism being voiced by twentieth-century political scientists. Besides, she contended, it was dangerous to allow senators and representatives to be continually reelected to office and serve for what amounted to lifelong terms. She also joined those who advocated the strong Bill of Rights, which was finally added to the Constitution as the first ten amendments in 1791.

Mercy Warren had at least one immediate protégée, Judith Sargent Murray, a fervent feminist writer in the late eighteenth century. On March 4, 1796, apparently referring to the 1790 volume by Mercy, *Poems, Dramatic and Miscellaneous,* which contained two verse dramas promoting human liberty, Judith Murray wrote that although she did not know Mercy personally, "yet having repeatedly perused with highly zested pleasure the volume with which you have obliged the world, I trace in this invaluable publication . . . the brilliant manifestations of genius so conspicuously displayed therein. . . ." She then submitted some of her own writing to Mercy for appraisal and criticism—including a series of essays that she called "The Gleaner" and had signed "Constantia" when they appeared in the new *Massachusetts Magazine.* Her subjects included politics, social mores, religion, and education.

Another Massachusetts feminist was Lucy Terry Prince (1730–1821), famous in her youth as the slave who wrote the poem about the Deerfield massacre of 1746. Her husband, Abijah Prince, whom she had married on May 17, 1756, and by whom she had six children, was a free Negro, and it is supposed that he paid her master, Ensign Ebenezer Wells, in order to buy her freedom. The couple moved to their own farm in Sunderland, Vermont, in 1764. Later, when a neighbor, Colonel Eli Bronson, claimed part of their property, Lucy went to the United States Supreme Court, probably in 1800, to argue the case herself. Deerfield historian George Sheldon reported presiding Justice Samuel Chase of Maryland as commenting that she had made a better argument than he had ever heard from any member of the Vermont bar.

At an unspecified date, sometime after the end of the Revolution, Lucy pleaded with the officials of Williams College in western Massachusetts to admit one of her sons as student despite his skin color. She went so far as to make a three-hour speech, in which she quoted law and the Bible, but was apparently unsuccessful, since Sheldon found no mention of any son of Lucy Prince in the register of Williams College. Obviously the Declaration of Independence—"all men are created equal"—was inspiring more than separation from England.

Also Massachusetts-born and -bred, Hannah Adams set a

precedent by becoming the first American woman to earn her living by writing. (Mercy Warren was subsidized by family wealth and by her husband.) The years of the Revolutionary War had brought bankruptcy to her father, a Medfield, Massachusetts, merchant, so that the family took in divinity students as boarders. Hannah, too sickly to have much formal schooling, was encouraged by her father, himself an omnivorous reader, to read poetry and novels. In addition, the boarding students taught her Latin, Greek, geography, and logic, and introduced her to *An Historical Dictionary of All Religions,* by Thomas Broughton, an English clergyman.

Taking notes for her private use, she soon compiled her own manuscript in 1784, *An Alphabetical Compendium of the Various Sects,* which she then published. This established her reputation; it appeared in three American editions—1791, 1801, and 1817—and three London editions—1795, 1814, and 1823.

In 1799, she published *A History of New England.* Though it is today more of a collector's item than a scholarly tome, the last third of her introduction to the work is worth quoting. Poignantly, she apologizes for intruding on that exclusive male domain, the writing of history:

> But though a female cannot be supposed to be accurate in describing, and must shrink with horror in relating the calamities of war, yet she may be allowed to feel a lively interest in the great cause for which the sword was drawn in America. The compiler is apprised of the numerous defects of the work, and is sensible it will not bear the test of criticism. Her incapacity for executing it has been heightened by a long interval of ill health, which has precluded much of that studious application which, in a work of this kind is indispensably necessary. She hopes, therefore, that generous humanity will soften the asperity of censure, and that the public will view with candor the assiduous, though perhaps, unsuccessful efforts of a female pen.

Never married, she supported herself while writing by making lace and braiding straw. The first woman allowed to use the prestigious Boston Atheneum—where her portrait now hangs on the walls—she published four additional books, including a *History of the Jews* (1812) and her *Memoir* (1831).

Susannah Haswell Rowson (1762–1824), born in Plymouth, England, came to Massachusetts with her recently widowed father when she was about six in 1768, and settled in Nantasket. By the age of twelve she was knowledgeable enough about Homer, Virgil, and Shakespeare to be dubbed "little scholar" by her summer neighbor, James Otis, Patriot activist and brother of Mercy Warren.

Her father, an official of the despised British revenue service, was arrested in 1775, held virtual prisoner for three years, and had his property confiscated. Finally, in 1778, he was allowed to leave Massachusetts, first for Nova Scotia and then for London, where at the age of sixteen Susannah hired herself out as governess for the children of the Duchess of Devonshire. Shortly afterward, she wrote her first novel, *Victoria.* Her second novel, *Charlotte Temple,* published in England in 1789 and in Boston in 1790, became the first best-selling American novel. There is a strong presumption that an unhappy marriage in 1787 to William Rowson, overly fond of pleasure and drink and out of his depth in business, inspired parts of the novel dealing with female trials and tribulations.

The failure of her husband's business in 1792 made both Rowsons turn to the stage, where after a season in Edinburgh, 1792–1793, they were booked to play in America, first with the Hallam Company at Philadelphia, and later at Annapolis, Baltimore, and finally Boston, where they settled in 1796 as members of the Federal Street Theatre. What Susannah lacked in acting ability, she made up in versatility, singing, dancing, and playing the harpsichord and guitar.

In addition, she wrote nine novels, many short poems, songs, and her most successful stage work, *Slaves in Algiers, or Struggle for Freedom* (1794), a comedy revolving around the eventual escape to freedom of a group of American women captured by North African pirates and held for ransom. Entertaining her audience and at the same time making strong points for women's ability, she included these words:

> *Well, ladies, tell me—how d'ye like my play?*
> *"The creature has some sense," methinks you say;*
> *She says that we should have supreme dominion,*
> *And in good truth, we're all of her opinion.*
> *Women were born for universal sway,*
> *Men to adore, be silent, and obey.*

She wrote and starred in two more plays before retiring from the stage in 1797 to open a private school in Boston, where she offered girls instruction above the elementary level, using textbooks she herself had written. Born into a Loyalist family, she became an ardent Patriot—a personal rebellion and Revolutionary attitude, which may well account for the protests against women's dependent role found in her writings.

Far away from New England, Eliza Wilkinson of Charles Town, S.C., in 1782 asserted vehemently that women had the ability to hold the highest political offices:

> Never were greater politicians than the several knots of ladies who met together. All trifling discourse of fashions, and such low little chat was thrown by, and we commenced perfect statesmen. Indeed, I don't know but if we had taken a little pains, we should have been qualified for prime ministers, so well could we discuss several important matters in hand.

(And of course her reference to "the several knots of ladies who met together," gives support to the contention that many females who never committed thoughts to paper for posterity or whose writings are yet to be uncovered were also feminists.)

Later in this same series of letters describing the British siege of her hometown in 1779, the young widow Wilkinson even takes on the legendary Greek poet Homer, solid in his 2500-year reputation as the first literary giant of the West:

> Homer gives us two or three broad hints to mind our domestic concerns, spinning, weaving, etc., and leave affairs of higher nature to the men; but I must beg his pardon—I won't have it thought that . . . we are capable of nothing more than minding the dairy, visiting the poultry-house, and all such domestic concerns; our thoughts can soar aloft, we can form conceptions of things of higher nature; and have as just a sense of honor, glory, and great actions, as these "Lords of the Creation." What contemptible *earth worms* these authors make us! They won't even allow us the liberty of thought, and that is all I want. I would not wish that we should meddle in what is unbecoming female delicacy, but surely we may have sense enough to give our opinions to commend or discommend such actions as we may approve or disapprove; without being reminded of our spinning and household affairs as the only matters we are capable of thinking or speaking of with justness or propriety. I won't allow it, positively won't.

But then in a somewhat chastened vein five pages later she blames her outbursts on what she calls her "unmanageable" pen:

> Before I am aware [my pen] flies from matters of fact or plain narration, and intrudes my poor opinion on the stage. What will the men say if they should see this? I am really out of *my sphere* now, and must fly to Homer for direction and instruction on household matters. Begone, pen: I must throw you by until I can keep you in proper order.

Fortunately, a descendant of Eliza Wilkinson, Caroline Gilman, published the letters in 1839, noting that posterity might well be interested in the thoughts of an articulate female who had lived through the Revolution.

Last in this admittedly small roster of late-eighteenth-century feminists is Hannah Lee Corbin of Virginia. Indignantly she complained to her brother Richard Henry Lee (famous for introducing the resolution in the Second Continental Congress of 1776 calling for independence from England) that widows were forced to pay taxes though they had no representation, not even a husband to speak on their behalf. His answer was that women were excluded from legislative sessions because men in the process of voting had a tendency to behave tumultuously and thus females, if allowed to attend such assemblies, would be quite out of character.

Hannah Lee Corbin has to be credited with making her powerful and famous brother think about women's place in society. However, it is only fair to note that she was asking for suffrage not for all women but just for "femes sole," the single women who had many of the same economic rights as men, but none of the political rights accorded to men. It would be pleasant to think that she was hoping to take one step at a time, but there is no more information available about her. In fact, even her original letter has been lost. Only her brother's reply is still in existence to give evidence of her questions.

Happily, women were not required to struggle for equal rights all by themselves in the era of independence. Their words, accomplishments, contributions—and plight—attracted the attention and considerable help from some members of the male power structure.

# CHAPTER SEVENTEEN

# *Men as Allies*

Some of women's best friends were men. For example, on the wave of the Enlightenment, flowing into America from Europe, Benjamin Franklin in 1747 composed "The Speech of Polly Baker" for the *London General Advertiser*. Writing under a female pseudonym—the hoax was not discovered for decades—he protested against prejudice toward women who led a free-and-easy sex life comparable to a man's. The words of "Polly Baker" made the rounds in England, America, and France, where she was hailed as a feminist Joan of Arc as she protested to the court trying her for the fifth time on charges of bastardy:

> Can it be a crime (in the nature of things I mean) to add to the number of the King's subjects, in a new country that really wants people? I own it, I should think it a praiseworthy rather than a punishable action. I have debauched no other woman's husband, nor enticed any youth. These things I never was charged with, nor has anyone the least cause of complaint against me, unless, perhaps, the minister of justice, because I have had children without being married, by which they have missed a wedding fee.
>
> . . . I readily consented to the only proposal of marriage that ever was made me, which was when I was a virgin; but too easily confiding in the person's sincerity that made

it, I unhappily lost my own honor by trusting to his; for he got me with child and then forsook me. That very person you all know. He is now become a magistrate of this country. . . . I must now complain of it, as unjust and unequal, that my betrayer and undoer, the first cause of all my faults and miscarriages (if they must be deemed such) should be advanced to honor and power in the government that punishes my misfortunes with stripes and infamy. . . .

How can it be believed that heaven is angry at my having children, when to the little done by me towards it God has been pleased to add his divine skill and admirable workmanship in the formation of their bodies and crowned it by furnishing them with rational and immortal souls. . . . The duty of the first and great command of nature and of nature's God is increase and multiply, a duty from the steady performance of which nothing has been able to deter me. But for its sake I have hazarded the loss of the public esteem and have frequently endured public disgrace and punishment, and therefore ought, in my humble opinion, instead of a whipping to have a statue erected in my memory.

Certainly, this was advanced thinking, but as far as giving women equal education or a voice in politics, Dr. Franklin remained a conservative eighteenth-century gentleman. Thus Sarah, his only daughter by his common-law wife, Deborah Read,[1] received no more nor less than the usual female education—the three Rs, needlework, penmanship, French, dancing, and instruction on the harpsichord.

Philadelphia, Benjamin Franklin's home base, was of course the site of both the Declaration of Independence in 1776 and the Constitutional Convention in 1787. And several men of Philadelphia were inspired to play a large role in

---

[1] Her first husband had deserted her and perhaps remarried. However, he might someday return, so that a legal marriage ran the risk of bigamy.

adding social revolution to the military, economic, and political aspects of the struggle for independence. Among other causes they embraced were improved status for women.

One statement published in Philadelphia was long ascribed to Thomas Paine, author of *Common Sense,* the pamphlet that had so effectively pleaded the cause of independence from England. Titled "An Occasional Letter on the Female Sex" and first distributed in August 1775, its author is now referred to only as "anonymous," but the letter remains a strong appeal on behalf of women, "surrounded on all sides by judges who are at once their tyrants and seducers."

Later while the Constitutional Convention was in session, the *Pennsylvania Gazette* on June 6, 1787, urged women to use "their influence over their husbands, brothers, and sons." The editors asserted:

> It is the duty of the American ladies, in a particular manner, to interest themselves in the success of the measures that are now pursuing by the federal convention for the happiness of America. They can retain their rank as rational beings only in a free government. In a monarchy (to which the present anarchy in America if not restrained must soon lead us) they will be considered as valuable members of society, only in proportion as they are capable of being mothers for soldiers who are the pillars of crowned heads. . . . As the miseries of slavery will fall with peculiar weight upon them, they are certainly deeply interested in the establishment of the influence, and the character in society, for which God intended them.

At about this same time, another Philadelphian, Dr. Benjamin Rush, emerged to improve the lot of women. On the side of humanity and morality, he may well have been one of the few true heroes of history. A Quaker who received his education at Princeton and Edinburgh, he signed the Declaration of Independence, advocated abolition of slavery, urged prison reform and the end of the death penalty, and proposed substantive education for women.

A member of the literary salon run by Elizabeth Graeme Ferguson, whose intelligence he greatly admired, he also had the highest praise for his own wife, Julia Stockton, telling John Adams:

> If there is a single philosopher in the cabinet of St. James's, he will advise immediately to make peace with America. "The Romans govern the world," said Cato, "but the women govern the Romans." The women of America have at last become principals in the glorious American controversy. Their opinions alone and their transcendent influence in society and families must lead us on to success and victory. My dear wife, who you know in the beginning of the war had all the timidity of her sex as to the issue of the war and the fate of her husband, was one of the ladies employed to solicit benefactions for the army. She distinguished herself by her zeal and address in this business, and is now so thoroughly enlisted in the cause of her country that she reproaches me with lukewarmness.

Perhaps as a consequence of his respect for these two women, Dr. Rush gave a lecture during the summer of the Constitutional Convention: "Thoughts upon Female Education, Accommodated to the Present State of Society, Manners, and Government in the United States of America." His audience on July 28, 1787, consisted of visitors to the recently opened Young Ladies' Academy at Philadelphia, for which he was serving as one of the original trustees.

Undoubtedly keeping the ongoing convention in mind, Dr. Rush emphasized the many reasons why an American education should be different from an English education for women. Women of the United States, he declared, had to be prepared to manage their busy husbands' property, to take extra responsibility while their husbands involved themselves in countless enterprises, and to assume many household chores in the absence of a permanent servant class and with the scarcity of domestic help. Also, "the equal share that every citizen has in the liberty and the possible share he may have in the government of our country make it necessary that our ladies should be qualified to a certain degree, by a peculiar and suitable education, to concur in instructing their sons in the principles of liberty and government." In other words, "our ladies" could be the instructors on the intricacies of government as well as the founts of idealism, though even Dr. Rush stopped short of urging their active participation in politics.

Coming down to details, Dr. Rush spelled out the requirements of a good education for young ladies. English grammar and spelling, and attractive, legible handwriting led the list. In addition, the well-educated female should have some knowledge of arithmetic, bookkeeping, geography, history, and biography, so that she would be qualified "not only for a general intercourse with the world but to be an agreeable companion for a sensible man." (This line of thought was so widely accepted that a hundred years later the same reason was adduced for female education in the founding of prestigious women's colleges—and it was reiterated long into the twentieth century.)

Gratifyingly, however, it can be reported that Dr. Rush ended his speech on an onward-and-upward note:

> I know that the elevation of the female mind, by means of moral, physical, and religious truth, is considered by some men as unfriendly to the domestic character of a woman. But this is the prejudice of little minds and springs from the same spirit which opposes the general diffusion of knowledge among the citizens of our republics. If men believe that ignorance is favorable to the government of the female sex, they are certainly deceived, for a weak and

ignorant woman will always be governed with the greatest difficulty.

Like Philadelphians, New Englanders, too, spoke out for women—probably because of the area's ancient Puritan heritage of nonconformity and intellectualism. Thus, sometime around 1782, as the Revolution was nearing its formal end, the Reverends Jeremy Belknap and John Eliot of Massachusetts helped to change the attitude toward publicly supported education for girls. They complained that Boston women learned only dancing and music, and that although some went to writing school, they barely learned to copy printed notes or to sign their own name.

At least a few men must have followed the lead of these ministers, because in 1789 Boston admitted girls to its public schools. (Previously, tradition rather than an actual law or ruling had kept them out.) In 1788, Northampton, Massachusetts, was fined for its failure to provide any kind of education for girls—a step in the right direction, but one that proved ineffective, since as late as 1818 the citizens of the town voted "that this town shall not be at any expense for schooling girls." Much better was the attitude of Gloucester, which in 1790 proclaimed officially: "Females . . . are a tender and interesting branch of the community but have been much neglected in the public schools in this town."

Also in Massachusetts, John Adams, no doubt influenced by the abilities of his wife Abigail, expressed his conviction that no art or science was too difficult for females. But reacting in a way his eighteenth-century male contemporaries would surely have understood, he encouraged his own daughter to learn French, but to refrain from mentioning her study of Latin grammar, "for it is scarcely reputable for young ladies to understand Greek and Latin."

In Connecticut, President Ezra Stiles of Yale proved himself willing to run ahead of public opinion on the subject of better education for females. Early in the 1780s, he included these two topics in his list of standard debate themes for seniors: (1) "Whether Women Ought to be Permitted to Partake in Civil Government Dominion and Sovereignty" and (2) "Whether Female Academies Would Be Beneficial."

And yet how far females still had to go is discouragingly illustrated in President Stiles's statement issued on December 22, 1783:

> Be it known to you that I have examined Miss Lucinda Foote, twelve years old, and have found that in the learned languages, the Latin and the Greek, she had made commendable progress, giving the true meaning of passages in the *Aeneid* of Virgil, the selected orations of Cicero, and in the Greek testament, and that she is fully qualified, *except in regard to sex* [italics added] to be received as a pupil of the freshman class of Yale University.

Postscript: President Stiles instead tutored Lucinda Foote in the complete Yale course of study. Later she married, mothered ten children, and disappeared from public view.

Again in Connecticut, America's first lexicographer, Noah Webster, included his ideas on female education in a small section of his 1790 essay, "On the Education of Youth in America." Webster saw women as important for spreading the ideas of liberty, for educating their own children, and for insuring the good manners of the American people. But he was unwilling to go too far. Underlining his judgments in italics he wrote: "That education is always *wrong* which raises a woman above the duties of her station. In America, female education should have for its object what is *useful*."

He recommended the study of arithmetic, geography, and poetry, and advised that females should read books about life and manners. Observing that in American cities music, drawing, and dancing were included in female education, he declared, "that no man ever marries a woman for her performance on a harpsichord or her figure in a minuet. However ambitious a woman may be to command admiration *abroad,* her real merit is known only at *home.* Admiration is useless when it is not supported by domestic worth. But real honor and permanent esteem are always secured by those who preside over their own families with dignity." And in a footnote, he adds drawing to the condemned list of the luxurious manners and amusements of England and France that must never be copied by Americans.

The very same year that Noah Webster was writing this essay, the sovereign state of New Jersey went off on an astounding frolic of its own. The exact facts are lost in a haze of anarchy and confusion, but somehow, beginning in 1790, an idea took flight that the newly revised state constitution allowed women the right to vote. Tradition alone should have barred women from the polls, but word was bruited about that the clause in question specifically used the words "he or she" in enumerating qualifications for the franchise. The explanation given was that a member of the drafting committee was a Quaker who took seriously his sect's insistence on equal rights for both sexes.

Thus for seventeen years, until 1807, each local election board in New Jersey had the power to accept or reject women voters, since the original state constitution had merely stated that all residents—no mention of sex—meeting certain standards should be allowed to exercise suffrage. Premature paradise came to a crashing end, however, when in Elizabethtown fraud ran rampant. Hordes of people—women, blacks, boys, and aliens—without the proper qualifications of age, residence, race, and property had been encouraged to vote. Hurriedly, the state legislature passed a law confining the franchise to free white males who were citizens of New Jersey.

One last resident American ally of women should be celebrated here, even though he was only five years old at the time of the Declaration and sixteen at the signing of the Constitution. He was Charles Brockden Brown (1771–1810), "father of the American novel," who in 1798 at the age of twenty-seven wrote the first significant tract for women's rights in America. He called his small book *Alcuin,* naming it for a philosopher and teacher in the early-ninth-century court of the Emperor Charlemagne. In form it is a dialogue between a scholar and a (female) intellectual on such subjects as the subjection of wife to husband in marriage, inferior education for women, and their exclusion from business and the professions as well as from politics: "Yes (said the lady); of all forms of injustice, that is the most egregious which makes the circumstance of sex a reason for excluding one half of mankind from all those paths which lead to usefulness and honor."

Though as in colonial days most spokesmen for social change came from New England or Philadelphia, some Southerners were also restive, especially in Virginia. No doubt Philip Fithian, tutor at Nomini Hall, who took the time and trouble to record his activities in a diary, was representative of many similarly minded but silent residents. In the years immediately preceding the Revolution, he assigned fifteen-year-old Priscilla, his oldest female pupil, readings in *The Spectator,* the erudite London journal published by Richard Steele and Joseph Addison.

*The Spectator* included essays on literature, the theater, and current mores—and was deliberately directed to women as well as to men. "There are none to whom this paper will be more useful than to the female world," Addison wrote in the tenth issue. Significantly, though the essays were widely read and discussed in the era of the Revolution, the publication dates were the years 1711 to 1712, the end of the reign of Queen Anne (1702 to 1714)—a time that had been particularly ripe for advocating a limited change of attitude toward women.

*Limited* is the key word here. Addison and Steele, while encouraging a brighter future for women, warned females to refrain from political partisanship and instead distinguish themselves as "tender mothers and faithful wives."

Apparently Thomas Jefferson of Virginia was in agreement with this philosophy. Long after the Declaration of Independence—he was the chief author—had proclaimed that "all men are created equal," he explained to his daughter that women should be educated not for their personal satisfaction or advancement but to teach their own daughters "and even direct the course for their sons."

Jefferson believed in an intellectual aristocracy for which most men would not even qualify. Therefore, it followed that women should certainly stay out of politics. In 1788, when serving as ambassador to France he wrote:

> Our good ladies, I trust, have been too wise to wrinkle their foreheads with politics. They are contented to soothe and calm the minds of their husbands returning ruffled from political debate. They have the good sense to value domestic happiness above all others. There is no part of the earth where so much of this is enjoyed as in America.

However, many women refused to view such writing as deathless prose, even from the pen of the great Jefferson. Besides, the American Revolution had been as much an overthrow of societies past as it was a political rebellion. Thus, numerous females watched restively as, contrary to Jefferson and his like-minded friends, the number of males qualified to vote and to hold public office grew larger and larger—until the time finally came when all *men* were considered eligible.

# Aftermath

Almost immediately, history followed America's struggle for independence with the French Revolution of 1789, preaching human emancipation and individual dignity through "Liberty, Equality, and Fraternity." Then, into the limelight on both sides of the Atlantic, came Mary Wollstonecraft's *Vindication of the Rights of Women,* written in England in 1792 and arguing for better education and increased opportunity for women to support themselves financially if they wished. Meanwhile, gathering enough steam to push females out of their homes and into factories was the burgeoning Industrial Revolution, which between 1800 and 1850 would recruit a labor force consisting of anywhere from two-thirds to three-fourths to nine-tenths girls and women, who would previously have stayed home to mind younger children or to work in cottage industry.

In this setting, two problems raised in colonial days and exacerbated by the lofty language of the Declaration of Independence came to the fore: abolition of slavery, and equality for women in the social, political, and economic life of the new nation. Not surprisingly, advocating the one taught lessons invaluable for arguing in favor of the other. Also, in an unexpected turn of events the two problems became closely interrelated.

Thus, Elizabeth Cady Stanton (1815–1902) was a staunch abolitionist who at the age of thirty-three took on leadership of the nineteenth-century women's rights movement. She had gained experience in public affairs as an anti-slavery activist under the tutelage of Quaker Lucretia Coffin Mott of Massachusetts, an organizer of the 1837 Anti-Slavery Convention of American Women. Horrified at the exclusion of women—half of humanity, they protested—from the World's Anti-Slavery Convention in London in 1840, Lucretia Mott, her sister Martha Coffin Wright, and Elizabeth Cady Stanton channeled their fury into launching the women's rights movement at a convention in Seneca Falls, New York, eight years later. On July 19, 1848, they issued a Declaration of Sentiments and Resolutions, resoundingly paraphrasing the Declaration of Independence (in the excerpts below, words and phrases that they altered have been italicized):

We hold these truths to be self evident: that all men *and women* are created equal. . . .
The history of mankind is a history of repeated injuries and usurpations on the part of *man toward woman,* having in direct object the establishment of an absolute tyranny *over her.*

Then, substituting examples of oppression by men over women for instances of tyranny committed by King George III against the colonists, they included women's lack of suffrage, the effect of the Blackstone Code making a woman legally dead upon marriage, her inability to own property, and the decidedly inferior education available to her.

In this connection, a further ramification of the Declaration of Independence was a call for equal education for women—a necessity made clear since early colonial days. Actually, the best way to appreciate the entrenched opposition to equal education for women is to look at the United States today. Even in the 1970s the United States shows traces of the tradition of withholding education from females, or at most allowing them an inferior substitute. While colleges for women finally came into existence a century ago, widespread admission of women to professional graduate schools dates only from the end of World War II. (Harvard Law School, for example, finally opened its doors to women in 1950.) The current decade has seen the almost universal establishment of coeducation, but accompanied by reluctance to drop sexual quotas. Harvard, the earliest American college and still considered the leader in the field of American education, continues to refuse to accept students on the basis of objective test scores, relying instead on a set ratio of men to women—recently decreased from 4 males to every 1 female to 2.5 men to each woman. And the numbers of female professors in all United States colleges, though increasing, are almost all but negligible. (Again, to cite the leader Harvard: less than two percent of tenured professors there were women as of April 30, 1974—15 out of 762.) Public-school education, now universal and compulsory for both sexes, has only recently begun to give women teachers equal pay with men teachers. A final break with the past. However, on the elementary level, women still predominate as teachers and principals, although—in a long-overdue wrenching from worn-out precedent—the qualifications for certification are gradually being upgraded.

In summary, then, three problems, all deeply involving women, originated long ago in colonial days, received a tremendous push for positive action from the Declaration of Independence and the post-Revolutionary period—but continue unresolved at this late date. Thus, abolition of slavery for men and women followed the Civil War in 1865, and almost one hundred years later Congress enacted civil rights legislation, which in the 1970s is both incompletely implemented and also insufficient. Women won the right to vote and to hold national office by 1920, but the Congress of 1975 includes only 19 women members out of 435 in the House of Representatives and not a single United States senator—and the struggle for ratification of the Equal Rights Amendment to the Constitution continues. As for equal education, it keeps coming tantalizingly closer to achievement, but never quite meets the goal fully.

The ancient struggle for utopia—or at least for equality—goes on.

# *A* N*ote on* D*ates,*
## *S*pelling, C*itations—*
### *and* G*ood* F*riends*

Though largely Catholic Europe had adopted the modern Gregorian calendar in 1582, in order to catch up with the true vernal equinox, Protestant England stubbornly resisted change until September 1752. At that time, eleven days were added to the old Julian calendar, which was then discarded both in the mother country and her colonies. This, of course, accounts for the confusion of such dates as Washington's birthday, frequently given as "February 11, 1732 (Old Style), February 22, 1732 (New Style)." However, since dates are not the pivot of *Demeter's Daughters,* they are simply reported as originally recorded, with no attempt to modernize those occurring before September 1752.

On the other hand, spelling and punctuation have been modernized, when necessary to avoid confusion. No sacrilege is involved here, since contemporary quotes of identical material seldom agree as to spelling and punctuation. In any case, there has been a special effort to preserve original sense and flavor of all quotations used. For example, the original spelling "Charles Town" is used for South Carolina's oldest and largest city, which changed to the modern "Charleston" after the Revolution.

For the further convenience of the reader, contemporary statements or writings that are an integral part of the text have been identified where they occur. Several sources that are already—or that deserve to be—classics are also named in the text. All sources are fully cited in the section that follows. Primary sources include firsthand writings and records involving the period under consideration, though occasionally dated both earlier (1486) and later (1808) than the time span covered by the book. Thus, Heinrich Kramer's encyclopedia of witchcraft, *Malleus Malifacarum,* though first published in 1486, illuminates the Salem hysteria of 1692. Similarly, Anne Grant's *Memoirs of an American Lady,* though finally published in 1808, was an account of observations made before the Revolution. Secondary sources include nineteenth- and twentieth-century books and articles, written on the basis of research rather than personal recollection.

The difficulty as well as the delight of writing this book has been the newness of the subject. As the book began to proliferate and to set its own style and outer limits, I was most fortunate to have three severe critics always ready to read a paragraph, a chapter, and finally the complete book—and, most importantly, to suggest additions, subtractions, and wholly new ideas. These true paragons are my lawyer-husband Burt, who particularly scrutinized the sections on law; my daughter Pamela, whose special interests and expertise are mythology, folklore, and legend; and my good friend Natalie Miller, who, as Massachusetts education specialist in charge of coordinating the state's efforts to eliminate sex discrimination within the school system, has known exactly where to suggest clarification.

I am also extremely grateful to Cary Memorial Library, Lexington, where the excellent colonial history resources are perfectly matched by the patience and helpfulness of every member of the reference staff.

# Bibliography

## Contemporary Sources, 1486–1808

(*Please note: Although the writings listed below were completed between 1486 and 1808, many were first published much later, and some have been reissued as recently as the 1970s. This accounts for the comparatively modern dates appearing in many of the citations that follow.*)

ADAMS, ABIGAIL. *Letters of Mrs. Adams, the Wife of John Adams.* Edited by Charles Francis Adams. Boston: Wilkins, Carter, 1848.

———. *New Letters of Abigail Adams, 1788–1801.* Edited by Stewart Mitchell. Boston: Houghton-Mifflin, 1947.

ADAMS, HANNAH. *A Summary History of New England from the First Settlement at Plymouth to the Acceptance of the Federal Constitution.* Dedham, Mass.: Privately printed for the author, 1799.

ADAMS, JOHN. *The Works of John Adams.* Vol. 9. Edited by Charles Francis Adams. Boston: Little, Brown, 1854.

BARCLAY, GRACE. *Diary, or Personal Recollections of the American Revolution.* Edited by Sidney Barclay. New York: Anson D. F. Randolph, 1859, 1866.

BOLTON, HERBERT EUGENE, ED. *Spanish Exploration in the Southwest, 1542–1706.* New York: Barnes and Noble, 1963.

BOSWELL, JAMES. *Life of Samuel Johnson, LL.D.* Chicago: Encyclopaedia Britannica, 1952.

BRADFORD, WILLIAM. *Of Plymouth Plantation.* Edited by Samuel Eliot Morison. New York: Modern Library, 1952.

BRADSTREET, ANNE. *Works.* Edited by John Harvard Ellis. Gloucester, Mass.: Peter Smith, 1962.

BROWN, ALEXANDER, ED. *The Genesis of the United States, A Series of Historical Manuscripts now first printed.* 2 vols. New York: Russell and Russell, 1964.

BROWN, CHARLES B. *Alcuin.* New York: Grossman, 1971.

BURR, GEORGE LINCOLN, ED. *Narratives of the Witchcraft Cases, 1648–1706.* New York: Barnes and Noble, 1968.

BYRD, WILLIAM. *Another Secret Diary, 1739–1741.* Richmond, Va.: The Dietz Press, 1942.

———. *The London Diary and Other Writings.* Edited by Louis B. Wright and Marion Tinling. New York: Oxford University Press, 1958.

———. *The Prose Works.* Edited by Louis B. Wright. Cambridge, Mass.: The Belknap Press of Harvard University, 1966.

———. *The Secret Diary.* Edited by Louis B. Wright and Marion Tinling. Richmond, Va.: The Dietz Press, 1941.

CAIRNS, WILLIAM B., ED. *Selections from Early American Writers, 1607–1800.* New York: Macmillan, 1927.

CLAP, ROGER. *Memoirs, 1630.* Freeport, N.Y.: Books for Libraries, 1971.

CLAYTON, JOHN. "A Letter." Vol. 3. *Tracts and Other Papers Relating Principally to the Origin, Settlement, and Progress of the Colonies in North America.* Edited by Peter Force. Gloucester, Mass.: Peter Smith, 1963.

CREVECOEUR, J. HECTOR ST. JOHN. *Letters from an American Farmer.* Garden City, N.Y.: Doubleday, reprinted from original 1782 edition.

COTTON, ANNE. "An Account of Our late Troubles in Virginia, Written in 1676." Vol. 1. *Tracts and Other Papers Relating Principally to the Origin, Settlement, and Progress of the Colonies in North America.* Edited by Peter Force. Gloucester, Mass.: Peter Smith, 1963.

CURWEN, SAMUEL. *Journal and Letters of an American in England, 1775–1783.* Edited by George Atkinson Ward. Boston: Little, Brown, 1864.

DANCKERS, JASPER. *Journal of a Voyage to New York, 1679–1680.* Edited by B. B. James and J. F. Jameson. New York: Barnes and Noble, 1913.

DRINKER, ELIZABETH. *Extracts from Journal, 1759–1807.* Edited by Henry D. Biddle. Philadelphia: J. B. Lippincott, 1889.

DYER, MARY. "The Justification of a Condemned Quakeress, 1659." Vol. 1. *American History Told by Contemporaries.* Edited by Albert B. Hart. New York: Macmillan, 1897.

FITHIAN, PHILIP VICKERS. *Journal and Letters, 1767–1774.* Edited by Hunter Dickinson Farish. Williamsburg, Va.: Colonial Williamsburg, 1957.

FRANKLIN, BENJAMIN. "The Speech of Polly Baker." Edited by John C. Miller, *The Colonial Image.* New York: George Braziller, 1962.

FRENEAU, PHILIP. *Poems Relating to the American Revolution.* Middleton, N. Y., 1865.

GRANT, ANNE. *Memoirs of an American Lady: with Sketches of Manners and Scenes in America as They Existed Previous to the Revolution.* Albany: Joel Munsell, 1876.

HALIFAX, GEORGE SAVILE, MARQUESS OF. *The Lady's New Year's Gift; or, Advice to a Daughter.* Edited by J. P. Kenyon. Baltimore: Penguin, 1969.

HALL, CLAYTON COLMAN, ED. *Narratives of Early Maryland, 1633–1684.* New York: Barnes and Noble, 1959.

HODGE, FREDERICK W., ED. *Spanish Explorers in the Southern United States, 1528–1543.* New York: Barnes and Noble, 1946.

HOTTEN, JOHN CAMDEN, ED. *The Original Lists of Persons . . . Who Went from Great Britain to the American Plantations, 1600–1700.* London, 1874.

HULTON, ANN. *Letters of a Loyalist Lady, Being the Letters of Ann Hulton, Sister of Henry Hulton, Commissioner of Customs at Boston, 1767–1776.* Cambridge, Mass.: Harvard University Press, 1927.

JAMESON, J. FRANKLIN, ED. *Narratives of New Netherland, 1609–1664.* New York: Barnes and Noble, 1959.

JOHNSON, EDWARD. *Wonder-Working Providence of Sion's Sa-*

*viour in New England, 1628–1651.* Edited by J. Franklin Jameson. New York: Barnes and Noble, 1910.

KAMINKOW, JACK AND MARION, EDS. *A List of Emigrants from England to America, 1718–1759.* Baltimore: Magna Charta, 1966. (Transcribed from microfilms of the original records at the Guildhall, London.)

KRAMER, HEINRICH, AND SPRENGER, JAMES. *Malleus Malificarum.* Translated by Montague Summers. New York: Dover, 1971.

LORANT, STEFAN, ED. *The New World. The First Pictures of America Made by John White and Jacques Le Moyne and Engraved by Theodore de Bry, with Contemporary Narratives of the Huguenot Settlement in Florida, 1562–1565, and The Virginia Colony, 1585–1590.* New York: Duell, Sloan, and Pearce, 1946.

MATHER, COTTON. *"Decennium Luctuosum." Narratives of the Indian Wars, 1675–1699.* Edited by Charles H. Lincoln. New York: Barnes and Noble, 1959.

———. *Selections.* Edited by Kenneth B. Murdock. New York: Hafner Library of Classics, 1965.

MAYO, LAWRENCE SHAW, ED. *The History of the Colony and Province of Massachusetts Bay.* 3 vols. Cambridge, Mass.: Harvard University Press, 1936. (Includes "The Examination of Mrs. Ann Hutchinson at the Court of Newton," vol. 2, appendix 2, pp. 366–391.)

MILLER, PERRY, AND JOHNSON, THOMAS H., EDS. *The Puritans.* 2 vols. New York: Harper Torchbooks, 1963. (Includes "The Journal" of Sarah Kemble Knight.)

MORRIS, MARGARET. *Her Journal.* Edited by John W. Jackson. Philadelphia: George S. McManus, 1949.

MORGAN, EDMUND S., ED. *Puritan Political Ideas.* Indianapolis: Bobbs-Merrill, 1965.

*Mourt's Relation, A Journal of the Pilgrims at Plymouth, 1622* Text. Edited by Dwight B. Heath. New York: Corinth Books, 1963.

MYERS, ALBERT COOK, ED. *Narratives of Early Pennsylvania, West New Jersey, and Delaware, 1630–1707.* New York: Barnes and Noble, 1959.

OLSON, JULIUS E., ED. *The Northmen, Columbus and Cabot, 985–1503.* New York: Barnes and Noble, 1934.

PIERCE, RICHARD D., ED. *The Records of the First Church in Boston, 1630–1868.* Boston: Colonial Society of Massachusetts Collections, vol. 39, 1961.

PINCKNEY, ELIZA LUCAS. *Letterbook, 1739–1762.* Edited by Elise Pinckney and Marvin R. Zahniser. Chapel Hill: University of North Carolina Press, 1972.

RICHARDSON, SAMUEL. *Pamela or Virtue Rewarded.* New York: Norton, 1958.

RIEDESEL, BARONESS FREDERIKA VON. *Journal and Correspondence of a Tour of Duty.* Edited and translated by Marvin L. Brown, Jr. and Marta Huth. Chapel Hill: University of North Carolina Press, 1965.

ROWLANDSON, MARY. *The Narrative of the Captivity and Restoration of Mrs. Mary Rowlandson.* Boston: Houghton-Mifflin, 1930.

RUSH, BENJAMIN. *Selected Writings.* Edited by Dagobert D. Runes. New York: Philosophical Library, 1947.

―――――. "Thoughts upon Female Education, Accommodated to the Present State of Society, Manners, and Government in the United States of America, 1787." *Essays on Education in the Early Republic.* Edited by Frederick Rudolph. Cambridge, Mass.: Harvard University Press, 1965.

SALLEY, ALEXANDER S., JR., ED. *Narratives of Early Carolina, 1650–1708.* New York: Barnes and Noble, 1959.

SAVAGE, JAMES. *A Genealogical Dictionary of the First Settlers of New England, Showing Three Generations of Those Who Came before May, 1692.* 4 vols. Baltimore: Genealogical Publishing, 1965.

SCOT, REGINALD. *The Discoverie of Witchcraft.* New York: Dover, 1972.

SEWALL, SAMUEL. *Diary, 1674–1729.* Edited by M. Halsey Thomas. 2 vols. New York: Farrar, Straus and Giroux, 1973.

STARBUCK, ALEXANDER. *The History of Nantucket.* Rutland, Vt.: Tuttle, 1969. (Includes 1701 journal account of John Richardson, a visiting Englishman.)

STONE, WILLIAM L., ANNOTATOR. *Ballads and Poems Relating to the Burgoyne Campaign.* Port Washington, N.Y.: Kennikat Press, 1970.

TYLER, LYON GARDINER, ED. *Narratives of Early Virginia, 1606–1625.* New York: Charles Scribner's Sons, 1907.

*Warren-Adams Letters,* 2 vols. Boston: The Massachusetts Historical Society, 1925.

WARREN, MERCY. "The Group." In *Representative Plays by American Dramatists,* vol. I. Edited by Montrose J. Moses. New York: Benjamin Blom, 1964.

———. *History of the Rise, Progress, and Termination of the American Revolution.* 3 vols. Boston: E. Larkin, 1805.

WEBSTER, NOAH. "On the Education of Youth in America, 1790." *Essays on Education in the Early Republic.* Edited by Frederick Rudolph. Cambridge, Mass.: Harvard University Press, 1965.

WELLS, LOUISA SUSANNAH, *The Journal of a Voyage from Charles Town, South Carolina, to London, Undertaken during the American Revolution by a Daughter of an Eminent American Loyalist in the Year 1778 and Written from Memory Only in 1779.* New York: Arno Press, 1968.

WHEATLEY, PHILLIS. *Poems and Letters.* Edited by Charles Fred Heartman. Miami, Fla.: Mnemosyne Publishing, 1969.

WILKINSON, ELIZA. *Letters during the Invasion and Possession of Charles Town, S.C. by the British in the Revolutionary War.* Arranged from the original manuscripts by Caroline Gilman. New York: Samuel Colman, 1839.

WINSLOW, ANNA GREEN. *Diary of a Boston School Girl of 1771.* Edited by Alice Morse Earle. Boston, 1894.

WINTHROP, HANNAH. "Letter after Battle of Lexington." *Massachusetts Historical Society Proceedings,* XIV, 1875.

WINTHROP, JOHN. *Journal History of New England, 1630–1649.* 2 vols. Edited by James Kendall Hosmer. New York: Barnes and Noble, 1959.

———. *Life and Letters.* 2 vols. Edited by Robert C. Winthrop. Boston: Little, Brown, 1869. (Includes letters to and from Margaret Winthrop.)

## Nineteenth-Century Sources

(*In the case of recently reissued books, the earlier date refers to original publication.*)

ADAMS, CHARLES FRANCIS. *Three Episodes of Massachusetts History: The Settlement of Boston Bay, The Antinomian Controversy, A Study of Church and Town Government.* 2 vols. New York: Russell and Russell, 1892, 1965.

BROOKS, GERALDINE. *Dames and Daughters of Colonial Days.* New York: Crowell, 1900.

BROWN, ALICE. *Mercy Warren.* New York: Charles Scribner's Sons, 1896.

CHILD, LYDIA MARIA. *The History of the Condition of Women, in Various Ages and Nations.* 2d ed. Boston: Otis Broaders, 1838.

CLEMENT, J., ED. *Noble Deeds of American Women.* Buffalo: George H. Derby, 1851.

CROCKER, HANNAH MATHER. *Observations on the Real Rights of Women with Their Appropriate Duties Agreeable to Scripture, Reason, and Common Sense.* Boston: Printed for the author, 1818.

EARLE, ALICE MORSE. *Colonial Dames and Good Wives.* Boston: Houghton-Mifflin, 1895.

————. *Home Life in Colonial Days.* New York: Macmillan, 1898, 1926.

————. *Margaret Winthrop.* New York: Charles Scribner's Sons, 1896.

EGLE, WILLIAM HENRY. *Pennsylvania Women in the American Revolution.* Cottonport, La.: Polyanthos, 1898, 1972.

ELLET, ELIZABETH. *Women of the American Revolution.* 3 vols. New York: Baker and Scribner, 1848.

FOWLER, WILLIAM W. *Woman on the American Frontier.* Ann Arbor: Plutarch Press, 1878, 1971.

GRISWOLD, RUFUS. *The Female Poets of America.* New York: James Miller, 1848, 1874.

MAY, CAROLINE. *The American Female Poets.* Philadelphia: Lindsay and Blakiston, 1848.

MORGAN, LEWIS H. *Houses and House-Life of the American Aborigines.* Chicago: University of Chicago Press, 1881, 1965.

NELL, WILLIAM C. *The Colored Patriots of the American Revolution.* New York: Arno, 1855, 1968.

POPE, CHARLES HENRY. *The Pioneers of Massachusetts, A Descriptive List Drawn from the Records of the Colonies, Towns, and Churches, and Other Contemporaneous Documents.* Boston: Charles H. Pope, 1900.

SHELDON, GEORGE. *A History of Deerfield, Massachusetts.* 2 vols. New Hampshire Publishing Co., 1895, 1972.

THOMAS, ISAIAH, *The History of Printing in America, with a Biography of Printers, and an Account of Newspapers.* 2 vols. Worcester, Mass.: Isaiah Thomas, Jr., 1810.

## Twentieth-Century Sources

### I. BOOKS

ADAMS, JAMES TRUSLOW. *Provincial Society, 1690–1763.* Chicago: Quadrangle, 1971.

ANTHONY, KATHARINE. *First Lady of the Revolution, The Life of Mercy Otis Warren.* New York: Doubleday, 1958.

ARIÈS, PHILIPPE. *Centuries of Childhood, A Social History of Family Life.* New York: Vintage, 1962.

BAILYN, BERNARD. *Education in the Forming of American Society.* Chapel Hill: University of North Carolina Press, 1960.
———. *The New England Merchants in the Seventeenth Century.* New York: Harper Torchbooks, 1964.

BARING-GOULD, WILLIAM S., AND BARING-GOULD, CEIL. *The Annotated Mother Goose.* New York: Clarkson N. Potter, 1962. (See especially Chapter 1, "All About Mother Goose.")

BATTIS, EMERY. *Saints and Sectaries.* Chapel Hill: University of North Carolina Press, 1962. (An interpretative biography of Anne Hutchinson.)

BEARD, MARY. *Woman as Force in History.* New York: Macmillan, 1946.

BENSON, MARY SUMNER. *Women in Eighteenth Century America.* New York: Columbia University Press, 1935.

BLUMENTHAL, WALTER HART. *Brides from Bridewell: Female Felons Sent to Colonial America.* Rutland, Vt.: Tuttle, 1962.

BONFANTI, LEO, ED. *Biographies and Legends of the New England Indians.* Wakefield, Mass.: Bonnell, 1968.

BOOTH, SALLY SMITH. *The Women of '76.* New York: Hastings House, 1973.

BOYER, PAUL, AND NISSENBAUM, STEPHEN. *Salem Possessed: The Social Origins of Witchcraft.* Cambridge, Mass.: Harvard University Press, 1974.

———, EDS. *Salem-Village Witchcraft: A Documentary Record of Local Conflict in Colonial New England.* Belmont, Calif.: Wadsworth, 1927.

BRIDENBAUGH, CARL. *Cities in the Wilderness, Urban Life in America, 1625–1742.* New York: Capricorn, 1964.

———. *Vexed and Troubled Englishmen, 1590–1642.* New York: Oxford University Press, 1968.

BRUCE, KATHLEEN. "Massachusetts Women of the Revolution (1761–1789)," Chap. 11, vol. 3. *Commonwealth History of Massachusetts.* Edited by Albert Bushnell Hart. New York: The States History Co., 1927/1928.

BURLAND, COTTIE. *North American Indian Mythology.* New York: Hamlyn, 1973.

CALHOUN, ARTHUR W. *A Social History of the American Family.* Vols. 1 and 2. Cleveland: Arthur W. Clark, 1917.

CLARK, ALICE. *Working Life of Women in the Seventeenth Century.* London: Cass, 1919.

CONDON, THOMAS J. *New York Beginnings, The Commercial Origins of New Netherland.* New York: New York University Press, 1968.

DEMOS, JOHN. *A Little Commonwealth, Family Life in Plymouth Colony.* New York: Oxford University Press, 1970.

DEXTER, ELISABETH ANTHONY. *Career Women of America, 1776–1840.* Boston: Houghton-Mifflin, 1950.

———. *Colonial Women of Affairs.* Boston: Houghton-Mifflin, 1924.

DOW, GEORGE FRANCIS. *Every Day Life in the Massachusetts*

*Bay Colony.* Boston: The Society for the Preservation of New England Antiquities, 1935.

————. *Slave Ships and Slaving.* Port Washington, N.Y.: Kennikat Press, 1969.

EARLE, ALICE MORSE. *Two Centuries of Costume in America, 1620–1820.* 2 vols. Rutland, Vt.: Tuttle, 1903, 1971.

FARB, PETER. *Man's Rise to Civilization, As Shown by the Indians of North America from Primeval Times to the Coming of the Industrial State.* New York: Avon, 1973.

FLEXNER, ELEANOR. *Century of Struggle.* New York: Atheneum, 1973.

FOREMAN, CAROLYN THOMAS. *Indian Women Chiefs.* Muskogee, Okla.: The Star Printery, 1954.

FRITZ, JEAN. *Cast for a Revolution.* Boston: Houghton-Mifflin, 1972.

GEORGE, M. DOROTHY. *London Life in the Eighteenth Century.* Harmondsworth, Middlesex, England: Peregrine, 1925, 1965.

GOODWIN, MAUD WILDER. *Dutch and English on the Hudson.* New Haven: Yale University Press, 1919.

GREEN, HARRY CLINTON, AND GREEN, MARY WOLCOTT. *The Pioneer Mothers of America: A Record of the More Notable Women of the Early Days of the Country and Particularly the Colonial and Revolutionary Periods.* 3 vols. New York: G. P. Putnam's Sons, 1912.

GREVEN, PHILIP J., JR. *Four Generations, Population, Land, and Family in Colonial Andover, Mass.* Ithaca, N.Y.: Cornell University Press, 1970.

HANSEN, CHADWICK. *Witchcraft at Salem.* New York: Signet, 1970.

HEWES, AMY. "Early Eighteenth Century Women (1689–1761)," Chap. 12, vol. 2. *Commonwealth History of Massachusetts.* Edited by Albert Bushnell Hart. New York: The States History Co., 1927/1928.

HILL, CHRISTOPHER. *Society and Puritanism in Pre-Revolutionary England.* London: Panther, 1969.

HOLLIDAY, CARL. *Woman's Life in Colonial Days.* New York: Frederick Ungar Publishing Co., 1922, 1960.

HUGHES, PENNETHORNE. *Witchcraft.* London: Pelican, 1971.

JAMES, EDWARD, AND JAMES, JANET, EDS. *Notable American Women, 1607–1950.* Cambridge, Mass.: Harvard University Press, 1972. (Biographical dictionary.)

JANTZ, HAROLD S. *The First Century of New England Verse.* New York: Russell and Russell, 1962.

JONES, RUFUS M. *The Quakers in the American Colonies.* New York: Russell and Russell, 1962.

JORDAN, WINTHROP D. *White over Black: American Attitudes toward the Negro, 1550–1812.* Baltimore: Penguin, 1973.

JOSEPHY, ALVIN M., JR. *The Indian Heritage of America.* New York: Alfred A. Knopf, 1968.

KANOWITZ, LEO. *Women and the Law.* Albuquerque: University of New Mexico Press, 1969.

KEEN, BENJAMIN, ED. *Readings in Latin American Civilization.* Boston: Houghton-Mifflin, 1955, 1967.

KITTREDGE, GEORGE L. *Witchcraft in Old and New England.* New York: Atheneum, 1972.

LEONARD, EUGENIE ANDRUSS. *The Dear Bought Heritage.* Philadelphia: University of Pennsylvania Press, 1965.

LEVIN, DAVID. *What Happened in Salem.* New York: Harcourt, Brace and World, 1960.

LOCKRIDGE, KENNETH A. *Literacy in Colonial New England.* New York; Norton, 1974.

McCORD, DAVID. *An Acre for Education. Notes on the History of Radcliffe College.* Cambridge, Mass., 1954.

MACFARLANE, ALAN. *Witchcraft in Tudor and Stuart England.* New York: Harper Torchbook, 1970.

MARKS, GEOFFREY, AND BEATTY, WILLIAM K. *The Story of Medicine in America.* New York: Scribner's, 1973.

———. *Women in White, Their Role as Doctors through the Ages.* New York: Scribner's, 1972.

MORGAN, EDMUND S. *The Puritan Dilemma.* Boston: Little, Brown, 1958.

———. *The Puritan Family.* New York: Harper and Row, 1966.

———. *Visible Saints.* Ithaca, N.Y.: Cornell University Press, 1968.

MORISON, SAMUEL ELIOT. *Builders of the Bay Colony.* Boston: Houghton-Mifflin, 1958. (See especially chapter 11, "Mistress Anne Bradstreet.")

——. *The Intellectual Life of Colonial New England.* Ithaca, N.Y.: Cornell University Press, 1960.

MORRIS, RICHARD B. *Studies in the History of American Law.* New York: Octagon Books, 1930. (See especially chapter 3, "Women's Rights in Early American Law.")

NICHOLSON, IRENE. *A Guide to Mexican Poetry, Ancient and Modern.* Mexico, 8 DF, Mexico: Editoria Minutiae Mexicana, 1968.

NOTESTEIN, WALLACE. *The English People on the Eve of Colonization, 1603–1630.* New York: Harper Torchbooks, 1962.

——. *A History of Witchcraft in England.* New York: Apollo, 1968.

NOYES, ETHEL J. R. C. *The Women of the Mayflower and Women of Plymouth Colony.* Ann Arbor: Gryphon, 1921, 1971.

PIERCY, JOSEPHINE K. *Anne Bradstreet.* New York: Twayne, 1965.

PLUMB, J. H., ED. *Studies in Social History: A Tribute to G. M. Trevelyan.* New York: Longmans, Green, 1955. (See especially chapter 3, "The English Woman, 1580–1650.")

PRIESTLEY, HERBERT INGRAM. *The Coming of the White Man.* New York: Macmillan, 1930.

PUTNAM, EMILY JAMES. *The Lady: Studies of Certain Significant Phases of Her History.* Chicago: University of Chicago Press, 1910, 1970.

QUARLES, BENJAMIN. *The Negro in the American Revolution.* New York: Norton, 1973.

ROCHE, O. I. A. *The Days of the Upright, A History of the Huguenots.* New York: Clarkson N. Potter, 1965.

ROWLING, MARJORIE. *Everyday Life in Medieval Times.* London: B. T. Batsford, 1968.

RUSSELL, JEFFREY BURTON. *Witchcraft in the Middle Ages.* Ithaca, N.Y.: Cornell University Press, 1972.

RUTMAN, DARRETT B. *Winthrop's Boston. A Portrait of a Puritan Town, 1603–1649.* Chapel Hill: University of North Carolina Press, 1965.

SCHLESINGER, ARTHUR M. *Prelude to Independence.* New York: Vintage, 1965.

SEYBOLT, ROBERT FRANCIS. *The Evening School in Colonial America.* Urbana: University of Illinois, 1925.

————. *The Private Schools of Colonial Boston.* Cambridge, Mass.: Harvard University Press, 1935.

SLOTKIN, RICHARD. *Regeneration through Violence: The Mythology of the American Frontier, 1600–1800.* Middletown, Conn.: Wesleyan University Press, 1974.

SMITH, ABBOT EMERSON. *Colonists in Bondage. White Servitude and Convict Labor in America, 1607–1776.* New York: Norton, 1947, 1971.

SPRUILL, JULIA CHERRY. *Women's Life and Work in the Southern Colonies.* New York: Norton, 1938, 1972.

STANTON, ELIZABETH CADY, ANTHONY, SUSAN B., AND GAGE, MATILDA JOSLYN. *History of Woman Suffrage, 1881–1922.* 5 vols. New York: Arno, 1969. (In this recently reissued work, volume one contains many references to colonial history.)

STARKEY, MARION L. *The Devil in Massachusetts.* Garden City, N.Y.: Anchor, 1969.

STENDAHL, KRISTER. *The Bible and the Role of Women.* Philadelphia: Facet, 1966.

TAPLEY, HARRIET SYLVESTER. "Women of Massachusetts ( 1620–1689)," Chap. 11, vol. 1. *Commonwealth History of Massachusetts.* Edited by Albert Hart. New York: The States History Co., 1927/1928.

THOMPSON, ROGER. *Women in Stuart England and America.* London: Routledge and Kegan Paul, 1974.

TREVOR-ROPER, H. R. *The European Witch-Craze.* New York: Harper Torchbooks, 1969.

VAN RENSSELAER, MRS. SCHUYLER. *History of the City of New York in the Seventeenth Century.* 2 vols. New York: Macmillan, 1909.

WHITE, ELIZABETH W. *Anne Bradstreet, The Tenth Muse.* New York: Oxford University Press, 1971.

WILLIAMS, CHARLES. *Witchcraft*. New York: Meridian, 1959.

WILLIAMS, SELMA R. *Kings, Commoners, and Colonists: Puritan Politics in Old and New England, 1603–1660*. New York: Atheneum, 1974.

WILLISON, GEORGE F. *Saints and Strangers*. New York: Reynal and Hitchcock, 1945.

WINSLOW, OLA ELIZABETH. *Meetinghouse Hill: 1630–1783*. New York: Macmillan, 1952.

WOODY, THOMAS. *A History of Women's Education in the United States*. 2 vols. New York: Science Press, 1929.


II. PERIODICALS

COMETTI, ELIZABETH. "Women in the American Revolution." *New England Quarterly* 20 (1947): 329–346.

DEMOS, JOHN. "Underlying Themes of Witchcraft in Salem." *American Historical Review,* June 1970.

HENRETTA, JAMES A. "Economic Development and Social Structure in Colonial Boston." *William and Mary Quarterly* 22 (1965): 75–92.

KEIM, C. RAY. "Primogeniture and Entail in Colonial Virginia." *William and Mary Quarterly* 25 (1968): 545–586.

MOLLER, HERBERT. "Sex Composition and Correlated Culture Patterns of Colonial America." *William and Mary Quarterly* 2 (1945): 113–153.

MORGAN, EDMUND S. "The Puritans and Sex." *The New England Quarterly* 15 (1942): 591–607.

OLDHAM, ELLEN M. "Early Women Printers of America." *The Boston Public Library Quarterly* 10, January and July 1958.

SCHLESINGER, ELIZABETH BANCROFT. "Cotton Mather and His Children." *William and Mary Quarterly* 10 (1953): 181–189.

*Women, A Historical Survey of Works by Women Artists*. Salem Fine Arts Center, Winston-Salem, N.C., 1972. (Exhibition catalog.)

# Index

347

# Selma R. Williams

IN HER UNDERGRADUATE days at Radcliffe College, Selma R. Williams bewailed the fact that she had been born too late to be a suffrage activist. Only after teaching U.S. history on the junior high and high school levels, and most recently to graduate students, did she finally discover what she wanted to be when she grew up—an activist uncovering deep female roots in history, and spreading the word.

Now she combines writing feminist history with work as partner in a professional consulting group set up to eradicate sexism from school textbooks, and at the same time to produce and deliver slide-lectures.

Author of a previous Atheneum book, *KINGS, COMMONERS, AND COLONISTS: Puritan Politics in Old and New England, 1603-1660,* she lives in historic Lexington, Massachusetts. Her husband Burt is a Boston lawyer, and their two daughters are college students.